The Global Nomad

TOURISM AND CULTURAL CHANGE
Series Editor: Professor Mike Robinson, *Centre for Tourism and Cultural Change,*
Sheffield Hallam University

Understanding tourism's relationships with culture(s) and vice versa, is of
ever-increasing significance in a globalising world. This series will critically examine
the dynamic inter-relationships between tourism and culture(s). Theoretical
explorations, research-informed analyses, and detailed historical reviews from a
variety of disciplinary perspectives are invited to consider such relationships.

Other Books in the Series
Irish Tourism: Image, Culture and Identity
    Michael Cronin and Barbara O'Connor (eds)
Tourism, Globalization and Cultural Change: An Island Community Perspective
    Donald V. L. Macleod

Other Books of Interest
Classic Reviews in Tourism
    Chris Cooper (ed.)
Coastal Mass Tourism: Diversification and Sustainable Development in Southern
Europe
    Bill Bramwell (ed.)
Dynamic Tourism: Journeying with Change
    Priscilla Boniface
Managing Educational Tourism
    Brent W. Ritchie
Marine Ecotourism: Issues and Experiences
    Brian Garrod and Julie C. Wilson (eds)
Natural Area Tourism: Ecology, Impacts and Management
    D. Newsome, S.A. Moore and R. Dowling
Progressing Tourism Research
    Bill Faulkner, edited by Liz Fredline, Leo Jago and Chris Cooper
Recreational Tourism: Demand and Impacts
    Chris Ryan
Shopping Tourism: Retailing and Leisure
    Dallen Timothy
Sport Tourism Development
    Thomas Hinch and James Higham
Sport Tourism: Interrelationships, Impact and Issues
    Brent Ritchie and Daryl Adair (eds)
Tourism Collaboration and Partnerships
    Bill Bramwell and Bernard Lane (eds)
Tourism and Development: Concepts and Issues
    Richard Sharpley and David Telfer (eds)
Tourism Employment: Analysis and Planning
    Michael Riley, Adele Ladkin, and Edith Szivas
Tourism in Peripheral Areas: Case Studies
    Frances Brown and Derek Hall (eds)

Please contact us for the latest book information:
Channel View Publications, Frankfurt Lodge, Clevedon Hall,
Victoria Road, Clevedon, BS21 7HH, England
http://www.channelviewpublications.com

TOURISM AND CULTURAL CHANGE
Series Editor: Mike Robinson
Centre for Tourism and Cultural Change, Sheffield Hallam University, UK

The Global Nomad
Backpacker Travel in Theory and Practice

Edited by
Greg Richards and Julie Wilson

CHANNEL VIEW PUBLICATIONS
Clevedon • Buffalo • Toronto • Sydney

Library of Congress Cataloging in Publication Data
The Global Nomad: Backpacker Travel in Theory and Practice
Edited by Greg Richards and Julie Wilson, 1st ed.
Tourism and Cultural Change
Includes bibliographical references and index.
1. Backpacking–Social aspects. I. Richards, Greg. II. Wilson, Julie. III. Series.
GV199.6.G55 2004
796.51–dc22   2003024106

British Library Cataloguing in Publication Data
A catalogue entry for this book is available from the British Library.

ISBN 1-873150-77-6 (hbk)
ISBN 1-873150-76-8 (pbk)

Channel View Publications
An imprint of Multilingual Matters Ltd

UK: Frankfurt Lodge, Clevedon Hall, Victoria Road, Clevedon BS21 7SJ.
USA: 2250 Military Road, Tonawanda, NY 14150, USA.
Canada: 5201 Dufferin Street, North York, Ontario, Canada M3H 5T8.
Australia: Footprint Books, PO Box 418, Church Point, NSW 2103, Australia.

Typeset by Wordworks Ltd.
Printed and bound in Great Britain by the Cromwell Press.

Contents

Preface

This volume is the product of the research programme on backpacking developed by the Backpacker Research Group (BRG) of the Association for Tourism and Leisure Education (ATLAS). The BRG was initiated in Hainan in October 2000 by a few ATLAS members who shared the general feeling that backpacker research was becoming an important field of enquiry, but that the research field was unstructured and ill-defined. The idea of forming the BRG, therefore, was to act as a platform for discussion and debate between backpacker researchers worldwide and to develop common research programmes and publications. The research programme is described in Chapter 1.

The structure and content of the book was finalised at Kasetsart University in Bangkok in July 2002, at a meeting attended by 15 members of the BRG, mainly researchers from universities in the UK, Germany, Australia and New Zealand. The meeting was addressed by Professor Erik Cohen of the Hebrew University of Jerusalem, and travel industry participation came from the International Student Travel Confederation (ISTC) and the Tourism Authority of Thailand (TAT). The two-day meeting generated intense discussion over the nature, meaning and form of backpacker travel, and the draft chapters in the present volume, presented at that meeting, acted as a catalyst for this discussion, though the range of debate was much wider and helped to identify those areas deserving of more research attention in future.

The meeting enabled feedback to be given to individual authors on their chapters and helped develop the common themes that run through this book.

In spite of the wide range of contributions, it is clear that large gaps remain to be covered. In particular, the geographical spread of the research presented here is mainly limited to Asia and Australasia. It is also clear that only some parts of the ATLAS BRG research programme have been covered (as discussed in the following chapter). In order to address these limitations, therefore, future meetings and research activities are being planned. At the time of writing, the second meeting of the BRG is planned for 2004, in India, and it is hoped to stage regular meetings in the future. Information about the ATLAS BRG activities can be found on the Internet (www.atlas-euro.org).

Acknowledgements

A large number of individuals and organisations were involved in the activities leading up to the production of this volume. It is impossible to mention all contributors individually, but some specific acknowledgements should be made.

Firstly the conception of the Backpacker Research Group owes much to late-night discussions held in Hainan. Thomas Bauer from Hong Kong, Brian King from Australia and Hans Wessblad from Sweden and others made important contributions to the structuring and development of the original research group. All those who subsequently became members of the group contributed to developing the research programme, through contributing either ideas or sources of information. Particular thanks are due to Irena Ateljevic for volunteering to undertake the literature review for the group, the fruits of which are presented in this volume. Developing the BRG would also have been impossible without the support of Leontine Onderwater of ATLAS, who helped to administrate the group and organise the first meeting. Reinier Straatemeier also helped to create the BRG discussion group and Internet page.

The Bangkok meeting at the International MBA school of Kasetsart University was a crucial step in bringing the group together and giving an impulse to the research programme. Our thanks therefore go to Nirundon Tapachai, who organised the meeting and provided invaluable support for our work there. Nirundon also helped to support the research programme by recruiting two of his students, Tisapan Kirdsuthi (Norna) and Prahpon Osodsamransook (Top), to assist in fieldwork undertaken in Bangkok. The MBA programme at Kasetsart also provided excellent facilities for the meeting. The meeting was also sponsored by the Tourism Authority of Thailand, who made useful contributions to our discussions of backpacker behaviour.

The Bangkok meeting also would not have been possible without the support of the International Student Travel Confederation (ISTC), who both provided resources for the meeting itself, and were also intimately involved in the development and implementation of the global nomad survey, the results of which are presented in Chapter 2 of this volume. David Jones, Helen Cunningham and Aafke van Sprundel helped to conceptualise, develop and implement the surveys.

While in Sydney in July 2002, Graeme Warring and Greg Cole kindly gave us the benefit of their extensive experience of the global 'backpacker industry', while fellow BRG member Ian McDonnell of the University of

Technology, Sydney supported us by recruiting two of his students, Jessica Djamil and Emma Hodson, as research assistants.

Dr Kate Gleeson of the School of Psychology at the University of the West of England deserves special thanks for her authoritative advice on research undertaken in Bangkok and Sydney on the social construction of backpacker travel; some of the findings of this are presented in Chapter 2. This particular study was made also possible by support from the UK Royal Geographical Society / HSBC Holdings, the UK Royal Society (Dudley Stamp Memorial Trust) and the Centre for Environment and Planning of the University of the West of England, Bristol (UK). Thanks are also due to Desiree Verbeek of Tilburg University (the Netherlands) who undertook the data entry task for this study.

Of course this volume would not have been possible without the hard work of the members of the Backpacker Research Group and particularly those who attended the inaugural meeting in Bangkok. Although not everyone who was present at that meeting is represented in this volume, nonetheless all who were there made a major contribution to developing the discussion on backpacking. Finally, thanks to Professor Erik Cohen for his insightful keynote address at the Bangkok meeting and our personal thanks also go to Erik and Nang for their hospitality in Bangkok and for introducing us to the various facets of local and global culture there.

Greg Richards and Julie Wilson
Gràcia, Barcelona
May 2003

Contributors

Dr Irena Ateljevic: Senior Lecturer, Travel & Tourism, Faculty of Business, Auckland University of Technology, New Zealand. E-mail: irena.ateljevic@ aut.ac.nz.

Jana Binder: PhD candidate, part-time lecturer and research assistant, Department of Cultural Anthropology and European Ethnology, Johann Wolfgang Goethe-University, Frankfurt am Main, Germany. E-mail: jana.binder@culture.in-flux.de.

Professor Erik Cohen: Department of Sociology, Hebrew University of Jerusalem, Israel. E-mail: mserik@mscc.huji.ac.il.

Dr Malcolm Cooper: Professor, Graduate School of Asia Pacific Studies, Ritsumeikan Asia Pacific University, Japan. E-mail: cooperm@apu.ac.jp.

Dr Stephen Doorne: Lecturer, Department of Tourism and Hospitality, University of the South Pacific, Fiji Islands. E-mail: doorne_s@usp.ac.fj.

Patricia Erfurt-Rauchhaupt: Associate Lecturer, Wide Bay Campus, University of Southern Queensland, Australia. E-mail: saratoga@ bigpond.net.au.

Tony Harrison: Research Officer, SLIMS Labour Market Intelligence Services, Glasgow, UK. E-mail: tony.harrison@slims.org.uk.

Denise Kain: Director of Sales & Marketing, Southern Cross Suites, Australia. E-mail: dkain@southerncrosssuites.com.au.

Professor Brian E.M. King: Head, School of Hospitality, Tourism and Marketing, Victoria University, Australia. E-mail: Brian.king@vu.edu.au.

Darya Maoz: instructor and PhD candidate, Department of Sociology and Anthropology, The Hebrew University of Jerusalem, Israel E-mail: daryariva@pob.huji.ac.il.

Kieran O'Mahony: Deputy Principal, Urangan State High School, Hervey Bay, Queensland, Australia. E-mail: kimah25@hotmail.com.

Ken Newlands: Lecturer, School Management and Entrepreneurship, UNITEC Institute of Technology, New Zealand. E-mail: knewlands@ unitec.ac.nz

Dr Greg Richards: Interarts Foundation, Barcelona, Catalunya, Spain. E-mail: grichards@interarts.net.

Clare Speed: Senior Lecturer in Tourism, Centre for Tourism, Sheffield Hallam University, UK. E-mail: c.speed@shu.ac.uk.

Dr Lee Slaughter: Associate Lecturer, School of Tourism and Leisure Management, University of Queensland, Australia. E-mail: ljslaughter@ uq.edu.au.

Paul Vance: Senior Lecturer in Tourism Management, Business School, University of Hertfordshire. E-mail: p.vance@excite.com.

Peter Welk, MA: Geographer/Ethnologist, Freiburg, Germany. E-mail: petewelk@yahoo.com.au.

Dr Julie Wilson: Research Fellow, Department of Geography, Rovira i Virgili University, Catalunya, Spain / University of the West of England, Bristol, UK. E-mail: jw@fll.urv.es.

Part 1

Introduction

Chapter 1

Drifting Towards the Global Nomad

GREG RICHARDS AND JULIE WILSON

According to James Clifford (1997: 1) travel is arguably an integral part of the postmodern 'new world order of mobility'. Society as a whole is becoming more restless and mobile, in contrast to the relatively rigid patterns of modernity. One of the cultural symbols of this increasingly mobile world is the backpacker. Backpackers are to be found in every corner of the globe, from remote villages in the Hindu Kush to the centres of London or Paris. They carry with them not only the emblematic physical baggage that gives them their name, but their cultural baggage as well. Their path is scattered with the trappings of the backpacker culture – banana pancakes, bars with 'video nights' and cheap hostels (Iyer, 1988). The questions that this book sets out to examine are why do so many people become 'global nomads', what do they gain from their travel, and what impact do they have on the places they visit? The varied contributions to this debate analyse both the theoretical implications of the backpacker phenomenon and the practical implications that it has for tourist destinations, local communities and policy makers.

According to some authors (e.g. Westerhausen, 2002) growing numbers of people are reacting to the alienation of modern society by adopting the lifestyle of the backpacker. Their nomadic existence is supported by the increasing ease of international travel, a growing network of budget hostels and travel companies, and the increasing flexibility of life path and work patterns. The growing demand for backpacker travel has stimulated a dense infrastructure of services dedicated to their needs, from backpacker hostels to companies organising bus trips, and the 'backpacker's bible'; the *Lonely Planet* guide books. As international conglomerates such as Accor begin moving into the backpacker market, the global nomad is also being incorporated into the 'McDonaldised' system of conventional tourism.

Academic interest in the motivations and experiences of backpackers has also grown in recent years, particularly as their economic, social and cultural significance for a range of destinations has become recognised.

Although the term 'backpacker' has been used in the travel literature since the 1970s, the backpacker phenomenon has only more recently been widely analysed by academic researchers. An analysis of the bibliography compiled by members of the Association of Tourism and Leisure Education (ATLAS) Backpacker Research Group (BRG) indicates that of 76 dated references relating to backpacker and youth travel, only 11 were published before 1990. This was the year in which the term 'backpacker' was first noted in the academic literature (Pearce, 1990). The growing interest in the topic is underlined by the fact that the ATLAS BRG alone now has more than 30 members in 11 countries.

At least until recently, much of the backpacker research has been under-taken in countries where the impact of backpacking is particularly evident, notably in South-East Asia, Australia and New Zealand (e.g. Elsrud, 1998; Hampton, 1998; Murphy, 2001; Ross, 1997). A second factor influencing the geographical distribution of backpacking studies has been the tendency for research to be undertaken 'on the road', usually in the more popular backpacker destinations in Asia and Australasia. Both of these patterns are reflected in the current volume, which draws most of its material from studies of popular backpacker destinations. It includes the first global survey of backpacking and combines diverse theoretical and empirical contributions to the study of this rapidly developing area.

In introducing the contributions in the rest of the volume, this chapter first considers the rationale for treating the backpacker as the 'global nomad'. An overview is then given of the research programme that stimu-lated the production of this volume, and finally the structure of the text and the individual contributions are outlined.

The Global Nomad

In the eyes of some commentators (e.g. MacCannell, 1976), tourism has become an icon of the rootlessness and alienation of modern life. The search for meaning in modern societies encourages pilgrimage to the sites of differentiation created by modernity and a search for the 'primitive' and pre-modern cultures it has displaced (MacCannell, 1992a). The disappear-ance of pre-modern cultures makes them all the more attractive as sites of tourism consumption and distinction – a chance to see the past before it disappears. Globalisation not only increases the speed at which cultures are marginalised, but also increases the speed with which the tourist can travel to see them. The presence of tourists around the globe is not only a sign of the progress of globalisation, it is also an integral part of the globalisation process. The presence of tourists ties more and more places into the global economy and modern communication networks. Tourists make the places they visit increasingly like home, which stimulates their restless search for difference still further (de Botton, 2002).

One of the cultures most under threat from the extension of modern society is that of the nomad. The nomad is:

> the one who can track a path through a seemingly illogical space without succumbing to nation-state and/or bourgeois organisation and mastery. The desert symbolises the site of critical and individual emancipation in Euro-American modernity; the nomad represents a subject position that offers an idealized model of movement based on perpetual displacement. (Kaplan, 1996: 66).

The nomad therefore represents not just the 'Other' to be visited, but also an idealised form of travel as liberation from the constraints of modern society. The global nomad crosses physical and cultural barriers with apparent ease in the search for difference and differentiation and in this way, the backpacker as nomad is placed in opposition to the 'tourist', caught in the iron cage of the modern tourist industry.

The sense of freedom offered by backpacking may well be one of its major attractions. As Binder and Welk show in their contributions to this volume, the ability to decide one's own itinerary, to change travel plans at will and not to be weighed down by cultural or physical baggage are features of travel important to backpackers (see also Chapter 2). The problem is, of course, that this freedom also has its own constraints, such as a lack of time or money, or the sheer physical impracticality of visiting all the sites one wants to see. The backpackers' freedom to travel also becomes a freedom to change the very places that they travel to see, as their own travel (however different it may be from that of the tourist) begins to impact on the 'unchanged' or 'authentic' cultures they want to visit. The backpacker is therefore forced into adopting a nomadic style of travel in an attempt to avoid other travellers – a strategy that is bound to fail, given the propensity of the _Lonely Planet_ and other guide books to open up new destinations to hordes of other travellers also seeking to escape from each other. Not surprisingly, what many backpackers regard as an 'authentic' destination is one untouched by other tourists (Timmermans, 2002).

Backpackers therefore seem to be driven into the far corners of the globe by the 'experience hunger' of modern society (de Cauter, 1995), which also forces them into becoming nomadic. Once they have consumed the experiences offered by one place, they need to move on to find new ones. Just like traditional nomadic peoples, the global nomad constantly moves from place to place. Patterns of movement are also cyclical; well-trodden routes emerge between 'enclaves', the arenas or stages of the backpacker subculture. The research programme established by the ATLAS BRG in 2000 was therefore entitled 'the Global Nomad'.

The Global Nomad Research Programme

The basic motivation for setting up the BRG stemmed from a perception among several members of ATLAS (particularly in Asia and Australasia) that backpacking was becoming an increasingly important social, cultural and economic phenomenon around the globe. In spite of this, there was felt to be a lack of research dealing with transnational or transcultural issues. Members of the group are drawn from a wide range of disciplinary backgrounds, including sociology, anthropology, geography, cultural studies, management and marketing. Current members of the group are drawn from eleven countries, with the UK, Australia and New Zealand having the biggest membership.

The first stage of the programme involved a review of previous research on backpacker tourism, which eventually provided the basis for the literature review by Ateljevic and Doorne in Chapter 4 of this volume. The bibliography underlined the fragmentation of the literature and indicated that many previous studies have been descriptive rather than analytical. The literature review also identified many gaps in previous research that the BRG has tried to address in its research programme.

Within the Global Nomad research programme, three main areas, or 'routes' were identified that were of interest to ATLAS BRG members, and these are described below.

Route 1: Where have the drifters gone?

In Cohen's (1973) classic typology of tourists the drifter is the archetypal backpacker, travelling to new destinations with no set itinerary. The restlessness of the drifter existence, with its attendant uncertainties, is arguably a good preparation for later life. Backpackers often see their travels as a form of self-development, in which they learn about themselves, their own society and other cultures. This knowledge can be used to advantage in the future – if you can survive as a backpacker, you can deal with any problems that life may throw at you later.

In theory then, backpacking should be a basis for success in later life. The ability to deal with uncertainty and change are arguably the very qualities required to operate effectively in postmodern societies. Backpackers might be expected to be more successful than their contemporaries who have not abandoned the security of their own society or culture. Yesterday's drifters should become today's movers and shakers.

But is this true? In order to test this proposition, it is important to look at the life history of former backpackers and see how their previous travel experience has impacted on their lives. Have backpackers been able to use their travel experience to develop their life chances? Does more travel experience lead to more success in life? Looking back, how do former backpackers reflect on their experiences? Are there common strands of experience to be identified?

In addition, backpackers can tell us a lot about how travel itself has changed. The journals that many backpackers keep are crammed with experiential and cognitive information about the reasons for their travels, the way in which they travelled, the people they met and the destinations they visited. By examining the travel diaries and stories of backpackers over a number of years, the changes in the nature of the backpacker experience in particular and of travel in general could be highlighted.

This route of the global nomad research concentrates on the following areas:

(1) Why do people become backpackers?
(2) What do they experience on their travels?
(3) How has the backpacking experience changed over time?
(4) What impact does backpacking have on later life?

These questions are particularly important given the perception that 'real' backpacking is a dying art (see Cederholm, 1999). Westerhausen (2002) also suggests that 'real' backpackers increasingly have to flee the onslaught of tourism. What changes in the nature of backpacking or its participants could explain this? What do these developments in backpacking tell us about the changing nature of society as a whole?

Route 2: On the beaten track

Backpackers, because of their 'nomadic' existence, are very difficult to monitor. In addition, the common image of backpackers as low-budget or even undesirable tourists has meant that there has been relatively little research on their activities in the past.

However, backpackers are an important element of the youth tourism market and growing incomes and freedom to travel are likely to make this market even more important in future. Backpackers are also crucial for certain destinations and certain types of travel products (such as coach travel, budget accommodation, 'student' travel - see Vance, Chapter 14). Backpackers also arguably set new travel trends, opening up new destinations and developing new markets, for example in developing destinations (Hampton, 1998; Scheyvens, 2002).

The decision-making process of backpackers is therefore arguably of significance for the tourism market as a whole. Because of the relatively long travel times and flexible itineraries of backpackers, they are far more likely than most other travellers to come into contact with previously-unknown tourist attractions.

To evaluate the activities and impacts of current backpackers in more detail, it is important to undertake transnational research that can track the movements of travellers between one destination and another, and examine their decision-making processes. This information should be of value to a wide range of tourism policy makers and marketeers.

This research route examines:

(1) Who are the backpackers?
(2) Why do they choose backpacking?
(3) Which destinations do they visit?
(4) How do they travel?
(5) What are their motivations for choosing specific destinations and travel routes?
(6) What sources of information do they use on their travels?

This research involves surveys of backpackers to different destinations, with standardised questionnaires to provide comparative data. In the current volume, the development of this questionnaire is discussed along with the findings of surveys of backpackers from different countries of origin (Richards & Wilson, Chapter 2) and a specific destination-based study in New Zealand (Newlands, Chapter 13).

Route 3: Tourists of the future

The global nomads of today are potentially the avid tourists of the future. Their backpacking experience will have an important influence on the destinations they choose to visit in later life, possibly with their families and friends. Attracting backpackers may therefore be seen as an important step in a long-term marketing policy for certain destinations.

In looking at travel by young people as part of the educational experience, this route will examine the role of backpacking in forming and changing destination image. Do backpackers have a more positive image of the destination as a result of their experience? Are they more likely to make a repeat visit in future?

By conducting a longitudinal study of backpackers before and after their travels in different countries, the effect of backpacking on destination image could be directly monitored. Attitudes to travel can also be analysed, such as the awareness of environmental, social and cultural issues in the destination and the impact of these on destination choice and modes of travel and accommodation.

The information generated by this research route could be used to assess the potential of backpacking as a learning experience for future travel, and the extent to which attitudes formed during youth travel are likely to influence future travel behaviour. The impact that working abroad has on on cultural attitudes is currently the subject of a joint study by ATLAS and the International Student Travel Confederation.

Figure 1.1 summarises some of the relationships being examined by the ATLAS BRG. In relation to this draft conceptual model, route 1 of the Global Nomad research programme is concerned with the activities and experiences of backpackers, as well as the contribution of backpacking to personal development. Route 2 focuses on the determinants and motivations of those participating, while route 3 focuses on feedback of experience into future travel choices (thus linking together routes 1 and 2). Taken

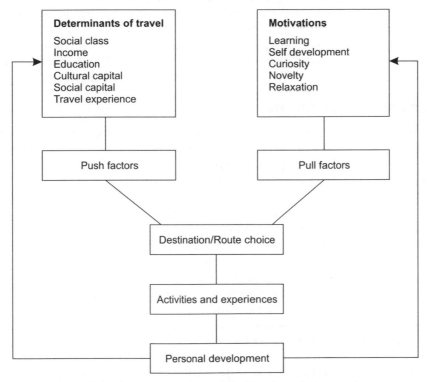

Figure 1.1 BRG draft conceptual model of backpacker travel

together, these different research themes can hopefully produce a more holistic view of the phenomenon of backpacking.

Developing the Research Programme

In order to launch the research programme and to provide a forum for discussion on backpacker research, an expert meeting was convened in Bangkok in July 2002. This meeting brought together 15 members of the BRG, and presentations were made of research from different countries and from different disciplinary perspectives. Given the distribution of BRG members, it is not surprising that contributions on backpacking in Asia and Australasia predominated. There was also a clear split between contributions that were largely theoretical (dealing largely with 'route 1' of the research programme) and those that were more applied ('route 2'). The applied papers tended to come from Australasia, where academics are helping practitioners deal with the practical consequences of the expansion of backpacker tourism. The European contributions generally tried to explain backpacking as a socio-cultural phenomenon. This division between theory and practice is clear in those papers that were developed into chapters for this volume. Researchers have also tended to concentrate on the first two routes of the research programme. This is an issue that will be taken up in the concluding chapter, which outlines potential areas for future research.

Structure of this Volume

The backpacking phenomenon has developed considerably over the past 30 years, progressing from a marginal activity of a handful of 'drifters' to a major global industry. Although backpacking is increasingly seen by many destinations as an important tourism market, our literature survey indicated that relatively little academic research has been undertaken on either the backpackers or the backpacker industry. This volume explores backpacking from a range of different disciplinary and spatial perspectives, in an attempt to shed light on the implications of backpacking for the travellers themselves and for the places they visit. The basic aim of the text is to draw together these different perspectives to provide an overview of the meaning, impact and significance of backpacking. Although the geographical coverage of the case studies presented is perhaps limited, the different perspectives collected in this volume provide a useful introduction to many facets of backpacking and backpacker (sub)culture(s) that are significant worldwide.

Following this introduction to the backpacker research programme, in Chapter 2 Richards and Wilson review data on the global backpacking market. A study of 2300 travellers in eight countries is used to analyse the behaviour, motivations and profile of backpackers across destinations worldwide. The findings of this study are compared with previous surveys of backpackers to try and gauge how representative these data are of backpacking as a whole. In addition, findings obtained from a study on the social construction of backpacker travel are examined.

The second part of the volume deals largely with route 1 of the research programme. It looks at the behaviour of backpackers 'on the road': how they travel, where and when, and examines the behaviour of backpackers in particular spatial contexts, drawing particularly on the rich backpacking experience of destinations in South East Asia, Australia and New Zealand. These analyses link a number of different theoretical perspectives, touching on sociological, anthropological, geographical and literary issues. This review of backpacking as a modern or postmodern phenomenon opens with Erik Cohen's review of issues in backpacker research over the past 30 years (Chapter 3). Based on his own vast experience in the field, Cohen argues that modern backpackers differ from the original 'drifters' of 30 years ago. Although many backpackers aspire to the ideology of drifting, they in fact resemble 'ordinary tourists' in terms of their travel-styles and behaviour. This underlines what Cohen sees as an emerging gap between the ideology and practice of backpacking. He also notes that, as backpacking has changed over the years, it has also diversified, making attempts to lump all travellers together as 'backpackers' more problematic.

In Chapter 4, Irena Ateljevic and Stephen Doorne provide a wider review of the backpacker literature. They pay particular attention to the relationship between backpacker travel, behaviour and identity, and demonstrate how the discussion about backpacking has shifted from the concept of backpackers as being marginal in terms of their behaviour and their treatment by the tourism industry, to being an attractive market. In Chapter 5, Peter Welk discusses the issue of identity formation among backpackers, based on field research in Asia and Australasia. He sees back-packers as developing their own 'scene' or 'culture' in which opposition between backpackers and conventional tourists becomes crucial to the self-identification of backpackers. In this way, Welk argues, backpackers distinguish themselves along symbolic lines, an important element of which is an anti-tourist attitude. Jana Binder adopts a qualitative anthropo-logical approach to the analysis of backpackers on the road in Chapter 6. Through a series of observations and conversations with backpackers in South-East Asia, she demonstrates the complex relationship between self-representation and backpacking practice, echoing Cohen's identifica-tion of a rift between the ideology and practice of backpacking.

A very specific aspect of the backpacking market is dealt with by Darya Maoz in Chapter 7. She analyses the behaviour and attitudes of young Israeli backpackers in India, and shows how socialisation processes in Israeli society have a profound impact on styles of backpacking. She sees a distinction between the younger 'conquerors' fresh out of military service, who often see backpacking as an extension of the harsh army regime, and the older 'settlers' who pay more attention to local people and local culture. Although these Israeli backpackers cannot be considered typical of the market as a whole, theirs is an important backpacking subculture, whose presence is often remarked upon by other backpackers.

In Chapter 8 Julie Wilson and Greg Richards use literary sources to analyse the cultural referents of backpackers. They trace the books and novels that have acted as models for the travel behaviour of backpackers, outlining the development from 'writers who travel' to 'travellers who write'. They argue that the major themes found in the writings of Ernest Hemingway, Bruce Chatwin, Paul Theroux, Bill Bryson and other key authors are resonant in backpacker culture. Among these themes are the subcultural norms of tourist angst, rebelliousness, authenticity and the rituals of indulgence.

As a whole, the chapters in this second part attempt to trace the contours of the emerging backpacker (sub)culture(s).

Part 3 of the text contains more applied studies of backpacking. Many of these studies are concerned with the extent to which backpacking has begun to be recognised by the tourist industry and policy makers. In Chapter 9 for example, Clare Speed and Tony Harrison analyse the development of backpacking in Scotland, and show how official recognition of backpackers as a market segment by the public sector has been relatively slow, underlining the contradictions of formalising an informal market.

In contrast, Lee Slaughter demonstrates in Chapter 10 how rapidly Australian entrepreneurs and policy makers have taken to backpackers, with a plethora of market studies in recent years. Using a meta-analysis of these studies she draws a profile of the backpacker in Australia, showing that the classic picture of a young budget traveller staying in cheap accommodation and having a flexible itinerary is still appropriate. In Chapter 11 Malcolm Cooper, Kieran O'Mahony and Patricia Erfurt show that backpackers have also become an important element of the Australian economy – not just through their tourism consumption, but also by working their way round the country. This chapter traces the 'Harvest Trail' taken by many backpackers as they follow the fruit harvests in search of work. The flexible labour force provided by these mobile travellers has become an integral part of the rural economy in many areas.

Denise Kain and Brian King, in Chapter 12, examine the basis of product purchase decisions by backpackers in Australia. They demonstrate that backpackers are very price-conscious (although they do not always place importance on discount programmes), while investing in a great deal of information searching prior to departure. Challenging the widely held idea that the Internet will rapidly replace the established distribution channels, they conclude that backpackers are not always influenced by the Internet in their choices and stress the importance of 'word of mouth' communication in backpacker information exchange.

The final two chapters in Part 3 look at the backpacker market in New Zealand, which is rapidly becoming an important backpacker destination in its own right rather than simply an extension of a trip to Australia. In Chapter 13 Ken Newlands presents the results of a survey of backpackers in the major travel hubs of New Zealand. He confirms the importance of pre-departure information search in an analysis of booking behaviour, although he emphasises that informal sources of information exchange are more important when 'on the road'. He also examines the links with home and the contradiction of being in close contact even when on the other side of the world.

Paul Vance concentrates on the transport modes used by backpackers in Chapter 14. Drawing on a conceptual framework of backpacker transport choice in the context of New Zealand, he argues that while backpacker decisions about transport are complex, travel patterns are to a large extent influenced by the development of an identifiable traveller transport infra-structure.

In the concluding section, Greg Richards and Julie Wilson draw together the major themes presented in the different contributions to the research programme and identify some major issues in backpacker research. They argue that the context of backpacking is changing rapidly as the market expands, and that different types or styles of backpacking are beginning to emerge. They also highlight the tendency for backpacking to involve a 'suspension' of cultural norms, rather than either a reversal or extension or everyday life. In making recommendations for further research, Richards and Wilson highlight the gap that has emerged between the qualitative, ethnographic tradition related to theoretical studies of backpacking and the marketing-based approaches developed in more applied studies – a division that is also reproduced in the current volume. They argue that the development of a range of research tools is required to capture the multidimensional nature of the increasingly complex backpacker 'scene' and its surrounding environment.

Chapter 2

The Global Nomad: Motivations and Behaviour of Independent Travellers Worldwide

GREG RICHARDS AND JULIE WILSON

Given the global nature of backpacking, the development of comparative research in different regions of the world was considered important for the ATLAS Backpacker Research Programme. One of the first steps was therefore to conduct a major global transnational quantitative survey of backpackers. The data generated by this survey provide a profile of backpackers and their motivations, behaviour and experience in different contexts. These data also help to contextualise the individual qualitative and quantitative studies presented in the rest of this volume.

As Ateljevic and Doorne illustrate in Chapter 4 of this volume, most previous studies of backpacking have tended to be snapshots of activity in specific places at particular moments in time. A more comprehensive view of backpacking can be obtained by undertaking a transnational study with a common methodology. This can generate comparisons of backpacking in different regions and provide a tool for conducting comparative research over time. This chapter presents the results of the first global transnational survey of young independent travellers, and serves to contextualise backpacking within the wider travel market. Later in the chapter, specific research on the social construction of backpacking is presented.

The first 'global nomad' survey was designed and executed with the support of the International Student Travel Confederation (ISTC), a global network of student travel organisations. Through their network of travel companies worldwide, they were able to provide access to young travellers, particularly students. As the studies of backpackers in the rest of this volume indicate, students are an extremely important segment of the backpacker market. As Slaughter shows in Chapter 10, for example, the proportion of students in the backpacker market as a whole is estimated to be between 26% and 36%. Students also have a strong presence in other related segments of the independent travel market. For example the ATLAS Cultural Tourism Surveys (Richards, 2001) have indicated that more than 50% of cultural tourists under the age of 30 are students.

The young independent traveller market is also an extremely important segment of world tourism. Young travellers tend to travel more frequently and for longer periods than many older tourists or those taking package holidays. They also represent a major growth segment, as incomes rise among young people and new markets are opened up in newly industrialising economies and in Central and Eastern Europe.

In the past, however, relatively little empirical research was done on the young independent traveller or the backpacker market. As Ateljevic and Doorne point out in Chapter 4 of this volume, governments were often negative or neutral as far as encouraging backpacker tourism was concerned. There were isolated attempts to study the youth travel market in Europe (e.g. Seekings, 1998), but such research was usually based on secondary sources rather than on original survey data. More recently a lot of attention has been focused on the growth of backpacker tourism, and this has spawned a number of surveys at national level, particularly in Australia and New Zealand (e.g. Bureau of Tourism Research, 2000b; Tourism New Zealand, 1999). The interest in backpacking in these countries seems to stem from the relatively important role played by backpackers in the total tourism market. Governments have therefore played a major role in stimulating research into the backpacker market, as Speed and Harrison show in Chapter 9 of this volume. Most of the information on the backpacker market therefore comes from surveys conducted by individual companies (e.g. TNT/Uni Travel, 2003) which are often not available to third parties, and from sub-analyses of national tourism surveys.

The predominance of individual commissioned surveys means that it is difficult to make comparisons between them. Some attempts have been made to compare studies in order to provide a longitudinal picture of market developments, as Slaughter has done in Chapter 10 of this volume. However it is usually only possible to compare a limited number of questions between surveys, and there are also problems of different wording and of categorising questions.

In order to develop a more consistent and detailed picture of the motivations and travel behaviour of backpackers and other young independent travellers, therefore, the ATLAS Backpacker Research Group (BRG) launched its first major survey in 2002. In collaboration with ISTC, the group developed a quantitative survey instrument based on a review of backpacking and youth travel literature and items contributed by BRG group members. The resulting instrument therefore combines both theoretical and applied perspectives on independent travel in general and backpacking in particular.

The survey combined the study of the social and cultural aspects of young travellers (their backgrounds, motivations and experiences) with data on the way in which the travellers purchased their travel and gathered information, as well as their destinations and previous travel experience. One of the important elements of the questionnaire is a self-definition question that asks respondents to classify themselves as 'backpackers', 'travellers' or 'tourists' during their most recent long trip. This self-definition approach is different from that used by most previous studies of backpacking, which usually attempt to use a series of external characteristics to identify backpackers. The basic characteristics used tend to be: use of budget accommodation, flexibility, independently arranged itineraries, an emphasis on social contact with fellow-travellers and relatively long travel duration (see Part 3 of this volume). Interestingly, the use of a backpack was not usually regarded as a defining characteristic of backpackers in previous studies (Timmermans, 2002). The problem with defining backpackers through their behavioural characteristics is that this does not uncover how the participants see themselves. By allowing the respondents to the global nomad survey to define their own travelstyle, it was hoped that more light could be shed on the relationship between previous definitions and the actual experience of travellers themselves.

The research was conducted during the spring of 2002, using mailing lists provided by travel company members of ISTC in different countries. The countries surveyed were chosen to give a range of different world regions and travel contexts. In total the survey generated over 2300 responses from eight countries: Canada, Czech Republic, Hong Kong, Mexico, Slovenia, South Africa, Sweden and the UK. Forty-two different nationalities were represented in the sample, emphasising the mobility of the international student population (although most of the respondents were nationals of these eight countries). These countries were selected to provide a range of different types of generating markets in Africa, the Americas, Asia and Europe.

Potential respondents were approached by email and asked to participate in the survey via the Internet. The survey population included individuals on the email lists of major student travel companies in the countries concerned. The survey made use of a special Internet survey system designed for ISTC. This system allows respondents to enter their responses to the questionnaire via a web page and the responses to individual questions are saved in a Microsoft Excel spreadsheet as well as being available for viewing in summary form via Internet. The Excel data were translated into SPSS format to allow for more detailed analysis.

While the methodology adopted for this survey has the advantage of generating a large amount of data on the global backpacking market, it also has a number of obvious limitations. The use of student travel companies to provide the survey population means that the sample consists predominantly of students, and that the age range is limited to relatively young travellers. The use of email and the Internet also limits the sample of travellers to those with access to the Internet, although in the student travel market this is unlikely to be as much of a barrier as in other travel segments.

One way of checking the generalisability of the sample is to compare the profile of respondents with those obtained in other surveys using different methods. In Chapter 13 of this volume, for example, Ken Newlands describes the use of an adapted version of the BRG survey with travellers in New Zealand. This survey was administered at backpacker accommodation, and should therefore provide a wider sample of those engaged in backpacking in New Zealand. A comparison of the two surveys (selecting only the backpackers to New Zealand in the ATLAS/ISTC survey) indicates that both samples have a high proportion of female respondents (over 60%), a high proportion of students (almost 30% in Newland's survey, 55% for the ATLAS/ISTC survey) and high education levels (with over half of the respondents having a degree in both studies). Newland's respondents have a higher average income, which is to be expected given the lower proportion of students. In terms of motivation, both samples listed exploring other cultures, increasing knowledge and mental relaxation in their top five motivations.

Comparisons with other studies also show a relatively high level of consistency. The Australian studies reviewed by Slaughter in Chapter 10, for example, indicate that students tend to be the largest occupational group. Research by TNT/UNI Travel (2003) in Australia also indicates that the educational level and age distribution of backpackers is similar to the global nomad survey sample.

In general terms, therefore, the global nomad survey might be considered to give a reasonable indication of independent traveller behaviour, particularly in the student travel market. While it cannot claim to be representative of all such travellers globally, it is a useful tool for comparing 'backpackers' with other young tourists and for comparing styles of backpacking in different world regions. The following sections describe the profile, motivation and activities of the travellers surveyed.

Who are the Travellers?

One remarkable aspect of the survey was that there were more female respondents (67%) than male respondents (33%). Many observations in the field and longitudinal surveys of travellers in Australia have indicated a more even distribution of female and male travellers (see Slaughter, Chapter 10 of this volume), although Speed and Harrison (Chapter 9), Kain and King (Chapter 12) and Newlands (Chapter 13) also found a predominance of women in their samples of backpackers.

The vast majority of respondents were students (70%), which is not surprising given the source of the survey population. The predominance of students is also reflected in the age profile of the respondents, more than 60% of whom were aged between 20 and 25. Only 5% of the sample was aged over 30. This age profile is, however, also typical for studies of backpackers, as data from Australia and New Zealand indicate (Slaughter, Chapter 10; Newlands, Chapter 13). The respondents had a relatively high level of education, with 34% having already gained a higher-education degree and a further 25% still studying for one.

The relatively low incomes of students were also reflected in the annual income of the respondents. Half of the total respondents had an income of US$5000 or less, although income levels were heavily dependent on the country of origin. This underlines the importance of saving for a major trip, as the average expenditure approached the usual annual income of the respondents in many cases. As Cooper, O'Mahony and Erfurt demonstrate in Chapter 11, working to earn money during the trip has become a major part of the backpacking experience.

Another important question regarding the 'identity' of the young travellers was the extent to which they considered themselves to be 'travellers' as opposed to 'backpackers' or 'tourists'. Over half of the sample identified with the label 'traveller', compared with almost a third who called themselves 'backpackers'. Less than 20% considered themselves 'tourists'. In general, older respondents were more likely to call themselves 'travellers', while the 'tourist' label was most popular among respondents under the age of 20. Self-designation also tended to change with travel experience, with those respondents who had taken more trips more often calling themselves backpackers or travellers (Table 2.1). The proportion of backpackers also varied significantly according to origin country. Almost half of the respondents sampled in Slovenia called themselves backpackers, compared with a third of those in Canada and Mexico and just over a quarter of respondents in Hong Kong and the Czech Republic. South-African-based respondents were particularly likely to see

Table 2.1 Traveller type by previous travel experience (%)

	Travel experience (number of trips)			
	1–3	*4–6*	*7–10*	*10+*
Backpacker	25.6	29.4	29.1	15.9
Traveller	26.3	31.1	29.5	13.1
Tourist	34.5	32.7	26.2	6.6

themselves as travellers (65%) whereas Hong-Kong-based respondents were much more likely to be tourists.

The identification with the 'traveller' concept was so strong among some respondents that they listed this as their occupation as well. This indicates that a definition of backpackers on the basis of external characteristics may differ considerably from the experience of the travellers themselves. As most previous studies of 'backpackers' (and most of the research in this volume) has been based on external definition, caution needs to exercised in generalising the researcher's perceptions of backpackers to the traveller population as a whole. The vast majority of the young travellers surveyed would be classified as 'backpackers' according to the definition of Pearce (1990), but there are many individuals who are not willing to identify themselves with this label. The social construction of backpacking research presented later in this chapter examines this issue in more detail.

Where do they Travel?

The survey respondents were asked to indicate the destinations they had visited during their entire travel career, as well as the destinations they had visited during their last major trip.

On average, the respondents had made six trips outside their region of residence over their entire travel career. Given the low average age of the respondents and the fact that these trips often involve inter-continental travel, the respondents demonstrate a high level of travel activity. Not surprisingly, however, the number of trips increases with age. Those under 20 had taken five trips on average, compared with eight trips for those aged over 30.

The destination of the trips taken was naturally strongly influenced by the country of residence. People tended to travel within their own world region more frequently. The pattern of destinations also generally reflected the distribution of international tourism, which is largely concentrated in the industrialised 'north'. Europe had been visited by more than 50% of respondents, North America by almost 50% and other world regions by less than 20%.

As travel experience increases, so people tend to travel further afield. The average visitor to Northern Europe had made only five major trips previously, compared with eight trips for visitors to Australia, and more than ten trips for those visiting India. This gives some indirect support for the idea of a travel career (Pearce, 1993) among the respondents, with Europeans, for example, tending to travel within Europe initially, and then to visit Australasia for their first big intercontinental trip before striking out for less developed Asian destinations.

There is some evidence of differentiation between destinations in terms of traveller types. Some destinations, such as South-East Asia, Australasia and South America were dominated by backpackers, whereas in North America travellers outnumbered backpackers. This pattern may in fact be caused by travellers being socialised into a particular group while they are travelling. It is likely, for example, that those visiting established backpacker centres such as Bangkok or Sydney will come across the term 'backpacker' far more often than other travellers will.

A selection of individual countries indicates that Asian destinations tended to have the highest proportion of self-defined backpackers, with the lowest proportion of backpackers being found in USA and Canada (Table 2.2). There seems to be a link between the phase of tourism development and the travelstyle. Relatively 'mature' destinations in North America and Europe have the lowest proportions of backpackers, while relatively 'new' destinations such as Vietnam have the highest. This may be an indication of the 'pioneer' function of backpackers, who arguably blaze a trail for the travellers or tourists who follow.

Backpackers also tended to visit more countries during their trips than travellers or tourists did. The average backpacker had visited 2.4 countries during his or her last major trip, compared with 1.8 for travellers and 1.7 for tourists.

Trip Characteristics

The main trips taken by survey respondents tended to be relatively long. The average trip length was more than 60 days, although most trips were less than 30 days and almost 30% were 14 days or less. Trip length tended to be related to factors such as occupation and income, with those in work and with higher incomes travelling longer than students. Trip length also differed with travelstyle, 'tourists' travelling for an average of 40 days, 'travellers' averaging 63 days and 'backpackers' 73 days. There was, however, no significant difference in trip length with age. It seems that travellers from different countries have constraints on travel at different ages, and this produced a fairly even pattern of trip length with age in the survey as a whole.

The general tendency for backpackers to favour budget accommodation was confirmed by the global nomad survey (Table 2.3). Backpacker hostels were used by almost 70% of 'backpackers', compared with only 19% of travellers and 8% of tourists. Table 2.3 shows that the vast majority of backpackers stayed at backpacker hostels, guest houses or with friends and relatives. Hotels were most favoured by tourists, while travellers tended to be more evenly spread across different accommodation types. Not surprisingly, the proportion of respondents staying in backpacker hostels varied strongly according to the destination. Over two-thirds of visitors to Thailand used a backpacker hostel, compared with just under half the visitors to Australia and only 16% in Spain. This tends to suggest that hostel use is strongly influenced by supply, with major backpacker centres such as Bangkok providing ample dedicated backpacker accommodation. Although backpackers predominated at backpacker hostels, about 30% of hostel users designated themselves as 'travellers' or 'tourists'. This points to the lack of a clear distinction between backpackers and travellers as far as the use of dedicated backpacker accommodation was concerned. This may contradict Westerhausen's (2002) idea that backpackers use a different travel infrastructure from other tourists. Perhaps, as Welk suggests in Chapter 5, the fact that tourists, travellers and backpackers use the same

Table 2.2 Proportions of backpackers, travellers and tourists visiting selected destinations

Destination	% visitors to destination		
	Backpacker	Traveller	Tourist
Australia	49.5	38.3	12.1
Canada	26.7	53.4	19.8
France	35.4	48.9	15.7
India	66.7	29.6	3.7
New Zealand	65.0	35.0	0.0
Thailand	75.4	20.3	4.2
Turkey	40.7	31.5	27.8
UK	30.8	52.2	17.0
USA	22.8	61.7	15.6
Vietnam	87.5	12.5	0.0

infrastructure might actually be a source of differentiation between these groups, as they use the same tourism facilities but in distinctive ways.

A further widely-quoted feature of backpacker travel is the flexibility of the travel itinerary. On the one hand, this may suggest that there is little planning of the trip, but it may also mean that backpackers need to gather more information about the destination in order to plan their own itineraries.

Young travellers tend to be information-intensive, consulting a wide range of information sources before departure. Unlike most other surveys of traveller information sources, the Internet is the main form of information gathering for these young people, outstripping family and friends (Table 2.4). The level of Internet use is likely to be higher than average among our sample given the survey method. However, a recent survey of backpackers in Australia indicated that 44% had used the Internet to gather information prior to arrival (TNT/Uni Travel, 2003). A comparison with Ken Newland's survey in New Zealand (Chapter 13) also shows that the Internet was used by more than half of his sample, which indicates that the overestimation in the global nomad survey may be relatively low. The type of information source used varies little with increasing travel experience, with the exception of guide books. Guide books were used by only 30% of those who had taken three trips or less compared with 50% of those having taken ten trips or more. This difference became even more marked during the trip, when 60% of the most experienced travellers had a guidebook with them. Guidebooks were also consulted by more than 60% of backpackers prior to departure, compared with less than 20% of tourists. This also matches the social construction of backpacking study results, which indi-

Table 2.3 Accommodation use by traveller type

Accommodation type	*% Respondents*		
	Backpackers	*Travellers*	*Tourists*
Backpacker hostels	69	19	8
Youth hostels	36	16	12
Friends and relatives	29	50	40
Independent guest house	23	13	9
Camping	19	11	7
Hotels	18	32	53
Bed and breakfast	14	16	12
Self catering	6	10	8
Campervan	1	1	1

cated a high level of recognition of the *Lonely Planet* as the 'backpacker's bible' (see Table 2.9 below). This distinction was also maintained in terms of the information sources consulted during the trip, with almost 70% of back-packers using guidebooks, compared with almost a third of tourists. This suggests that backpackers are far more likely to buy a guidebook prior to travel and then use the same guidebook as an information source while travelling. The portability of guidebooks is clearly one of the major advantages for backpackers. Not only was *Lonely Planet* the most frequently used guidebook, but backpackers were far more likely to use it than other travellers were. Backpackers were also more likely to use accommodation providers and fellow travellers for information, which emphasises the prevalence of information and story-swapping on the backpacker 'scene'.

In terms of the intensity of information use, most respondents used a range of different information sources both prior to departure and during their trip. Experienced travellers consulted significantly more sources, both pre- and post-departure. Backpackers were also likely to consult more sources of information than other respondents were, usually because of their use of personal recommendation from fellow travellers.

For travel booking, most respondents used travel agents, although again this is likely to have been affected by the sourcing of respondents from travel agency lists. Backpackers were more likely than other respondents to go to specialist youth or student travel agents than other types of travellers

Table 2.4 Information sources consulted prior to departure by traveller type

Information sources consulted	Backpacker	Traveller	Tourist	Significance level
Internet	77.3	70.7	64.0	0.000
Family, friends	66.8	72.3	74.5	0.008
Guide books	60.5	29.9	19.1	0.000
Travel agency	28.5	36.3	43.1	0.000
Previous visit	21.7	33.3	27.8	0.000
Newspaper, magazine	20.6	24.1	23.9	ns
Tour operator brochure	12.3	11.0	15.9	0.048
Tourist board	11.5	11.8	11.3	ns
TV, radio	10.2	9.9	12.3	ns
Airline	8.6	10.6	13.1	ns
Trade shows	1.4	1.4	1.8	ns

were. In terms of accommodation, however, very few booked in advance, and this was particularly marked for backpackers. In spite of the growth of specialists offering at least one night's accommodation as an add-on to flights, it seems most people are happy to arrive in the destination and organise things themselves. In particular more experienced travellers were less likely to book in advance.

Booking lead-time was not significantly different for the different types of travellers, all of whom tended to plan their travel an average of six weeks in advance. Travel booking lead-time rose for longer trips, reaching almost two months for trips of four to six months' duration.

Information on expenditure during the trip was particularly interesting given the current discussions about the benefits and costs of developing tourism and the emerging view of backpackers as a lucrative new market (e.g. Bureau of Tourism Research, 2002b; Tourism New Zealand, 2000). The average daily spend of respondents was relatively low, with over half the sample estimating their spend to be less than US$20 a day (Table 2.5). The level of daily spend is inversely related to the length of stay. However in terms of total spend, young travellers still make an important contribution to the economy of the destination they visit. The average total spend in the destination is at least US$1200, which is more than most 'high-spending' tourists spend during a shorter stay in the destination. The total spend including travel to the destination is almost US$2200 for a backpacker, which is higher than for either travellers (US$1800) or tourists (US$1470). Expenditure is also clearly influenced by income, with those on incomes over US$20,000 a year spending almost twice as much on average as those earning less than US$5000.

Table 2.5 Average daily spend in destination by traveller type

	Traveller type (%)			
Average daily expenditure (US$)	*Backpacker*	*Traveller*	*Tourist*	*Total*
$50–10	23.4	21.9	19.8	22.0
$11–20	34.3	32.5	29.9	32.7
$21–30	22.4	20.2	22.7	21.3
$31–40	9.9	12.1	10.2	11.1
$41–50	7.1	7.5	7.3	7.3
Over $50	2.8	5.8	10.2	5.6
Total	100	100	100	100

The level of expenditure is also heavily influenced by the destinations visited as well as by the length of the trip. The average total spend for a trip to Australia, including travel, was more than US$4600, whereas the average visitor to Thailand spent US$2200 and the average spend for Turkey was US$700.

There is also some indirect evidence against the idea that hardened backpackers tend to be more careful with their money. In fact those backpackers with more travel experience spend more per day than relatively inexperienced backpackers do. This is probably because they are older and have higher incomes, and may support the idea that people who travel to countries as relatively poor backpackers return later as wealthier travellers and spend more money.

Motivations and Activities

The basic motivations for travel among the respondents are a mixture of exploration, excitement and relaxation (Table 2.6). Some respondents were highly oriented towards experiencing as much as possible during their trip. This seems to be particularly true for backpackers, who tended to be motivated by experiential factors, whereas tourists were more likely to be in search of relaxation. The fact that a relatively high proportion of travellers were visiting friends and relatives perhaps explains the fact that they tended to place more emphasis on visiting friends and relatives and developing close friendships than other groups did. A relatively small proportion of respondents said they were travelling for more altruistic motives, such as contributing something to the places they visit. What is clear, however, is that trips usually combine at least two different main motives, often relaxation and excitement or lazing on the beach and cultural encounters.

The different traveller types exhibited significant differences in motivation. Backpackers in particular tend to emphasise items related to experience seeking and are relatively less concerned about relaxation. In accordance with Pearce's (1990) definitional characteristics, backpackers are motivated more by a desire to meet fellow travellers than other respondents are. Travellers were particularly more likely to be visiting friends and relatives, and tourists tended to emphasise relaxation-related motives.

Perhaps surprisingly, there was relatively little difference in motivation between travellers in terms of length of stay. Motivations also varied little with increasing travel experience, perhaps reflecting a relatively stable set of basic travel motives. It is likely that motivations will differ more widely between different trips taken by the same individual, but this could not be measured in the current survey.

Table 2.6 Motivation for undertaking last main trip by traveller type (scale: 1 = of no importance, 5 = very important)

Motivation: I went on trip to:	Traveller type			
	Backpacker	Traveller	Tourist	Total
Explore other cultures	4.6	4.4	4.2	4.4
Experience excitement	4.3	4.1	4.0	4.2
Increase my knowledge	4.1	4.0	3.8	4.0
Relax mentally	3.9	3.8	4.0	3.8
Have a good time with friends	3.7	3.7	3.7	3.7
Interact with local people	3.9	3.7	3.4	3.7
Challenge my abilities	3.9	3.7	3.2	3.7
Build friendships with others	3.6	3.6	3.3	3.6
Visit friends and relatives (VFR)	2.9	3.7	3.5	3.4
Use my imagination	3.7	3.4	3.0	3.4
Avoid hustle and bustle	3.5	3.4	3.4	3.4
Find myself	3.4	3.3	3.0	3.3
Relax physically	3.2	3.3	3.5	3.3
Develop close friendships	3.1	3.3	3.0	3.2
Associate with other travellers	3.5	3.0	2.9	3.1
Be in a calm atmosphere	3.1	2.9	3.1	3.0
Use my physical abilities/skills	3.2	2.9	2.7	3.0
Gain a feeling of belonging	2.8	3.0	2.9	2.9
Contribute something to the places I visit	2.7	2.8	2.5	2.7

A factor analysis of the motivations expressed by the travellers indicated the existence of four main factors, which could broadly be characterised as experience seeking, relaxation seeking, sociability and contributing to the destination. In general terms the first three of these factors can be associated closely with the Leisure Motivation Scale of Ragheb and Beard (1982). In particular, the experience-seeking scale includes both the intellectual and competence-mastery components of the scale, while a search for relaxation indicates stimulus-avoidance. There was a clear difference in terms of the factors that were important for each of the travelstyles, with backpackers scoring higher on the experience-seeking factor and tourists emphasising the relaxation factor. Travellers, on the other hand, tended to combine experience and relaxation seeking with sociability. These results are fairly similar to those obtained by Newlands (Chapter 13, Table 13.3), which may again indicate a fairly stable set of basic motives for backpacking.

Activities

As a search for experiences features strongly in the motivations of young travellers, it is not surprising that most respondents indicated that they had undertaken a wide range of activities during their trip. Backpackers in particular tended to undertake more different activities than other travellers (even when controlling for length of stay), perhaps pointing to the expectation that backpacker trips should be seen as a 'once in a lifetime' experience that requires that every possible experience be sampled. There was also a relationship between the motivation of the respondents and the number of different activities undertaken during the trip. In general terms those who were motivated more by experience-seeking motivations such as exploring other cultures or developing skills were more active than those with relaxation-related motives such as avoiding hustle and bustle and physical relaxation.

In spite of the argument that backpackers are keen to distinguish them-selves from other types of tourists, their activities tended to be fairly similar to those that might be expected of tourists in general. The activities mentioned most frequently were visiting historical sites, walking, sitting in cafes and restaurants and shopping, which were practiced by over 70% of respondents (Table 2.7). Observing wildlife and nature was a far more popular activity for backpackers, perhaps indicating the tendency for many to go trekking in wilderness areas. Backpackers were also more likely to indulge in fairly passive activities such as 'hanging out on the beach' as well as more 'extreme' sports and adrenaline-inducing experiences. This may suggest that the backpacking experience consists of relatively long periods of passive activity interspersed by intervals of more active and intense experience. The time backpackers spend apparently 'doing noth-ing' or 'hanging out' may also be an important part of the backpacking experience, providing time to reflect on life and 'find oneself', although this is difficult to confirm via a quantitative survey. This also underlines the need to combine different research methods in order to gain a more complete picture of the experience of backpacking.

Some activities did show stronger differentiation, for example by travel experience, length of stay and types of travellers. Backpackers, for example, tended to do more of everything, whereas tourists were the least active. This is probably related to an expectation among backpackers have

Table 2.7 Percentage of respondents undertaking activities on last main trip by traveller type

Activity	Traveller type (%)			
	Backpacker	Traveller	Tourist	Total
Visiting historical sites, monuments	84.5	74.6	72.7	77.3
Walking, trekking	86.5	73.4	67.1	76.4
Sitting in cafes, restaurants	68.4	74.3	71.8	72.0
Shopping	62.6	74.1	80.3	71.6
Visiting museums	72.3	66.4	62.5	67.6
Cultural events	68.0	66.5	60.8	66.0
Hanging out on the beach	63.8	54.2	54.2	57.2
Nightclubs	58.8	57.8	51.3	57.0
Observing wildlife/nature	64.9	49.7	40.4	52.9
Sports activities/adrenaline	33.2	25.5	22.0	27.3
Watching sport	21.6	22.8	17.7	21.6
Learning language	11.6	18.9	10.8	15.3
Academic study	12.3	15.1	8.1	13.1
Working as volunteer	8.5	7.6	4.3	7.3
Earning money	2.6	3.8	2.0	3.1
Total	100	100	100	100

that they need to experience a lot in order to justify their trips. As travel experience increased, so did the number of activities undertaken, which may mean that the need to justify the travel experience increases with the number of trips taken. This finding tends to support the idea of back-packers in particular as 'experience hungry' tourists. However, as we know little about the home context of the backpackers, it is difficult to say whether the search for experience is driven by alienation, as many authors have suggested. The motivations stated by the respondents tend to emphasise a search for difference in other cultures, rather than alienation from their own. Motives such as 'finding oneself' or 'avoiding hustle and bustle' were not scored particularly highly by most respondents. In general the activity patterns of backpackers and other respondents were not as different as one might have expected from a reading of the literature. The fact that backpackers, just like tourists, visit cultural sites most frequently

Table 2.8 Benefits gained from last main trip (scale: 1 = very little benefit, 5 = very much benefit)

Benefits gained from travel	Mean score			
	Backpacker	*Traveller*	*Tourist*	*Total*
Thirst for more travel	4.6	4.4	4.3	4.5
Appreciation of other cultures	4.4	4.3	4.0	4.3
More interest in learning about other cultures	4.4	4.3	4.1	4.3
More tolerance of cultural difference	4.3	4.1	3.8	4.1
Self knowledge and self awareness	4.2	4.1	3.7	4.1
Self confidence	4.1	4.0	3.6	4.0
Understanding of own culture	4.1	4.0	3.6	3.9

does not tend to support Westerhausen's (2002) idea of a separate set of activities for backpackers.

Table 2.8 indicates that the main benefit that the respondents gained from their travel was a thirst for more travel. As the most popular motivation for travel was 'exploring other cultures', the main benefit seems to come from the exploration itself, rather than the specific culture visited. This may also mean that once people start travelling they find it difficult to stop, underlining the importance of attracting backpackers early in their travel careers, as they are likely to remain avid travellers. Even though most survey respondents might be regarded as relatively young travellers, about 25% of the respondents indicated that they were on repeat visits to another country.

Culture appears to play an important role in the satisfaction that people get from travelling. In particular, those with more travel experience said they gained more appreciation of other cultures through their travel and were more likely to be motivated by interaction with local people. The fact that visits to historical sites and monuments were the most frequent activities underlines the importance of culture in the travel experience, but tends to indicate a fairly traditional view of cultural experiences.

The picture that emerges from this first transnational survey of backpackers is that backpackers are generally on long-duration, low-budget trips, and that they try and pack a wide range of activities into their travels. Travel experience is a major factor in determining travelstyles and destinations. There is some evidence to back up the idea of an emerging 'traveller career', as more experienced travellers tend to visit more distant regions or more 'adventurous' destinations. Travel experience is not necessarily directly related to age, so the level of travel experience seems to be a useful indicator to include in future backpacker research.

The profile of the backpackers in the survey largely accords with that presented in the backpacker literature (e.g. Pearce, 1990). In general terms, backpackers do show a higher preference for budget accommodation (particularly 'backpacker hostels') and are more likely to be motivated by a desire to meet fellow travellers. Backpackers make less use of the travel industry to book transport or accommodation in advance, underlining the flexible nature of their itinerary. The average length of stay is highest for backpackers, confirming the tendency towards 'longer rather than very brief holidays'. In terms of the 'informal and participatory' activities that Pearce suggests are characteristic of backpackers, there is evidence that they do undertake more 'informal' activities such hanging out on the beach or sitting in cafes as well as participation in sport and voluntary work. On the other hand, they are also the most frequent visitors to historical sites and monuments, which might be seen as a more 'formal' type of cultural experience. Pearce's definitional criteria therefore seem to be generally supported by the survey data. However, the distinction between backpackers and other travellers is not always clear cut; for example other young travellers also favour budget accommodation, and make use of 'backpacker' hostels.

In addition, those who identify with the 'backpacker' concept are a minority in the survey. It is clear that many individuals who might be identified as backpackers on the basis of external criteria do not see themselves in this way. This emphasises the need to examine the backpacking phenomenon from different perspectives, and to understand how the backpacker concept is constructed not only by the backpackers, but also by those around them. The social construction of the notion of backpacking is dealt with in more detail in the following section.

The Social Construction of the Backpacker Phenomenon

Perspectives of the backpackers

To date, only a limited number of studies have moved beyond backpacker motivations and behaviour to look at popular characterisations of backpacking by attempting to 'tap' into backpacking as a socially-constructed phenomenon. Typically, interviews and participant observation studies have been conducted 'on the road', and conclusions about backpackers' self-representations have been drawn inductively from the responses gathered. While this can be strong as a qualitative, interpretative technique, it has often been open to misuse, and findings have often been sporadic, anecdotal and put forward as generalised global norms that are assumed to be specific to most backpackers. More recent studies have begun to subdivide the scene and those participating in it (e.g. Binder, Maoz and Welk in this volume; Uriely *et al.*, 2002). As a contribution to this developing 'emic' approach to backpacking analysis, a semi-qualitative study of social constructions of backpacking was undertaken within the ATLAS BRG research programme.

One way of structuring qualitative findings is to adopt a stimulus-response approach where the stimulus is derived from qualitative, interpretive sources while responses take the form of reactions to this qualitative material. *Q methodology*, a social constructionist technique, is one such way of achieving this as it can arguably reduce the tendency for over-generalisation and researcher-driven analysis.

What is Q methodology?

Q methodology is a quintessentially alternative approach for those dealing with discourse and text (Stainton Rogers, 1995). The data from Q methodology are, literally, what participants make of a 'pool of items' germane to a given topic of concern. It is not, however, the constructors (i.e. the participants) who are the focus of the approach but the 'constructions' themselves. According to Stainton Rogers:

> ... the range of topics that can be studied using this technique is almost unlimited, but typical examples would be 'representations' of social objects (e.g. selves, Others, objects); understandings (e.g. of social issues or cultural artefacts such as books, movies or works of art); and policies and strategies (e.g. towards social issues). What these three have in common is that they are socially contested, argued about ... matters of taste, values and beliefs about which a limited variety of alternative stands are taken. (Stainton Rogers, 1995: 180)

In essence, all 'understanding' is socially constructed and heterogenic, while each understanding is informed by a broader world view or cosmology. Owing to the 'finite diversity' of opinions that it seeks to extract, Q methodology permits us to 'hear the muted voices as well as the dominant ones' (Stainton Rogers, 1995: 183). As such, the approach fits well with those research questions concerned to hear many different voices. It is therefore ideal for examining the socially-constructed parameters, or the 'concourse' of attitudes (Stephenson, 1978) surrounding (or embedded within) a given issue or phenomenon.

The basis of Q methodology is the Q-sort technique, which involves the sorting of a set of 'construct' statements (textual or pictorial) along a simple, face-valid dimension, for example from 'most agree' to 'most disagree'; from 'most characteristic' to 'least characteristic'. The statements are generally derived from a diverse range of sources and collectively are known as a 'Q pack'. By sorting or scoring this Q pack, participants can configure positions and express holistic points of view, including ones that were not in the expressive experience of the researcher.[1] Interpretation of the data is typically undertaken using factor analysis, and recourse is also made to the open-ended comments made by participants in explaining the particular position or score they allotted to a given construct. This can elicit rich qualitative material with which to contextualise the analysis of the statement scores.

Parameters of the study

The Q study aimed to allow exploration of backpacker representations based on the 'concourse' of the global backpacking phenomenon. This involved three phases:

(1) *Construction of a 'concourse' of assumptions, stereotypes, ideas and research-derived norms of the nature of the backpacker phenomenon and related activities:* Sources for this varied widely, and included findings from the global nomad survey, theoretical underpinning derived from an academic literature review, applied research findings, industry experts, members of the ATLAS BRG, novels, popular culture, film, videos and other media. This eclectic range of sources helped to iden-tify commonly-held assumptions and stereotypes about backpacking as well as those aspects of backpacking that have been formally researched. In this way, it was possible to include anyone with any kind of grounded perception about backpacking – not just the 'central' individuals (i.e. the backpackers themselves).

(2) *Building a series of 'constructs' based on this concourse:* The resulting material was sifted, ordered and condensed to yield a diverse pool of constructs. The constructs, or statements, were made as simple and as short as possible and did not contain more than a single idea in any one construct statement. The final Q pack contained 78 short construct statements.

(3) *Testing the theoretical constructs empirically via a study of visitors to popular backpacker enclaves:* For this initial analysis of the social construction of backpacking, a sample of 'travellers only' ($n = 166$) was taken from a larger sample ($n = 251$) containing responses from a much wider group of informants, including tourism providers and those working in the service sector in backpacker enclaves, tourism industry

representatives and policy makers, residents, student/independent travel agency staff and academic commentators. Additional data on respondents' profiles were sought and respondents were also asked to specify anything that might have affected their attitudes towards backpacking, for example: religious or political beliefs, or experiences from childhood.

The 'traveller-only' responses were collected in cafes / bars, backpacker hostels and other forms of accommodation, and open spaces in Bangkok and Sydney. Specific locations were the Banglamphu / Khao San Road area of Bangkok and King's Cross / Darlinghurst, Bondi Beach and Glebe in Sydney – popular 'enclaves' with an overt backpacker infrastructure and a prominent backpacker presence. As year-round destinations for travellers, these fieldwork locations were ideal for collecting large numbers of detailed responses, particularly in view of the English-language orientation of most visitors.

There are three considerations that we should mention prior to presenting selected findings from this study. First, we should emphasise that, under usual circumstances, eliciting representations only from backpackers themselves in a study about the backpacking phenomenon would limit it significantly. This is because, the more diverse the range of opinions in the sample, the better the Q study will be at conceptualising how the phenomenon is socially constructed by all those with a role in it. So, for this chapter we have not presented the findings in their usual Q-methodology form, as the purpose is to illustrate specifically how backpackers themselves construct their own understanding of the phenomenon and to test some of the assumptions common in previous research. This format therefore does not reflect a conventional Q study, in that we have used the constructs for a slightly different purpose to look only at representations of the backpackers and not at the representations of the whole 'concourse' of opinions involved.

Second, for practical reasons, the Q sort was not undertaken in the more conventional manner of asking respondents to sort statement cards into different piles and then to re-sort and score them on to a scaling 'grid' with a quasi-normal distribution. Rather, the task was adapted to fit transient, time-restricted respondents, who were requested to score the statements on a five-point scale. The 're-sort' therefore did not feature; but in effect this meant that a larger list of statements could be 'sorted' once, rather than having a shorter list 'sorted' twice. Third, for this chapter we have used mean values, standard deviation and variance as a way of evaluating the opinions of the group as a whole, rather than using factor analysis. [2]

Respondent profile: Travellers only

More than 80% of the travellers were interviewed in Bangkok. This was largely because the language problems involved with contacting service providers in Bangkok led to a conscious decision to obtain more responses from service providers in Sydney to balance the overall sample.

More than 80% of the respondents were under 30 years of age, with the largest single age group being between 22 and 25. Their incomes reflected those of the quantitative research, with more than 37% having an annual income of US$10,000 or less. In total 21 nationalities were represented, and the sample included 56 British, 18 Irish, 15 Australians, 10 North Americans, 4 Asians and 5 Israelis. More than half (56%) were male, many more than in the global nomad survey. In terms of education, more than 60% of the travellers had a university degree and more than a third were students, which indicates a similar, if slightly older, respondent group to that obtained in the quantitative research.

Even though the study was conducted within established 'backpacker enclaves', by no means all the respondents identified themselves as 'backpackers'. Just under 64% of the respondents identified themselves in some way with the term 'backpacker'. Less than half of these used the term backpacker as the sole description of their travelstyle. Interestingly, there was a large degree of overlap within the sample between the categories 'backpacker', 'traveller' and 'tourist'. Almost 40% of the 'backpackers' also called themselves tourists, and almost half also used the term 'traveller'. This illustrates the complexity of the use of such terms within the group that academics would usually refer to as 'backpackers'. By no means all of these individuals identify closely with the term, and many see themselves as having multiple travelstyles, probably depending on the type or stage of their journey. It is clear that, when given the choice, many backpackers will assume multiple or flexible identities. Just as we found in the global nomad survey, those who choose to identify only with the label 'backpacker' are in a minority, accounting for only about a third of respondents.

The responses also indicated a field of tension between 'backpackers', 'travellers' and 'tourists'. Some respondents exhibited the backpacker rejection of tourists often noted in the literature (see Welk, Chapter 5, for example): 'buses are for grannies ... P.S. Please don't tell my granny'. On the other hand, one German student who identified himself as a backpacker, traveller and tourist said:

> after seeing a lot of backpackers who got stuck in foreign countries, because they liked [the feeling of being] someone 'special' for the local

people as a backpacker, so much I avoid trying to be a 'real backpacker' because if you [exceed] your limits the only thing you are is ridiculous.

One traveller also said '[there are] too many hippy "new age" type backpackers, but we're not all like that!!' A Swedish architect admitted 'I'm travelling with a backpack, so I guess I'm both a backpacker and a traveller', but then went on to say 'I never understand the backpacker uniform. Hippie style clothing, piercings, tattoos, dreadlocks. A lot of these people would never dress like this at home so why do it while travelling abroad!'

Other respondents were aware of the changing nature of the backpacking experience. One Australian commented 'backpackers were probably traditionally known to rough it and be "hippies" ... [but] now I think a wider group of people backpack to get a better insight into local culture, meet other backpackers and do it cheaply'. A 35 year old Dutch airline pilot 'traveller' said:

between the age of 20 and 30 we were backpacking, travelling very basic through countries which were just 'opening up'. Nowadays it looks like there are not [so many] countries to discover, unless they are dangerous (e.g. Afghanistan). So backpacking nowadays is becoming so easy and accessible even for naïve travellers. So backpacking has become travelling for most people coming to Thailand ... the real 'edge' from fifteen years ago is gone.

These responses frame the definition of 'backpacking' as a much more dynamic field of discourse than has been supposed in much previous research. It seems that backpackers are defined not just by their own rejection of conventional tourists, but also by increasingly negative reactions from travellers and tourists – a form of 'backpacker angst' (Wilson & Richards, Chapter 8).

Attitudes to Backpacking

The statements with which respondents agreed most not surprisingly tended to reflect the positive aspects of backpacking as a relatively free, creative means of travel that allows you to meet other people and get to know more about the places you travel to (Table 2.9). In terms of socialising, backpackers are seen mainly as getting on well with other travellers, who also become an audience for the travel stories picked up along the way. Social contacts and the freedom offered by backpacking also aid the process of self-development, and make backpackers more self-confident. In spite of the freedom and independence offered by backpacking, however, travellers themselves are quick to agree that *Lonely Planet* is the backpacker's

Table 2.9 Ten statements most agreed with in the social construction study
(1 = strongly agree, 5 = strongly disagree)

Construct statement	Mean score	Standard deviation
A good way to make friends	1.59	0.81
More freedom	1.65	0.89
Backpackers like talking about their travel	1.65	0.88
A more creative way of travelling	1.76	0.95
Learn more about the country than other tourists	1.82	1.00
Always looking for the cheap option	1.87	1.02
Looking for authentic experiences	1.92	0.85
Turns you into a confident person	1.95	0.98
Get on well with other people	2.02	1.01
Lonely Planet is the backpacker's bible	2.08	1.19

bible, suggesting that they may be aware of the role of the '*Lonely Planet* Bubble' (Giesbers, 2002) in circumscribing their freedom. The fact that backpackers are also looking for the 'cheap option' must also curtail the actual degree of freedom experienced.

Interestingly, the search for authentic experiences is also seen as an important element of backpacking. For example, one 'kiwi' female backpacker/traveller/tourist in Bangkok commented 'my experiences while travelling in Asia are always uplifting and very inspiring. Asian people seem to have such a strong belief system ... and to me this keeps each culture so strong and true and also very much alive'. This suggests, as Cohen argues in Chapter 3, that many backpackers are still relatively 'modern' in their approach to travel: 'As a child my parents were very strict and never let me out of the house. This may have affected my view of the freedom of backpacking' (20 year old British male backpacker). 'My father travelled when he was young and I've always had a desire to get out and see the world' (Canadian traveller, female, aged 24).

In terms of the statements most disagreed with (Table 2.10), there was a strong reaction against the 'traditional' image of backpackers as hippies, which is strengthened by a rejection of the idea that backpackers never wash. There was also strong rejection of the idea that backpackers are all the same. It seems that people feel that the image of the backpacker has not only changed since the early years of the 'hippie trail', but also that backpackers have become more diverse.

Table 2.10 Ten statements most disagreed with in the social construction study (1 = strongly agree, 5 = strongly disagree)

Construct statement	Mean	Standard deviation
Is more fun if you take drugs	4.04	1.27
Carry mobile phones	4.10	1.06
Don't visit museums/art galleries	4.13	0.98
Never wash	4.26	1.07
Only listen to rock music	4.35	0.98
Don't take photos	4.40	1.03
Don't use the Internet to contact home	4.47	1.02
Never use guidebooks	4.55	0.87
Backpackers are all the same	4.56	0.93
All backpackers are hippies	4.58	0.85

The respondents also disagreed strongly with the idea that backpackers don't use guidebooks, which is consistent with the idea of the *Lonely Planet* as the backpackers' bible. Backpackers are also seen as using the Internet to stay in touch, which also explains the important role of the Internet as a source of information. In contrast to the idea put forward by Ureily *et al.* (2002) that backpackers don't take photos because this is considered a 'tourist' activity, the respondents clearly asserted that photos are an important part of the backpacking experience.

The important role of museums as cultural attractions for backpackers identified in the global nomad survey is also confirmed by the respondents, who rejected the idea that backpackers don't visit museums and galleries. There was also some evidence of an anti-hedonistic element in the traveller community, as many also reacted against the idea that backpacking is more fun if you take drugs.

Looking at the significant differences between those who saw themselves as backpackers and other respondents (Table 2.11), backpackers were far more likely to agree that they were seeking extreme experiences and that thrill seeking is an essential part of backpacking. They tended to reject more negative images of backpackers, such as laziness or a lack of contribution to the local community. In general, the backpacker respondents see backpacking more in terms of a relatively free, creative form of travel, and agreed that they were inspired by Jack Kerouac's novel *On the Road* (see Wilson & Richards, Chapter 8). It is clear that backpackers have a

Table 2.11 Comparison of backpackers and other travellers (significant differences only)

	Mean score		Significance level
	Backpackers	*Others*	
Backpackers seek extreme experiences	2.15	2.59	0.00
Backpackers are lazy	3.94	3.36	0.00
Thrill seeking is essential	2.25	2.71	0.01
Don't give anything back to local communities	4.05	3.56	0.01
Jack Kerouac is a backpacker role model	2.95	3.40	0.01
Never go on organised tours	2.16	2.59	0.02
Can go wherever and do whatever they want	2.26	2.77	0.02
Get on well with other people	1.89	2.25	0.03
Know how to handle themselves in tricky situations	2.61	2.97	0.03
A more creative way of travelling	1.65	1.97	0.04
Want to help local people	2.83	3.17	0.04

more positive or socially desirable image of themselves than travellers or tourists do.

There were also a number of significant differences in reactions to the statements by gender and age. In particular, women tended to disagree far more with statements that suggest a macho, 'sexy' or rebellious role for the backpacker. Women disagreed much more firmly than men that back-packers are sexually promiscuous, lazy or never wash. Women tended to agree that thrill seeking is important in backpacking, but to a lesser extent than men did. Interestingly, there was no significant difference between men and women in their reactions to the statement 'backpacking is dangerous'. The major difference in attitudes with age was in response to the statement 'bad experiences make backpacking more interesting', where younger backpackers (under 25) were significantly more likely to agree with this statement. Perhaps older backpackers have already had their share of 'bad' experiences and feel they don't need any more to enhance the experience. Older backpackers were also less likely to agree that 'back-packers like home comforts' and that 'backpackers are fit and strong'. Interestingly there was no difference with age in the reactions to the statement 'older backpackers are more sophisticated'.

Conclusions

The quantitative and qualitative research presented in this chapter provides some interesting insights into the profile, behaviour and attitudes of the 'backpacker'. Most clearly, the research indicates that many people who would fall within widely-accepted academic definitions of back-packers do not identify themselves with the term and that the boundaries between 'backpackers', 'travellers' and 'tourists' are far from clear. In spite of the commonalities between the respondents, including being relatively young, predominantly middle class and well educated, 'backpackers' are a heterogeneous group, with different motivations, attitudes activities and reactions to the term 'backpacker'. The field of meaning that is created by the 'backpacker–traveller–tourist' triad is clearly more complex than has previously been supposed. These and other issues raised by the surveys presented here will be examined in more detail in the chapters that follow.

Notes

1. Q methodology can therefore also be ideal as one part of a triangulated study.
2. For the principal Q methodology study, see Wilson & Richards (forthcoming), which includes the factor analysis of the data and the full range of respondents, rather than 'travellers only'.

Part 2

Backpacking as a (Post)modern Phenomenon

Chapter 3

Backpacking: Diversity and Change

ERIK COHEN

Introduction

Backpacking is a controversial subject: while often imagining themselves as the 'real' travellers as against the conventional tourists (e.g. Uriely *et al.*, 2002; Welk, Chapter 5 of this volume), backpackers are often condemned for their appearance, conduct – especially sexual freedom and use of drugs – superficiality, stinginess and seclusion in backpacker enclaves. While tourism officials and the tourist industry depict backpackers as exploiters of poor locals from whom they seek to live on the cheap, researchers have recently highlighted their neglected but significant economic contribution to marginal communities in less developed parts of the world (Scheyvens, 2002). Governments of many developing countries have in the past sought to upgrade the tourism services of localities that are popular with backpackers (e.g. Wilson, 1997) or to put restrictions on backpacking visits. While some Thais have recently begun to recognise the economic potential of this type of tourism (*The Nation*, 2001), the Thai authorities are still disinclined to backpackers, and seek to develop luxury tourism (e.g. Niyamabha, 2002).

While research on tourism generally lagged behind the rapidly expanding industry, research on backpacking was particularly tardy to pick up with the growing phenomenon – perhaps since it lacked the support of the tourism industry, which had little interest in its exploration. The earliest articles devoted specifically to the topic appeared in the 1970s (Cohen, 1973; Vogt, 1976), but the 1980s – the period of a major expansion in tourism studies – saw relatively few publications on backpacking (except studies such as Cohen, 1982; Riley, 1988; Teas, 1988). Recently, however, research has begun to pick up, with a growing number of publications (e.g. Loker-Murphy, 1996; Murphy, 2001; Spreitzhofer, 1998; Westerhausen, 2002).

The time thus seems appropriate for a more systematic approach to the accumulating knowledge, and for the direction of research beyond the presently prevalent themes of backpackers' motives, conduct and relationships or of their impact upon host communities (but see Elsrud, 1998, 2001). This chapter is intended as a first step in these respects.

From Tramp to Drifter: From Drifter to Backpacker

Youth nomadism, as Judith Adler (1985) reminds us, has been a widespread phenomenon in the pre-modern West. She argues that the lower-class tramp, wandering in quest of employment, became the formative model or trope for the emergent modern middle-class youth traveller; travelling for enjoyment and experiences. While some degree of historical continuity thus apparently exists between the 'tramping' of the past and contemporary backpacking, the emergence of the latter as a large-scale touristic phenomenon is, in my view, related to some distinctive traits of modern Western societies (Cohen, 1973) and the position of youth within them. These traits in turn may have engendered the desire to adopt 'tramping' as a model for this mode of travelling, which in its aims, style and consequences differs markedly from all Western precedents. Chief among these traits was the widespread alienation of Western youths from their societies of origin, especially in the United States and Western Europe; which culminated during the 1960s, and led to the (failed) 'student revolution' and the various attempts to create alternative lifestyles. While the extent of alienation may have receded to a significant extent towards the end of the last century, the stresses and uncertainties of late modern life are certainly a disorienting factor that induces young men and women to take time out (Elsrud, 1998) to gain a new perspective on their own life and future (Noy & Cohen, forthcoming), while having a challenging but enjoyable time in the world of others.

I propose to call the earlier, alienated individuals roaming the world alone, common in the 1960s and 1970s, 'drifters', and the more recent youth travellers, following well-trodden paths in large numbers 'backpackers'. If the model for the drifter was the tramp, the drifter is the model for the backpacker; but I wish to stress that this chronological division is not strict: the Vermassung of drifting had started already in the 1970s (Cohen, 1973); and even today, individual drifters can be found in remote localities as yet untouched by mainstream 'backpacker' tourism. The very remoteness of the drifters, indeed, appears to hide them from the fieldworker studying backpackers on the more popular itineraries and enclaves.

My own conceptualisation of the original 'drifter' was to a significant extent influenced by a personal encounter in the later 1960s. While on fieldwork in Ayacucho, a town in the central Andes of Peru, I was approached on the street by a tall, athletic young German, a student of chemistry, who asked to lodge in my flat for a day or two. It turned out that he had arrived in the central Peruvian Sierra all the way from the Atlantic coast of Brazil via the Amazon River and its tributaries, part of the time travelling alone in a small boat and curing himself of the tropical illnesses he suffered from in the wilderness. His trip took about seven months, during which he was sometimes alone for such a long time that he talked to himself.

This self-reliant individual served as the prototype of the 'original drifter' in my article on the Nomads from Affluence, in which I claimed, that in order to preserve the freshness and spontaneity of their experience, drifters travel deliberately without either itinerary or timetable, without a destination or even a well-defined purpose (Cohen, 1973: 176).

However, in this rather ideal-typical characterisation, I overlooked two significant constraints that impact on even the most independently-minded traveller. On the one hand, there are external constraints on his or her unrestrained freedom of travel, such as temporal restrictions on the validity of visas and passports or of airline tickets, or limitations on access to some countries, or to sensitive areas within them, imposed by the authorities. On the other hand, and probably more important, are inward constraints: drifting, as I have conceived it, appears to take much more competence, resourcefulness, endurance and fortitude, as well as an ability to plan one's moves, even if they are subject to alteration, than I had originally surmised. Not many young travellers have the ability to cure their illnesses in the midst of a tropical forest as that German did.

The 'original drifter' (Cohen, 1973) may have been an ideal to which many youths were attracted, but only very few succeeded. Therefore I had already at an early stage qualified the concept and suggested several sub-types of drifters (Cohen, 1973: 100–101), emerging just as contemporary youth tourism became a mass phenomenon; those who at present would be loosely called 'backpackers'. I also described the alternative tourism infrastructure of itineraries, transportation services, accommodation and other facilities which had begun to emerge in response to the growth of this kind of tourism (Cohen, 1973: 95–97).

However, I did not in that early paper relate the concept of the drifter to what has emerged as the dominant paradigm in tourism research from the mid-1970s to the 1990s: MacCannell's (1973, 1976) conceptualisation of the tourist as a secular pilgrim in quest of authenticity, which is in turn staged for them by their obliging hosts. However, it would follow from my later work on the phenomenology of tourist experiences (Cohen, 1979) that drifters – assumed to be the most alienated kind of tourists – would tend toward the most intensive types of experiences, and especially the 'experimental' or 'existential' ones, as they sought an alternative 'elective centre', which they could substitute for that of their home society. The drifter would thus strive more than the ordinary tourist to reach places and people that are 'really' authentic, and would display considerable touristic angst that places or events that appear authentic are in fact staged (see Wilson & Richards, Chapter 8, and Welk, Chapter 5).

It is hard to check this hypothesis regarding the early drifters, and there do not appear to be any systematic studies on the contemporary drifters who seek to set themselves apart from conventional backpackers, just as the latter seek to distinguish themselves from conventional tourists. Contemporary backpackers tend to embrace the ideology of drifting (Elsrud, 2001: 601), and imitate the style or form of travel characteristic of the drifter; but the mode or type of experience they pursue varies widely, with only a minority travelling in an existential or experimental mode. Many indeed resemble the ordinary tourists in that they seek diversionary or recreational experiences (Uriely *et al.*, 2002). Israeli backpackers at least are rarely alienated from the 'centre' of their own society (Uriely *et al.*, 2002; Mevorach, 1997; Noy & Cohen, forthcoming). While the drifter remains the model for the backpacker, few backpackers seek to realise it in practice, or show a great concern for profoundly 'authentic' experiences of sites, events or people on their trip. This may partly reflect the change in the nature of backpacking that came with its Vermassung, and partly also the broader changes in the nature of tourism in late modernity or 'postmodernity', to which I shall return later in the chapter.

In my early article, I distinguished between outward-oriented and inward-oriented drifters – those who seek to reach faraway locations and live with the locals, and those who primarily seek out the enclaves of their own kind (Cohen, 1973). While this distinction still appears to be significant, it should be used to distinguish between different kinds of backpackers' conduct, rather than to define types of backpackers. Contemporary backpackers combine, to varying degrees, both outward- and inward-directed conduct (Elsrud, 1998).

Though we do not possess adequate statistical information, it appears that the great majority of the young contemporary backpackers spend significant periods of their time, perhaps even most of it, in various backpacker enclaves, or on the road from one such enclave to the other – even though these enclaves may serve as bases for trekking, riding or rafting trips, and for tours or excursions to natural sights, ethnic communities or various events in the vicinity of the enclaves. There is therefore a parallel between backpacker and conventional tourism, the enclaves fulfilling a function parallel to that of vacationing resorts, in which most conventional tourists tend to spend their holidays. Only a minority of backpackers travel off the beaten backpacker tracks, or spend much of their time staying with local people.

Many backpackers travel to remote localities just to reach enclaves such as the district township of Pai (Emmons, 2000) on the Chiang Mai–Mae Hong Son road in northern Thailand. Backpackers apparently tend to share 'mental maps' of backpacker destinations that are reinforced by way of oral communication in backpacker enclaves, and where travel routes and plans are a principal theme of conversation (Murphy, 2001) that are updated as the popularity of countries and enclaves changes (Teas, 1988).

While most backpackers travel alone or in pairs, they primarily seek out the company of other backpackers. However, they do not form lasting groups; rather their enclaves are places of fleeting, spontaneous, but friendly and pleasant (and frequently even intimate) encounters between individuals belonging to a shared, but loosely-defined subculture (Murphy, 2001). When talking about 'people' on the trip, backpackers generally refer to other backpackers, rather than to the locals (Elsrud, 2001; Murphy, 2001). Though 'friendly' local staff are appreciated by back-packers (Murphy, 2001), relations with the locals in the enclaves are of secondary importance in comparison to those with other backpackers.

Despite basic similarities between backpackers as well as between their enclaves, some significant differences can be discerned, although these have not yet been documented systematically in the literature:

(1) There appear to be significant differences between urban and rural enclaves in the degree of their demarcation, the kinds and quality of services provided, and their role and function in the backpackers' trip. Urban enclaves such as Khao San in Bangkok are less demarcated than rural ones such as Pai in the north of Thailand (Emmons, 2000), and are much more commercialised (Maneerungsee, 2001, Spreitzhofer, 1998). They are central nodes via which backpackers arrive in the country, or through which they are forced to pass, rather than overt destinations of choice (as are remote rural enclaves). Urban enclaves therefore serve instrumental purposes: within them, the new arrivals orient themselves, organise their travels and make purchases, activi-ties that are less important in rural enclaves. Both kinds of enclaves, however, also serve as meeting places and provide for the hedonistic desires of backpackers for food, drink, drugs, rest and 'having a good time', although the rural enclaves appear to be preferred to the urban ones for these purposes, and some, like Ko Pangan in southern Thai-land, have acquired a worldwide reputation as sites of virtually unre-strained hedonism; epitomised in the Full Moon Party (Jidvijak, 1994).

(2)   There appear to be differences between backpackers from different
      countries in the scope of their interactions with other backpackers:
      while most interact with members of all countries with whom they
      have a common language, others tend to restrict interaction to their
      co-nationals; this is particularly the case with Israeli backpackers, as
      several studies have found (Maoz, Chapter 7 of this volume; Noy &
      Cohen, forthcoming), and possibly also with Japanese and other Asian
      backpackers.
(3)   Distinct variants appear to exisit within the general, vaguely-defined
      backpacker subculture, based primarily on the kind and intensity of
      the use of drugs and on preferred musical fashions. The possibility of
      subcultural differences between the middle-class backpackers and the
      growing numbers of backpackers of working class origins should also
      be investigated.
(4)   Finally, there appear to be important differences between younger
      backpackers and those in older age groups. While the former tend to
      stay in backpacker enclaves for relatively short periods of time[1] and
      use them as a basis for short excursions and longer tours, the older
      ones appear to settle down for prolonged periods of time – up to
      several months – in local communities that may not be particularly
      popular with young backpackers (Maoz, 1999 and Chapter 7).

Backpacker Ideology and Practice

My analysis indicates that the actual practice of most backpackers is at
considerable variance with the predominant image of the young traveller
who roams far off places all alone. How is this discrepancy between the
image or ideology and actual practice of backpacking resolved by the backpackers themselves?

As Scheuch (1981) pointed out a long time ago, the discrepancy between
the intentions of tourists and their practice is endemic to tourism itself. This
does not appear to be a matter of concern to ordinary tourists. But backpacking, as a travel practice studiously contrasted with conventional
tourism, is more ideologically 'loaded' (see Welk, Chapter 5) and hence
necessitates some express mechanisms that may help to maintain the
identity of the backpackers in the face of the discrepancy between their
ideology and their practice.

While these mechanisms have not yet been explicitly addressed in the
literature, some recent work helps us to detect them. Such work goes
beyond the mere descriptions of backpackers' motives and conduct, and
looks into the ways in which they themselves emically perceive their trip

and construct their identity. Important in this respect is Elsrud's recent article on 'risk creation' in backpacking tourism, which aimed to show ' ... how the risk and adventure narrative ... is [still] being manifested and expressed within backpacker communities' (Elsrud, 2001: 598). Elsrud's approach shows how risk and adventure on the trip are constructed by the backpackers; thus deflecting the focus of research from the question of whether the backpackers have 'real' adventures and face 'real' risks, to the manner in which they perceive and narrate their experiences, thereby narrowing and closing the discrepancy between the model and actual behaviour (see Binder, Chapter 6).

The creation of risk and adventure appears to be facilitated by the institutional structure of backpacker tourism, especially by the backpacker-oriented tour companies who represent themselves as alternatives to conventional tourism, and advertise their tours in such terms as eco-tourism, soft tourism, 'green' tourism or adventure tourism, and the localities and people on their tours as 'non-touristic' or 'authentic' (Cohen, 1989). They thus create the impression of offering 'real' adventure in unexplored areas. The 'staged authenticity' of such tours is more ingeniously concealed than it is in similar advertisements directed to conventional tourism, and appears more credible, precisely because of the allegedly alternative character of such tours. Many backpackers seem to take such representations at face value, thereby gaining external endorsement for the construction of their trip as risky and dangerous.

There also exists, then, an ironic parallel between backpacker tourism and conventional tourism: both thrive on fantasy, supported and exploited by different sectors of the tourist industry. But while contemporary, increasingly sophisticated 'mass' tourists often tend to relate sceptically and ludically (playfully) to the enchanting images offered them in touristic advertisements (Perkins & Thorns, 2001), 'mass' backpackers appear to be more easily taken in by the apparently credible images conjured up for them by the establishments serving this market segment, presented as an alternative to the mainstream tourist industry.

Backpackers: Modern and Postmodern

From the 1990s on, several researchers began to identify a 'postmodern' trend in tourism (e.g. Ritzer & Liska, 1997; Rojek, 1993; Urry, 1990), reflecting broader transformative tendencies in contemporary Western society. For present purposes, the most important of these tendencies are: the devaluation of 'origins', the alleged disappearance of 'originals', the concomitant growing salience of 'surface' experiences, the growing legitimisation of the quest for 'fun' and of a ludic (playful) attitude to the world. Since in the postmodern world there are allegedly no genuine 'primitives' any more (MacCannell, 1992b), nor 'untouched' cultures or environments, it follows that a quest for authenticity would be a futile enterprise.

Under the circumstances, the quest for authenticity loses its primacy as a culturally legitimising principle of (sightseeing) tourism. Rather, hedonistic enjoyment and fun tend to take its place in postmodern tourism. Postmodern tourists, or 'post-tourists' (Ritzer & Liska, 1997) acquiesce with this predicament, turning from the serious quest for experiences of the authentic, to a ludic enjoyment of surfaces, irrespective of their genuineness. But they may consciously and reflectively play an 'as if' game, imagining that simulated and otherwise contrived attractions are the real thing (Cohen, 1995). Contrived attractions, such as theme parks, amusement centres, malls, reconstructed environments and touristic festivals increasingly become the principal attractions of postmodern conventional tourism. Rather than seeking the experience of the 'Other', post-tourists often seek familiar experiences on their trip (Ritzer & Liska 1997: 99), deriving enjoyment from the quality of the offerings, rather than from their strangeness.

These general tendencies raise a question with regard to backpacking: are backpackers immune to the transformations of postmodern tourism, or are they amenable to their influence? In other words, are the backpackers the 'rear guard' of modern tourism, attached to its ideals in opposition to the postmodern trend in tourism? Or are they, contrariwise, the trend-setters of postmodern tourism, creating a mode of travelling to be followed by more conventional tourism, just as the drifters have served as the spearhead of penetration into new and hitherto marginal 'authentic' destinations?

While backpacker studies do not address these questions directly, an outline of an answer can be formulated using the available information: it appears that backpackers profess to various degrees the ideals of modern tourism, such as the experience of non-touristic, 'authentic' sites, but their actual practices are marked by many traits of postmodern tourism.

The quest for authenticity was, according to MacCannell (1973), closely related to the alienation of moderns from their own society; by extension it can be argued that, the more alienated an individual, the more intensive will his or her quest for authenticity be, motivating the most alienated moderns to seek and attach themselves to an 'elective centre' beyond the boundaries of the modern world (Cohen, 1979: 189–191).

Backpackers appear to differ in the degree of their alienation, and hence travel in quest of different modes of touristic experiences, as Uriely and his colleagues have recently demonstrated empirically for Israeli backpackers (Uriely *et al.*, 2002). But, while many may be to different degrees critical of Western civilisation (Spreitzhofer, 1998), or of their own society, the overall degree of their alienation has apparently diminished with time. Few contemporary backpackers will make pronouncements of the kind I heard from a drifter about 20 years ago: 'You don't know why you travel until you return home!' The great majority perceive their trip as a 'break' or 'time bubble' (Elsrud, 2001: 605) within their otherwise routine life-path: between school and college, college and university, university and a job, or between jobs. Few see in travel an alternative to a 'normal' career or seek an 'elective centre' abroad. Within this limited period, they primarily desire the achievement of unlimited freedom to do their own thing, which may include the unrestricted hedonistic quest of enjoyment and fun; as embodied iconically in the much-maligned 'Full Moon Parties' on Pangan (Jidvijak, 1994). At the height of the ecstatic rush of such events, the participants may indeed experience 'existential authenticity' (Wang, 2000: 56–71), which in contrast to the 'objective authenticity' allegedly sought by the modern tourist (MacCannell, 1973) is basically a postmodern experiential mode: a heightened internal state of exaltation or excitement unrelated to any external referent, such as an 'authentic' sight, event or object. 'Existential authenticity' is a state of 'real living', which may be induced by an appropriate environment, but unlike 'objective authenticity' it does not derive from its own contemplation.

There is an irony inherent in the backpacker's quest for freedom: while each might seek to do 'his or her own thing', most do very similar things; like the conventional tourists, from whom they desire to distinguish themselves (Welk, Chapter 5 of this volume), most backpackers pursue highly conventional lifestyles, characteristic of their subculture; following similar itineraries, staying in the same currently-popular enclaves, and participating in similar sightseeing, vacationing and partying activities – though the places that are currently 'in' may change over time (Teas, 1988).

The 'freedom' pursued by backpackers does not lead to the personal individuation of travelling styles that marked the earlier drifter. Rather, the freedom that most backpackers desire is that of unrestrained permissiveness found in the enclaves, which enables them to pursue similar hedonistic enjoyment, experimentation and self-fulfilment under relatively simple (and affordable) circumstances. The state of liminality, facilitated by their 'out-there-ness' (Lengkeek, 2001: 179–180), enables backpackers to gain a novel perspective on their own society (Noy & Cohen, forthcoming) and to reflect upon their own identity. Several researchers therefore approach backpacking as a contemporary *rite de passage* (Teas, 1988; Mevorach, 1997).

While the *rite de passage* is, in many respects, a useful and adequate model for the interpretation of backpacking, the extent of its applicability ought to be examined critically.

Backpacking as a *Rite de Passage*

Backpacking is often related to life crises and transitions – especially, but not exclusively, the transition from late adolescence to early adulthood in Western societies, characteristic of the 20–30 age group from which the great majority of backpackers originate. The attempt to apply the *rite de passage* model – as initially formulated by van Gennep (1960) and later elaborated by Victor Turner to backpackers (Turner, 1973; Turner & Turner, 1978) – derives from this affinity between life transitions and the backpacking trip. The backpacking youths can be said to 'exit' their normal life, separating themselves from their family and community to enter an unfamiliar, 'liminal' situation abroad. They have to prove themselves by resolving the problems encountered on their trip and making independent decisions without the direction, assistance or advice of parents or other authoritative adults. Their successful resolution of the problems and the eventual accomplishment of their trip is indicative of their competence in managing their own affairs autonomously. This is a significant marker of adulthood in Western societies, and the young people will thus be reincorporated into their society; after returning from their travels, as 'adults'.

The case of Israeli backpackers as analysed by Mevorach (1997) is a particularly enlightening example of the successful application of this model. It is widely assumed in Israel that the compulsive military service, with its exertions, dangers and responsibilities, constitutes the formative stage in the transition from adolescence to adulthood for (Jewish) Israeli youths. Mevorach, however, claims that the youths remain closely linked to, and supported by their parents throughout their military service. Indeed, the Israeli army purposely fosters the link between the parents and the army by means of a number of institutionalised practices. In contrast, according to Mevorach (1997), on the extended trip abroad, usually engaged upon after the completion of their military service, the youths find themselves for the first time in their lives on their own, and have to rely on their own wits, without the advice or support of parents or other adults. It is under these conditions that they learn to act autonomously, thus achieving one of the principal marks of adulthood.

More recent work by Maoz (1999) on older Israeli backpackers indicates that backpacking plays a similar role as a *rite de passage* in other life crises, especially in the transition from early to late adulthood of individuals who did not have the occasion for a moratorial break earlier in life.

While the model of the *rite de passage* is a useful heuristic device to interpret the dynamics and function of backpacking, several points should be noted that mitigate its applicability to this phenomenon.

First, the model of the *rite de passage*, as proposed by Turner, comprises a middle stage between separation from the community and re-entry into it in a new status: a liminal stage at which the youths lose their individuality and constitute an undifferentiated *'communitas'* (Turner, 1973: 216–218). Such a complete immersion of backpackers with their co-travellers has not been reported in the literature, nor is it in fact to be expected. Rather, backpackers remain very much egocentrically concerned with their own fun, enjoyment and experiences, even if they are gregarious, easily approachable and engage in a superficial camaraderie with the constantly fluctuating membership of their enclaves. While honing their social skills by interacting with many different strangers (Murphy, 2001), the fleeting nature of these encounters precludes the emergence of lasting intimate ties, not to mention an embracing communitas.

Second, the apparent inversion of home on the trip and the need to deal alone with strange and dangerous situations – though highlighted in backpackers' narratives (Elsrud, 2001) – has been largely ameliorated by the emergence of an institutional structure that serves the needs of the backpackers, ensconcing them in a familiar 'environmental bubble', paralleling that particular characteristic of conventional tourism. Hence, contemporary backpackers need to develop fewer skills and invest less effort in their trip than did the earlier drifters (Cohen, 1973).

Third, the separation from home, which Mevorach (1997) stressed, is presently less severe than it used to be when Mevorach conducted his study. Since then, the cumbersome means of communication at that time, the mails and international calls, have been largely supplanted by cell phones and email. The latter is especially popular among backpackers, who keep in touch with home and friends by means of the Internet cafés that have recently proliferated rapidly in most tourist destinations, and especially in the backpacker enclaves.

Fourth, the parent–child relationship in contemporary Western societies is very different from that prevailing in tribal or traditional societies, where *rites de passage* were commonly practiced. Adolescents in contemporary society seek independence at an early stage, and engage in activities of which the parents are often unaware – especially in the widespread drug subculture and the associated cults of techno, rap and other musical fashions. The departure on a backpacking trip is decided upon by the youths themselves, often in contradiction to parental wishes – unlike in tribal or traditional societies, where the *rite de passage* was conducted in full concurrence and often with the active participation of the parents.

Fifth, though backpacking may in a sense be a *reversal* of the ordinary conditions of the youths' life in their society of origin, and in that respect resembles the *rite de passage* in tribal societies, the reversal is not complete. Rather, it is in many respects an *extension* and intensification of the prevalent youth subcultures widespread in those societies. This is particularly observable in the backpacker enclaves, which (owing to their very remoteness from home and their isolation from the local society) make possible a fully-fledged blossoming of these subcultures to an extent that (owing to legal restrictions, parental and social controls and the high prices of drugs and drinks) cannot be as fully realised at home.

Under the prevailing conditions of liminality, although backpackers may use their freedom to experiment with new experiences, such experimentation appears at present to be less oriented to the novel and strange ways of life of the locals at the destinations. Rather, it is more oriented to possibilities offered by the enclaves, which the backpackers have already been aware of from home, and which may have constituted a major motive for their trip – such as the availability and affordability of various drugs. Even the spiritual quest of some backpackers, which may induce them to spend some time in an Indian ashram[2] or a Thai Buddhist temple, appears to be frequently based on a predisposition, deriving from New Age spirituality, that constitutes a significant component of many contemporary Western youth subcultures. The 'reversal' at the destination is thus, unlike in *rites de passage*, not complete. This, as Richards and Wilson suggest in Chapter 15, may be a reason to consider much backpacking experience to be a state of 'suspension' rather than either reversal or extension.

Finally, the uses that backpackers make of their freedom, and their experimentation with new experiences (some of which may involve the over-stepping of normative boundaries to which they have been committed at home) are formative factors in the constitution or re-constitution of the backpackers' sense of identity. This may, in some cases, influence their view of the world, their attitude to their society, and their choices regarding studies, occupation and sexual relations that they make when they return home. A significant number may adopt a 'postmodern' hybrid identity, embracing concomitantly two centres or cultural worlds – that of their own Western society and that of the country of their choice, such as India, Nepal or Thailand (Ateljevic & Doorne, Chapter 4; Uriely *et al.*, 2002). Unlike in the case of the *rite de passage*, the re-aggregation of the youths in the home society is thus not necessarily complete; and insofar as the number of such individuals increases over time, their hybrid worldviews may exert an influence on their home society. Backpackers who have returned from the 'Orient' thus appear to serve to no small extent as agents of the 'Easternisation' (Campbell, 1999) of the contemporary West.

Diversity of the Historical and National Contexts of Backpacking

Up to now I have dealt with (Western) backpacking as an undifferentiated phenomenon, as does most of the literature. Indeed, one of the shortcomings of that literature is that it tends to disregard the particular historical backgrounds within which drifting and backpacking emerged, or the differences between backpackers, engendered by the specific problems and tensions experienced in their various home societies. Most of the current literature takes backpacking for granted, and disregards the social forces in the backpackers' societies of origin that may have motivated them to depart on extended trips.

Contemporary backpacking as a massive movement of youths to the less developed regions of the world began in close association with the major social and political upheavals of the 1960s: the student revolution and the Vietnam War. It could be argued that the failure of the student revolution and the frustrations of the Vietnam War drove many Western youths to seek personal redemption elsewhere, having failed to achieve social salvation at home.

This historically-based resentment against Western society led me at the time to see drifting as grounded in the counterculture (Cohen, 1973) and thus as impelled by alienation from the home society. The changing socio-cultural circumstances of the contemporary West, associated with the emergence of postmodernism (with its greater openness to multiculturalism, multiple identities, and growing separation of the public and private spheres of life), make it implausible to continue to link contemporary backpacking with alienation.

As noted above, contemporary backpacking may be a 'time out' from the pursuit of an ordinary career, but it is perhaps not a quest for an alternative way of life or of an 'elective centre'. Indeed, none of the Israeli backpackers studied by Uriely *et al.* (2002) sought to opt out of his or her own society. But, as Elsrud (1998) has shown, backpacking is also a 'time frame' free of obligations, within which backpackers can 'create' their own time and which thus helps to further the process of personal growth and development – one of the principal life goals of contemporary individualistic Western society.

While we can thus discern a general historical trend in Western backpacking, the more specific contextual circumstances prevailing in particular societies that influence the relative magnitude of the phenomenon (and more significantly, the particular motives and travelstyles of their respective backpackers) remain largely unexplored. Virtually none of the existing studies pays any particular attention to the origins of the backpackers studied, nor to the differences between backpackers of different nationalities. The only case I know where the relationship between the social context and the magnitude and style of backpacking has been extensively investigated is the Israeli one. But this case illustrates exceptionally well the close connection between particular social and backpacking. Without going into too much detail, a series of studies on Jewish backpackers from Israel (Noy & Cohen, forthcoming) demonstrates that an extended trip abroad is usually taken by Israeli youth after the completion of their army service, when they are in their early twenties. The trip is typically both a reversal and a continuation of military service. While it often involves intensive and strenuous activities in which the youths can make use of their skills and stamina acquired during the service, it also offers them relief from the strains of that service – and from the wider strains of their society. They enjoy the freedom to live on their own and make personal decisions, rather than having to follow directions or orders of authoritative adults. As pointed out above, the trip – rather than the army – can thus be seen as the principal *rite de passage* for Israeli youth, in which they prove their autonomy and consolidate their identity (Mevorach, 1997). This process, however, only proceeds under constant preoccupation with Israeli affairs.

In contrast to other Western youths, Israeli backpackers spend most of their time with other Israelis, and their conversations revolve to a considerable extent on their military experiences and the complexities of the Israeli society. The trip thus offers them an opportunity to reflect upon their recent past and re-evaluate at a distance their perceptions and attitudes regarding their society and their own place and future within it.

While basically committed to their society and not alienated from it, the Israeli youths are often critical of various aspects of it. However, the studies do not specify the extent to which their criticism is influenced by their encounter with other ways of life on the trip, rather than by their reflections and conversations with other Israelis under the unrestrained conditions of backpacker enclaves.

Detailed studies of backpackers from other countries would enable us to formulate a comparative framework relating the crucial experiences of the youths in their different countries of origin – reflecting wider endemic social strains and problems – to the magnitude and style of their backpacking travel. It would also show to what extent the Israeli case is exceptional, or merely exemplifies (perhaps in an intensified manner) some general preoccupations current among contemporary Western backpackers.

Future Research Directions

In this chapter I have dwelt on three major points, which appear to me important for the formulation of a strategy for future research on backpacking:

(1) the dynamic and diverse nature of backpacking phenomena;
(2) the difference between the image and the practice of backpacking;
(3) the historical and social context that generates the motivation for backpacking and influences the particular style of travel of backpackers from different backgrounds.

It follows that future research should desist from referring to backpacking as if it were a homogenous phenomenon, and should pay much more attention to its diverse manifestations, in terms of differences in age, gender, origins and particular subcultures. The complex relationship between the domestic, class, ethnic, national and cultural background of the backpackers and their trip should be given much more systematic attention than it has received up to now.[3] The simple assumption that backpacking is a consequence of alienation is not borne out by contemporary research – but that does not mean that there are no subtle linkages between stresses in the home society and the motivation and style of backpacking. The application of the model of the *rite de passage* to backpacking has proved more suitable than that of alienation. However, as I have attempted to show, it suffers from several limitations, and its applicability is diminished further in 'postmodern' situations, where owing to backpacker openness to global influences, their hybridities and internal heterogeneity, the concept of 'reversal' (central to the model of the *rite de passage*) does not seem to make much sense any more.

There is also a need for a reorientation of research on backpackers from the currently prevalent concern with their itineraries, travelling style and interactions to a more 'emic' and reflexive approach concerned with the manner in which they themselves construct, represent and narrate their experiences (e.g. Elsrud, 2001; Noy, 2002). Such an approach would help us to understand the gap between the model and practice of backpacking which is at present merely noted as a curious fact.

Studies on backpackers have to a large extent been conducted by researchers who have themselves often had considerable backpacking experience (e.g. Binder in Chapter 6, Maoz in Chapter 7, and Welk in Chapter 5 of this volume; Teas, 1988; Westerhausen, 2002). The researchers' background has doubtlessly coloured their orientation to their research and the interpretation of their findings, and this is particularly visible in the (even when covert) desire of most researchers to defend backpacking from its critics in the tourism establishment and to stress its value for the backpackers as well as for their hosts (e.g. Scheyvens, 2002). Another consequence of the researchers' background is that few, if any, possess any in-depth acquaintance with the host societies and communities popular with backpackers, even if they have conducted fieldwork in those sites and have not merely interviewed their subjects after the latter have returned home. The focus of most studies is thus almost exclusively on the back-packers, with the locals merely constituting a background – mostly as service personnel (e.g. Murphy, 2001); but they are usually not studied as subjects in their own right (Saldanha, 2002). I suspect that this focus on the backpackers has led to an overestimation of the closure and exclusiveness of the enclaves, and has overlooked the extent and significance of their interaction with the host community.

We therefore need anthropological community studies of popular backpacker destinations in which the researcher will achieve a grasp of the local situation and study the backpacking visitors within its context. Such a turn will not only enhance our understanding of backpackers' interactions with the locals, but also give us a better picture of the locals' perceptions and attitudes to the backpackers, which hitherto have been given little systematic attention in the literature. It would also contribute to a direction of research that I have not dealt with in this chapter, and is not merely of academic but also of practical significance: the economic contribution of backpacking to the often marginal and impoverished host communities (Scheyvens, 2002).

Up until now researchers have focused almost exclusively on Western backpackers belonging to the middle classes of the white majority of their respective countries. It is therefore necessary to extend the scope of research to the emergent backpacking from non-Western countries (espe-cially from East and South-East Asia[4] as well as from Latin America) and from the working classes and the ethnic minorities of Western countries. Such an extension would complement a wider effort to expand research on tourism by nationals of non-Western countries and by ethnic minorities, which has up until now has suffered from considerable neglect in tourism studies. Although the scope of backpacking from non-Western countries (with the exception of Japan) and ethnic minorities is as yet apparently limited, early attention to it would enable us to follow its growth and dynamics in 'real time', an opportunity that has been largely missed with respect to backpacking from the West.

Backpacking research is as yet in its early stages. I have attempted in this chapter to outline some of the directions in which it could profitably develop, and some ideas that could advance our theoretical understanding of backpacking phenomena. A more systematic, discerning comparative approach to backpacking is called for, and some progress towards it will hopefully be made in the future. But it should not block alternative approaches; the most important and original ideas in tourism research came from researchers following their own lights and this was and will probably also remain the case with the study of backpackers.

Notes

1. A study of Byron Bay, a popular backpacker enclave in Australia, for example, found that the average stay of backpackers is about 3.5 days (Firth & Hing, 1999).
2. Originally referring to the four stages of life through which a 'twice-born' Hindu ideally passes, the word 'ashram' has come to mean a place for the pursuit of spiritual or religious disciplines, often under a guru.
3. The domestic context of backpackers before, during and after the trip, and particularly the changing parent–offspring relationship, is an almost neglected issue in backpacker research. The only study I am aware of in which this topic is extensively dealt with is Mevorach's (1997) dissertation, which is in Hebrew and remains unpublished.
4. In Thailand, for example, the Thai Youth Hostels Association started a series of eco-tour programmes to overseas destinations to enable young travellers to learn how to adapt and live with other people (Jariyasombat, 2001).

Chapter 4

Theoretical Encounters: A Review of Backpacker Literature

IRENA ATELJEVIC AND STEPHEN DOORNE

Introduction

The backpacker phenomenon as a metaphor of mobility has in the contemporary context become representative of a travel lifestyle and an expression of identity, as well as a coherent industrial complex in its own right. The growth of backpacker tourism has been accompanied by a corresponding proliferation of research and scholarship. This chapter takes an evolutionary approach to reviewing the broad range of research-based literature on backpacking over the last three decades. First, we discuss the role of early seminal works on long-term budget travellers, which were instrumental in informing theoretical and conceptual foundations for subsequent research. Second, we provide an overview of studies that have contributed to a shift from the 'drifter' as a de-marketing concept to the 'backpacker' as a marketing niche. Finally, we discuss interpretations of backpacker tourism that have built upon critical perspectives associated with issues of postmodernity, metaphor and representation. In conclusion, we argue that the prevailing political, economic and socio-cultural environment remains a core context for both the manifestation of backpacker tourism and the continued evolution of research perspectives.

Theoretical Encounters: A Review of Backpacker Research

The term 'backpacker' has over the last decade become synonymous with a travelstyle that emphasises freedom and mobility. Not only does the backpack as a luggage item facilitate these actions far more effectively than, for example, the more traditional suitcase, it has come to assume a symbolic status. As a subject of study, backpacker travel features as a common denominator for a diverse range of studies seeking both to unravel the internal complexities of its cultural form, and to interpret the phenomenon as a research context.

This chapter presents an overview of the literature related to backpacker tourism, and is devoted to identifying the breadth of material and diversity of research perspectives. The review follows an evolving conceptualisation of the phenomenon from early seminal works to more applied studies, reflecting a shift from a de-marketing concept to a marketing label, to those studies that explore associated issues of cultural and economic development. This proliferation of research interests has in recent years produced new hybrid discourses, informed by broader theoretical perspectives outside the now 'traditional' focus of tourism-studies literature.

In this sense, we begin with an overview of the largely conceptual and historically focused literature that emerged in the early 1970s. We argue that the conceptual foundation established during this period was instrumental in informing subsequent research and theoretical trajectories that continue to the present day. During the 1980s investigations into the backpacking phenomenon drew heavily on these early conceptual approaches and, in the context of economic significance, entered a process of defining and re-defining backpackers as a coherent, dynamic and evolving 'market segment'. Within this body of literature, a number of core areas have been explored including motivations, behaviours, and decision-making processes. Further to these, social interactions and issues of gender, class and identity have been discussed by some in the context of an overarching capitalist system: in particular, the process of institutionalising backpacker activities. The proliferation of these internally-focused studies and the complexity of issues has laid the foundation for the development of a range of perspectives that are informed by issues external to the backpacker, such as the dynamics of cultural and economic development. Following this, we discuss interpretations of backpacker tourism that have built upon critical perspectives associated with issues of postmodernity, metaphor and representation. We conclude by reviewing the material presented, identifying characteristics and gaps, which point to an emerging research agenda for continuing research of the backpacker phenomenon.

Seminal works and early conceptualisations

The conceptual origins of the contemporary backpacker emerged in the early 1970s, and were informed by disciplinary perspectives from the humanities. In sociological terms Erik Cohen, in his seminal works on tourist activity (Cohen, 1972, 1973, 1974), developed a typology of tourist roles around a major distinction between institutionalised and non-institutionalised travellers. Institutionalised roles are typified by the organised mass tourist showing a preference for being confined to the 'Western cultural bubble' in which decisions are made on behalf of the traveller and his or her needs are met by the tourist infrastructure. Institutionalised roles also feature the individual mass tourist who makes arrangements for transportation and accommodation through an agency and chooses low-risk, familiar situations when planning itineraries.

Non-institutionalised roles identified by Cohen include the 'explorer' and the 'drifter'. The primary shared values of these groups are novelty, spontaneity, risk, independence, and a multitude of 'off the beaten track' options. The primary distinction between the two centres is not only the drifter's lack of a fixed itinerary and a more limited budget, but reflects a more socio-political stance of a counterculture being 'an individualist, disdainful of ideologies ... he [sic] is at best un-patriotic...is hedonistic and often anarchistic' (Cohen, 1973: 91–92). Cohen's discussion of drifters is a significant departure from the 'constructive' youth movement and the earlier tradition of 'tramping', which originated in preceding centuries and was related to class-based activities ranging from the Grand Tour, to 'working holidays', to the *Wandervogel* youth movement. These earlier forms of nomadic travel reflected the social structure of the period, just as Cohen's description of the drifter reflects the emergence of affluent middle classes of the West. Following Cohen's discussion of the origins of the drifter phenomenon he proceeds to identify in detail a broad range of sociological motivations and behaviours, which he classifies into three areas: cultural, political and economic forces. With respect to the cultural context of their activity, he observes the counterculture of:

> the loosening of ties and obligations, the abandonment of accepted standards and conventional ways of life, the voluntary abnegation of the comforts of modern technological society, and the search for sensual and emotional experiences ... [that motivates them] to travel and live among different and more 'primitive' surroundings. (Cohen, 1973: 93).

Cohen also notes a strong connection with drifting and drug culture, particularly with respect to the 'Third World' of Asia and Latin America. On this subject Stuart Hall (1968) made similar observations with respect to the influx of Western youth to South-East Asia in search of the spiritual meaning often tied to drug culture. The mix of drug culture and the search for spiritual enlightenment saw hippies publicly criticised in India for inappropriate behaviours against local normative codes (Turner & Ash, 1975; see also Mehta, 1979 who provides a comprehensive view of the hippie era in South Asia).

With respect to economic forces Cohen notes:

> the relative affluence of modern society makes competition for an

occupational career less urgent and less challenging. Many youths, completing their studies at a relatively early age, show little enthusiasm to engage immediately on a routine occupational career. (Cohen, 1973: 94)

His discussion of the economic background of drifters suggests their need to experience 'real life' beyond familiar economic security, yet he also observes their abilities to travel for extended periods through careful budgeting and skilled financial management.

Politically, Cohen (1973: 94) identifies drifting as 'both a symptom and an expression of broader alienative forces current among contemporary youth', particularly with reference to the Vietnam War and 'the modern political system, in general. Despite the political context of drifting he observes the paradox of a corresponding institutionalisation of budget travel in the form of fixed travel patterns, established routines and increasing development and commodification. Most importantly, Cohen's observations identify the inevitable sequence of production and reproduction following the drifters' attempts to escape the political economy of tourism. In essence, they take with them that which they try to leave behind, permeating the further reaches of the globe, as Cohen (1973: 96) neatly summarises, 'as drifter-itineraries coagulate, a separate infrastructure, serving drifter-tourism, gradually comes into existence'.

Vogt (1976) prefers the term 'wandering', and observes a similar set of motivating characteristics, particularly with respect to their class-based origins. His anthropological perspective provides considerable substance to the behavioural dynamics and internal culture of the activity. With respect to decision making and personal control Vogt (1976: 30) sees this travelstyle as an opportunity to be creative and to generate 'feelings of mastery over the self and the environment' by creating strategies and taking choices. Complexity, novelty and diversity are important motivating factors in the choice of activities and destinations, yet Vogt reiterates Cohen's observation that such activities become standardised into routine. He (Vogt, 1976: 34) identifies the opportunity to engage in new and different sets of interpersonal relations as a key element driving the temporal and spatial dynamics of the activity where 'the awareness of brevity encourages a sense of immediacy'. Finally, he provides some insight into decision-making processes with respect to gathering places and resting periods. The reproduction and institutionalisation identified by Cohen provide wanderers with opportunities to match shared values and aesthetic preferences with accessibility and cost through the process of articulating identity through consumption. Indeed Cohen's (1982) later work raises arguments illustrating the extent to which these routinised behaviours have resulted in the 'traditional backpacker' exhibiting more conventional tourist characteristics.

We argue that the complementarity of Vogt and Cohen's observations in the 1970s provided the foundation for a bifurcation of subsequent research trajectories. Whereas Cohen's discussion provides a foundation for context-ualising behaviour in terms of society and change, Vogt's contribution has opened the door for the exploration of the internal dynamics of backpacker culture and consumer psychology. Subsequent research in this area has proceeded to define and redefine the evolution of drifters and wanderers in terms of 'budget travellers' and 'backpackers'.

From de-marketing to marketing

The transition from early conceptualisations of long-term travellers to their conceptualisation as a coherent 'market niche' has occurred through the exploration of the internal complexities of the subculture principally in terms of motivation, behaviour and socio-psychological characteristics.

Adler (1985) argues that contemporary tourism originates from the 'Grand Tour' taken by young European aristocrats in the seventeenth and eighteenth centuries. She goes on to identify the modern low-budget, extended-period travel phenomenon with 'tramping', an eighteenth and nineteenth century religious or labour-related travel practice that provided opportunities for sightseeing, adventure and education through first-hand experience. Tramping was the Grand Tour of the lower classes and provided the opportunity for individuals to gain and share skills by plying their craft from village to village while finding accommodation at inns or labour-related societies. Although the practice was commonly associated with work, it also functioned as a *rite de passage* to full (usually male) adult-hood through separation from home and family. By the 1930s tramping had all but passed as a labour-related practice and began to be viewed as socially-deviant behaviour. As Adler (1985: 341) comments, 'their mobility was conceived as a social problem, and their motivation explained in individual, psychological terms as *Wanderlust*' (see also Gray, 1981).

Riley (1988) introduced more terminology to describe the phenomenon. In rejecting Cohen's (1972; 1973; 1974) earlier definitions, Riley (1988: 326) asserts that 'today's typical youthful traveller is not accurately described as a "hippie", a "bum", or an adherent to "counter-culture". Western society has undergone some major changes and the contemporary long-term trav-eller reflects them'. Riley's study has significantly changed the conceptuali-sation and 'negative' connotations associated with 'drifters'. She described these individuals:

... as likely to be middle class, at a juncture in life, somewhat older than the earlier travellers on average, college educated, and not aimless drifters. They travel under flexible timetables and itineraries. Most expect to rejoin the work force in the society they left. (Riley, 1988: 326)

Riley's observations were later supported by Meijer (1989) and van der Berghe (1994) who in their studies from Central America both identify similar demographic and behavioural characteristics.

It was Pearce (1990) whose interpretation of the travelstyle introduced the term 'backpacker' into the academic literature. Pearce's analysis is primarily concerned with motivational aspects, particularly related to extending one's education: travel as escape from pressing life choices, and 'occasional work' to extend travel time. Most significantly, Pearce identifies a fourth theme related to the emergence of a subculture focused on the pursuit of health and outdoor activities. Pearce attributes the growth of this market specifically to the development of a corresponding industry in the form of the Youth Hostel Association in Australia throughout the 1990s. Pearce's work is significant in that the emergence of the term backpacker is not simply semantic variation, but indicates the fundamental shift of the term from a de-marketing label to a marketing tool – in the context of the growing economic significance of this market. The concept of the back-packer has rapidly become a firm foundation around which a range of research agendas has focused on defining and re-defining the phenomenon.

Further explorations of the characteristics, motivations and behaviours of backpackers emerged in the 1990s. Loker-Murphy and Pearce (1995), for example identify a number of common characteristics including high levels of interaction with hosts, low organisation, and the use of low cost, less comfortable facilities. These observable travel traits together with low average age, lack of travel structure, and a high degree of independence are together bound in, and to some extent facilitate, the search for 'more authentic' travel experiences. In a similar vein, other studies around this period used destination-specific studies to explore issues of decision making, motivation and the dynamics of backpacker behaviour, particularly with respect to the emergence of the phenomenon in Australasia (Doorne, 1994; Garnham, 1993; Murphy, 1999; Parr, 1989; Ross, 1992). These lines of enquiry spawned a raft of industry- and market-oriented quantitative and qualitative research that attempted to isolate and understand this increasingly prominent tourist segment with respect to their specific destination perceptions and their characteristics (see for example, Bureau of Tourism Research, 2000b; Murphy, 1998; Tourism New Zealand, 1999; South Australian Tourism Commission, 1999).

The broad concepts of motivation and behaviour provided the basis from which most contemporary studies on backpacker travel have emerged, principally dealing with the internal cultural issues of the travellers themselves. Ross (1993), for example, explores ideal and actual images of authenticity related to desires to achieve higher levels of personal fulfilment. Loker-Murphy (1996) segmented a backpacker population according to their motivational psychographics. Drawing on Pearce's concept of travel careers, she identified four different segments: social/ excitement seekers, escapers/relaxers, achievers and self-developers. Although Loker-Murphy (1996) challenges the homogenous treatment of the backpacker, her analysis remains firmly tied to Pearce's concept. Ross also (1997) explores motivators for travel such as achievement, affiliation and power in the context of education and relaxation preferences. Similarly, Ryan and Moshin (1999) use a leisure motivation scale to examine backpackers' activities as being reflections of attitudes and motivation. They identified four key groups including, 'mainstreamers', 'passive viewers', 'explorers' and 'the not keen'.

Hyde (2000) explores decision-making processes by drawing on two perspectives of consumer psychology, namely the 'consumer as a problem solver' and the 'consumer as a hedonistic person', in which backpackers make purchases in order to create feelings, experiences and emotions. An integral feature of independent travel is the enjoyment of consumer experiences when not having planned the details of the vacation gives rise to the unknown and the unexpected. Murphy (2001) explores the social interactions of backpackers, focusing on word of mouth communication and conversations. Although Murphy observes essential qualities that differentiate backpackers from other tourists, such as tolerance, openness and independence, the study identifies no corresponding language or vocabulary unique to backpacking culture. Murphy (2001) also notes that the social aspects and opportunities to meet people were second in importance only to choosing to backpack because it was a cheap way of travelling. It should be noted that all of the studies discussed above draw on research in Australasia in which the internal dynamics and culture of predominantly-European travellers are examined. Research by Shipway (2000) is the notable exception, as it examines the activities of Australasian backpackers in Europe and the UK.

Elsrud (1998) adds further depth to motivational backpacker studies by focusing on Swedish women backpackers and identifying their desire to go 'back in time' in the search for 'authenticity'. She discusses the notion of travel as 'time out', as a withdrawal from clock time and the routines of contemporary daily life. Hillman (1999: 1) similarly looks at issues of authenticity, particularly with respect to female backpackers in Australia and the way they 'use travel as a way of positioning themselves through a "rites of passage" perspective'. She also observes the role of backpacker travel in the re-establishment of independence following personal crises, particularly relationship break-ups. Hottola's (1999) study of women backpacker travellers in India and Sri Lanka observes the heterogeneity of the contemporary backpacker, and provides a comprehensive typology of these people. She identifies: 'students' (including globe trailers with an interest in seeing the world), 'professionals' (including academics, journalists, musicians, photographers, writers on working vacation), 'specialists' (particularly 'eco-packers' seeking pristine, natural environments), 'outcasts' (people seeking to start a 'second' life), 'freaks and neo-hippies' congregating primarily on beaches and counterculture communities, 'root diggers' or 'old hippies' revisiting past travel experiences and places, and 'army discharges' (predominantly Israelis in the void between the army and the return to civilian life – see Maoz, Chapter 7).

Despite producing even further segmentation of the backpacker population, Hottola's discussion reminds us of the human condition inherent in such research, as she states: 'the idea of creating typologies of people remains an enigma to me ... [m]ore than once I have found myself quite amused when reading about typologies which resemble a set of paper dolls rather than living beings' (Hottola, 1999: 79). Her observations are bounded within broader conceptualisation where travel is seen as a: 'flexible discourse which seeks to understand the human life worlds as they are in the empirical reality without artificial epistemological limitations' (Hottola, 1999: 373). This approach has similarly been acknowledged in the work of others seeking to move towards the more abstract terrain of identity.

Desforges (1998), for example, explores the notion of identity through the practice of 'collecting places' as a way in which travellers relate to the 'Other'. With respect to authenticity, Desforges identifies markers of authenticity as the absence of the travel industry and other tourists. He observes two effects: first, these travellers determine which places are brought into and excluded from the tourist economy, and second, they determine the terms by which people and places are included in the tourist trade. This economic power serves to reshape cultures, employment practices and economies that are all part of tourism's role in the production of place. In line with the motivational studies of the internal backpacker culture, Desforges (1998), drawing on Bourdieu's (1984) concept of cultural capital, discusses travel as a form that enables (as a sign of distinction) the traveller to gain access to a social class and its privileges. Munt (1994: 108) similarly discusses the relationship between class and the 'new petite bourgeoisie' who are 'best conceived as ego-tourists who search for a style of travel which is both reflective of an alternative lifestyle and which is capable of maintaining and enhancing their cultural capital'.

Desforges (2000) explores these issues in a later paper where he refers to Giddens (1991) notion of self-identity and a 'fateful moment' of life in which travel is drawn upon to re-imagine the self. Elsrud (2001) also uses Giddens' notion that identity is left to individuals to conceive through the means they are offered by society, and the notion that Western travellers undertake 'risky' travel because they come from a society that demands from them the ability to cope successfully with risk. A sense of difference (differentiation) is usually based on the 'primitive Other', and this provides the context in which Elsrud discusses risk associated with certain places, as well as the practice of telling stories about risks associated with the physical self (e.g. illnesses, dangerous foods, malaria). These narratives are used to position the storytellers and others within a hierarchy, and functions also as a form of cultural capital. The process of 'Othering' primitive ethnic groups has been examined by several authors in the context of backpacking in peripheral and marginal environments (see for example, Cohen, 1989; van den Berghe, 1994). A key process of 'Othering' occurs through travel media. For example, McGregor (2000) examines texts of backpacker guidebooks and their re-interpretation through word of mouth from the perspective that texts have no intrinsic meaning separate from the process of interpretation, itself informed by cultural capital.

Retracing the steps of earlier research in South-East Asia, Spreitzhofer (1998) adds a range of significant terms that illustrate the changing context of backpacker motivations. The drivers were egocentrism, self-affirmation and prestige, whereby he recognises 'elitism' and 'anti-tourist' attitudes. In this context, Spreitzhofer (1998: 982) argues that backpacking cannot be highlighted as a genuine alternative to mainstream tourism; ' ... in fact, it seems to be still no more than a variant of mass tourism on a low budget level itself ... '. This issue of institutionalisation through which the backpacker has come full circle to resemble 'the tourist' can also be identified in the context of motivations and values in a study by Ateljevic and Doorne (2001). This study revealed a continuum of backpacker values, which are articulated as travellers' styles and consumer behaviour. Through their juxtaposition of the traditional with the contemporary context, Ateljevic and Doorne reveal that, whilst the 'traditional backpacker' seeks to escape the Western consumer model, the 'contemporary backpacker' transplants that model. These findings are supported by Moran's (2000) focus on structured backpacker tours in New Zealand. Indeed both studies reveal the institutionalisation of the market that itself provides a point of departure for a discussion of issues external to the backpacker.

External issues: Cultural and economic dimensions of backpacker tourism

One of the features of backpacker travel is exploration, both of self and of new 'peripheral' places. Beyond the range of research focusing on the internal dynamic and culture of backpacker travel is a body of literature that focuses on the impacts and the activity of backpacking and its relationships in the context of development. Gray (1981), for example, identifies infrastructure problems emerging from wanderlust tourism. He argues that the costs of infrastructure associated with wanderlust (i.e. backpacker) tourism exceed those of a resort industry, and he outlines some of the problems of infrastructure policy that face planners in poor nations that have backpacking industries. Cohen (1982) provides a place-specific focus on the impact of youth tourism on two beaches in southern Thailand. He discusses the relationship between travellers and local hosts, particularly with respect to the values and the dynamics of business and infrastructure development. He also noted that, at that time, the youth tourist industry was regarded as undesirable and not included in planning processes owing to the negative impact of Western youth culture within which the 'traditional backpacker', searching for the meaning of life, wishes to experiment with different ways of life.

Cohen (1982) takes the pessimistic view whereby the future of a 'craft' tourism industry based on youth tourists is not positive. As the islands become better known, they will be incorporated into mainstream tourism, with ensuing changes in tourism infrastructure. Cohen (1982) notes that, on the beaches where local ownership remains predominant, development for higher-end tourism is restricted by lack of capital. In the long term, Cohen argues, this could make them more vulnerable to being taken over by outside interests. Smith (1990) shares similar views with respect to the social, economic and ecological impact of drifter tourism on Boracay Island in the Philippines. She observes that significant ecological and social damage has already been caused by drifter tourists on the island, and argues that negative impacts could be ameliorated through the targeting of the market segment and the type of tourist that will most benefit the area. Westerhausen (2002) shares these views, arguing that a sustainable tourism product and maximisation of economic return is an ephemeral condition, given that alternative tourism sectors face the inevitability of take-over by mainstream tourism.

Environmental sustainability is a critical focus of impact studies of backpacking. Firth and Hing (1999) examined attitudes and behaviours of hostels and their guests towards sustainable tourism. Their observations reveal that, although price is the most significant element in backpacker decision making, a number of hostels failed to advertise their eco-friendly practices, and so there was little awareness about them. Firth and Hing (1999) conclude that communicating pro-environmental practices can provide opportunities for niche-positioning of local tourist businesses. Zurick (1992) similarly explores issues of sustainability in peripheral economies of Nepal with respect to 'adventure tourists'.

In contrast to these predominantly pessimistic observations, many recent studies provide different views. For example, Wilson (1997) inverts the traditional critique of the socio-cultural relationships between backpackers and locals, arguing that low-budget tourism provides a major economic contribution to the local economy (unlike the current trend towards the 'high-end' tourism). Other advantages include wide local ownership of resources, and broad distribution of benefits throughout the local community. Low-budget tourism also requires relatively little additional infrastructure to accommodate visitors, and puts less pressure on existing water resources.

Low-budget tourists can also contribute to local communities by assisting in finding solutions to some of the problems created by 'mainstream tourism'. Similarly, Hampton (1998) argues that backpacker tourism has the potential to be framed as 'alternative' tourism, which is small scale, offering more local opportunities for employment, fewer economic leakages and overall fewer negative impacts. In his study of Lombok/Gilli Islands Hampton (1998) observed that backpacker tourism has developed certain characteristics: communication networks, demand for cheap accommodation, and a parallel structure of transport, restaurants, accommodation and support services. He describes these as 'minimalist' infrastructure, and argues that the development of backpacker tourism requires further in-depth research and careful planning. In one of the few studies of backpacking in Africa, Scheyvens (1999) argues that backpackers may be a more appropriate market for community tourism in Africa, as local people and products can meet the needs of backpackers because they do not demand luxury. She also observes economic benefits (such as the fact that enterprises are small and remain in local ownership and control), plus the revitalisation of cultural practices through meeting backpacker interest in local cultures.

Erb (2000) takes a further step into the external environment by examining 'who' tourists are for local people in communities in Western Flores in Indonesia and how the local people strive to accommodate these tourists, who enter their world as outsiders. The study argues that local communities are not 'victims of circumstances', but actively and strategically adapt to tourism. This relationship can have a contradictory nature. On one hand guests are honoured, respected and shown deference; but there is a degree of dependency created by the debt incurred by being a guest. Therefore, the host is able to wield an element of power over the guests, and control is exerted over 'outsiders'. Similarly, Cohen's (1989) study of hill tribe trekking in Thailand shows that this 'alternative tourism' offers commercial opportunities for enterprising locals, who seek to cash in on the alleged authenticity of the attractions that they offer. The fact that conventional tourist attractions are seen by many as overtly staged and inauthentic, 'opens to these local entrepreneurs a chance for a more subtle, covert and insidious form of staging' (Cohen 1989: 57). Doorne *et al.*'s (2003) study of local tourism entrepreneurship in China identifies an unfolding of multi-layered contexts and meanings through which tourism production and consumption take place. They argue that, far from ethnic identities being commodified to satisfy consumer demands for 'Othering', locals are proactive in identifying market segments and producing differentiated products to enhance their local and personal economies. In other words, it is the locals who commodify consumer culture by reproducing their identity to meet the Western preoccupation with 'primitive Otherness'.

This concept of production processes and 'niche' market opportunities has also been explored in respect of lifestyle entrepreneurship. Focusing on former backpackers who settled in New Zealand, Ateljevic and Doorne (2000) identified their business activities as facilitating more extended immersion experiences with landscape and culture, as distinct from entrepreneurship for material and financial gain. The rejection of the market-driven paradigm by these individuals in favour of reciprocity and environmental values created its own market niche aligned to consumers actively seeking products that convey these values and an eco-social orientation. Paradoxically, the search to distance themselves from a 'suffocating' market environment provided a niche opportunity to simultaneously engage with that market but on their own terms. Nimmo (2001) similarly observed the search for more immersed, 'authentic' socio-cultural experiences by backpackers stepping outside of their consumer role. Focusing on Willing Workers on Organic Farms (WWOOF), Nimmo (2001) explores this form of backpacking in New Zealand as de-commodified ecotourism. As WWOOFers, backpackers engage in voluntary work while at the same time satisfying their individual needs for structure and routine, thereby challenging the assumption that tourism is a strict bifurcation between work and leisure. Also on this theme, Uriely and Reichel (2000) explore working tourists and observe that in postmodern tourism the dichotomy between work and leisure is breaking down. Their study of kibbutzim, for example, identifies volunteering as an integral part of the tourism experience and provides opportunities for more 'authentic' social relationships through extended periods of social engagement.

Discourses of Hybridity: Re-contextualising Perspectives of Backpacker Tourism Research

Whilst the preceding discussion has reviewed the diversity of research foci, it is equally important to reflect on their theoretical perspectives which are increasingly informed by the emergence of a revived, reconstituted and more diverse cultural terrain throughout the wider environment of tourism studies (see for example Ateljevic, 2000; Crang, 1996; Dann, 1996a; Morgan & Pritchard, 1998; Pritchard & Morgan, 2000; Selwyn, 1996). Further dimensions of the backpacking context have emerged in the form of a critical re-interpretation of the phenomenon, particularly with respect to discourse analysis and the postmodern condition. In this respect the analysis of backpacker tourism forms an integral part of a broader theoretical discussion of tourism as a contemporary cultural and social practice.

Key contextual references have provided a foundation for discussion in this research trajectory. Clifford (1992, 1997), for example, provides the conceptual lenses through which we can explore issues of mobility and culture as a contemporary social condition. He draws on ethnographic perspectives to explore ideas about how anthropology can be reworked to examine the phenomenon of travel (Clifford, 1992: 101). In particular, he focuses on how difference is politically articulated and challenged and where communities draw lines between insiders and outsiders. Clifford poses a series of questions: 'How do groups negotiate themselves in external relationships and how is a culture also a site of travel for others? How are spaces traversed from outside? How is one group's core another's periphery?' One of Clifford's core arguments concerns the way in which metaphors of travel can be deconstructed to produce a notion of knowledge articulating an accumulation of history of locations and locations of history. Urry (1999) also explores the connotation of metaphors and their gender basis/orientation. For example, the very notion of 'nomadism' from a feminist perspective reveals that different people have different access to 'being on the road'. Conversely, the male metaphors of nomadic travel could be rewritten differently as, for example, the 'homeless drunk' or the 'sex tourist'. Bird *et al.* (1994) use a similar metaphor approach and explore the notion of displacement to discuss the narratives of travellers' tales. Cloke and Perkins (1998), exploring representations of adventure tourism in New Zealand, unravel these activities as a 'performance' metaphor, associated with an active body, heightened sensory experience, risk and vulnerability. In this sense, touristic experience is embodied, rather than limited to sight. Rojek and Urry (1997: 19) also explore representations of meaning and the 'ways in which tourist sensibility is produced and maintained'. They point to critical areas of understanding in terms of the 'tourist sign economy and the images of escape, freedom and relaxation which it produces' (Rojek & Urry, 1997).

Such perspectives are also discussed in specific backpacker studies; McGregor (2000), for example, explores relationships between juxtaposed cultures and the meanings derived from touristic narratives, particularly backpacker texts. Desforges (1998; 2000) examines issues of identity and representation with respect to the global–local nexus. Hottola (1999) provides the postmodern feminist perspective of the Western woman backpacker in India and Sri Lanka in the context of intercultural adaptation. Doorne *et al.*'s (2002) cultural analysis of economic relations in backpacker tourism explores the commodification of consumer culture from the perspective of the 'Other'. Erb (2000) similarly examines the ways that local communities actively engage in their backpacker tourism encounters. This range of perspectives seeks to go beyond the exploration of the backpacker tourism per se, and to challenge and invert the accepted 'neutrality' of traditional concepts and myths.

This trend is itself a reflection of the so-called 'crisis of representation' and (re)construction of the 'Other' (Marcus & Fisher, 1986) that has emerged within the social sciences. These perspectives have raised theoretical debates across all disciplines, yet these debates have only recently emerged within the mainstream of tourism literature. Social researchers are increasingly being asked to identify their 'position' within their writings, as texts are revealed as epistemological representations (see for example, Barnes & Duncan, 1992; Clifford & Marcus, 1986; Johnston, 1993). This 'crisis of representation' has encapsulated many of the concerns encountered in the feminist critique of the all-pervasive hegemonic dominance of the masculinist Western academic approach (see for example, Gilligan, 1982; Harding & Hintikka, 1983).

In this context, the number of studies that analyse discourses of tourism imag(in)ing and mythologising has increased (for example, Ateljevic & Doorne, 2002; Brown, 1995; Bruner, 1991; Cohen, C., 1995; Cohen, E., 1993; 1995; Crang, 1996; Hughes, 1992; Mellinger, 1994; Silver, 1993; Squire, 1994). Issues of text and the wider context of power relations feature as an enduring undercurrent in these contemporary critical perspectives. Bruner

(1991) for example takes a Lacanian perspective, arguing that tourism marketing discourse generates an 'imaginary' about indigenous people, which is not based on any real assessment of indigenous people, but rather on a projection from Western consciousness. Whilst previous work on tourist signs typically explained promotional imagery in terms of the economic interests of advertising (for example, Goodrich, 1978; Woodside & Lysonski, 1989) or the social psychology of consumption (for example, Mayo & Jarvis, 1981), this emerging tradition identifies the importance of deconstructing the cultural discourses of tourist destinations in the wider context of social and political processes.

Conclusion

This chapter has provided an overview of what is an inherently diverse, fluid and dynamic research environment. The approach we have taken has been to broadly describe approaches and studies in terms of their commonalities and distinctiveness, whilst attempting to acknowledge their often-multifaceted nature. Whilst we acknowledge the complexity and interrelatedness of issues, our descriptions here have highlighted their principal focus and the themes to which they contribute.

The discussion has identified a range of research trajectories in the form, first, of seminal works and early conceptualisations. Here, the emphasis on freedom and mobility was encapsulated by the early conceptualisation of the 'drifter' whose travelstyle articulated a semi-political statement against a growing political dominance and cultural homogeneity of the Western developed world. This motivation emerged during the 1960s alongside events such as the Vietnam War and represented a significant departure from earlier travel to the periphery that was characterised by 'explorers'. The images associated with the phenomenon became synonymous with derogatory associations of drug culture and anarchic values, yet simultaneously embodied an often nostalgic search for meaningful cultural existence.

During the 1980s, there emerged a raft of studies articulating a shift of backpacking interest from a demarketing to a marketing concept. The dominance of global markets and consumerism changed the guise of the 'hippie' drifter in favour of budget-oriented independent travellers seeking lifestyle enhancement and travel as an agent of personal growth. This transformation of the backpacker has more recently become a segmented and fragmented marketplace where the contemporary backpacker has become symbolic of myriad identities, markets and cultural forms. In the contemporary context, the original hippie drifter is juxtaposed with adrenalin junkies, within a dynamic, rapidly evolving marketplace. Concurrent with this phenomenon, a similarly diverse body of research has emerged, seeking to explore internal complexity as well as external development issues. Finally, the subject has been contextualised through the integration of disciplinary perspectives with respect to broader issues of culture, society, economy and space/place.

What is significant about the juxtaposition of early conceptualisations and those that define and re-define the backpacker is the prevailing political and economic context through which these perspectives have emerged. It can be argued that early conceptualisations, with the conventional tourism complex as a backdrop, were principally exploratory in their abstraction of the phenomenon to its socio-cultural context. The 'drifter' hippie movement and its rejection of the prevailing political ideology provided the principal reference against which the dynamics of change could be analysed. The apparent semantic shift to 'the backpacker' reflects a more significant agenda through the identification of a new and coherent 'market niche'.

Despite the obvious emphasis of industrialisation and commodification of the phenomenon, the significance of the ideological context cannot be understated. The transformation of the 'drifter' as de-marketing to the 'backpacker' as marketing tool mirrors the penetration by the industry of peripheral places and marginal environments in both the developing and the developed world. In the last decade a number of studies have emerged against this backdrop that seek to explore issues of cultural and economic development arising from backpacker tourism. These perspectives directly reflect the economic significance of the broader tourism phenomenon, which has itself been translated to the academic and institutional environment. In this respect, our discussion of a new trajectory of hybridised discourses of backpacker tourism has sought to integrate broader discussions of culture, economy and society. In doing so, it presents an important departure in the context of the 'political economy of signification' (Baudrillard, 1981) and the 'culture of consumption' (Featherstone, 1987; 1990). This shift can be seen as a disciplinary cross-fertilisation through which a broader philosophical transformation can be observed.

Our review of the literature is by no means definitive or exhaustive, but identifies both coherent and well-developed areas of interest, and also reveals a number of areas where further research would make a valuable contribution to the literature:

- Given the rapid changes of the industry and culture of backpacking over the last two decades, there is a continuing need for 'market' research that reveals even more heterogeneity and is context-specific. It should be noted also that the majority of motivational studies and the associated typologies are largely derived from a limited Australasian context.

- Gender perspectives can also be identified as demanding more attention, particularly the metaphorical associations commonly applied in backpacking discourses.
- The spread of the phenomenon to peripheral places and marginal environments demands ongoing research into relationships that articulate host perspectives in the context of institutionalisation.
- The relationship between work and leisure, particularly with respect to working holidays, is a rapidly-changing element of the backpacker phenomenon and in many respects can be integrated with longitudinal studies of consumer identity and culture.
- Finally, the subject of texts and discourses can be seen as an interpretative lens through which the above research agendas can be further explored and discussed.

The recent integration of diverse theoretical interpretations has had a dramatic effect in contextualising the broader debate as well as specific discussion on the subject of backpacking, and points the way to new understandings and critical perspectives on the phenomenon.

Chapter 5

The Beaten Track: Anti-Tourism as an Element of Backpacker Identity Construction

PETER WELK

Introduction

Globalisation is the dominant driving force of our age. Although it has been prevalent in the world economy since the times of the Silk Road, its dominance has never such an extensive part of people's lives as it is today. A recent addition to the all-encompassing presence of globalisation is its democratisation: never have so many people (though mainly in the industrialised world) been able to actively participate in this process, to become 'global players'. Freely and almost without restriction, we communicate with the world via the Internet, receive the world in our living rooms via television, travel it via land, air and sea, and have its full range of goods available in our supermarkets. Distances and borders do not seem to matter any more – 'distance is just something in your mind", says a Spanish interviewee. Francis Fukuyama would probably call it 'the end of geography'.

Meanwhile, globalisation has extended far beyond domination only of the economy; because of our continual involvement with it, it has oozed into our minds. We 'think' globally and establish numerous transnational contacts; we perceive processes in global contexts and relish ideas and ideals from foreign places that we have never visited. Our local cultures become more and more penetrated by global influences, which in turn become part of us. In short: we create 'global identities'. At the same time, the disappearance of a territorial consciousness makes us feel lost and isolated. The compartmentalisation of our minds by globalisation is met by the need to dissociate ourselves from others while belonging to a community that makes us feel 'at home'. Thus, reverse processes of localisation have emerged around the world over the last few decades; as reflected in the upsurge of territorial ethnicity.

But how does a global (or cosmopolitan) community such as the backpacker scene[1] cope with 'their' need to 'belong' somewhere, this community that cannot claim a place of origin or a geographical space that could be called 'home'? How do backpackers construct a 'space' they can identify with and where they can re-establish some kind of territoriality? Why do backpackers focus on mainstream tourism as a major counterpart from which to differentiate themselves? And how does this opposition affect the values and behaviour of the scene?

I will argue in this chapter that backpackers construct their dissociation from conventional tourists along symbolic, i.e. ideological, lines. We will see that, through this dissociation, the backpacker community – while neither a real subculture nor an ethnic group – displays characteristic features of both, because mainstream tourism puts a constant assimilative pressure on the backpacker scene. This in fact causes a symbolic territorial segregation, which takes place on a micro level. Finally I will argue that these same processes of distinction through which backpackers relate to other tourists have also started to emerge within different factions of their own community.

The Symbolic Construction of Communities

Cohen (1985) leaves out the territoriality principle entirely when arguing that many communities construct themselves not along any *objective* criteria of selection (such as geographical boundaries) but along *subjectively* perceived symbolic lines:

> [Symbols] are ... ideal media through which people can speak a 'common' language, behave in apparently similar ways, participate in the 'same' rituals, pray to the 'same' gods, wear similar clothes, and so forth ... (Cohen, 1985: 21)

Thus, a community does not necessarily have to consist of similar people but of people sharing the same set of particular values. 'The reality of community in people's experience thus inheres in their attachment or commitment to [this] common body of symbols' (Cohen, 1985: 16). However, 'the "commonality" which is found in community need not be uniformity' (Cohen, 1985: 20). The meaning ascribed to these values (and to the ways of behaviour) varies with their interpretation by the community's individual members, an internal differentiation that takes place within the limits that define the boundaries of the community. These boundaries have to be set wide enough to ensure that: 'although they recognise important differences among themselves, they also suppose themselves to be more like each other than like the members of other communities' (Cohen, 1985: 21).

So 'the boundaries [of a community] are *relational* rather than absolute; that is, they mark the community *in relation to* other communities' (Cohen, 1985: 58). Inclusive membership of one community meets the exclusion of others, 'to be an "x" means 'not being a "y"'' (Sollors, 1989: 241).

Concluding this point, we see that: 'this relative similarity or difference is not a matter for "objective" assessment: it is a matter of feeling, a matter which resides in the minds of the members themselves' (Cohen, 1985: 21). In lacking any other means to manifest a commonly shared identity, the backpacker community instead constructs itself along these symbolic lines.

Research method

The fieldwork for my Master's thesis (Welk, 2003) – on which parts of this chapter are based – was conducted in Queensland and Sydney in 1999 as well as in Penang in Malaysia in late 2000. I applied qualitative research methods by first using standardised questionnaires that were distributed in backpacker hostels and then conducting guideline interviews based on the questionnaire. Responders were offered flyers to exchange for a free meal. The questionnaire consisted of 45 questions designed to investigate backpackers' traveller profiles, behaviour and expenditure patterns, their interests, ideals, travelling experiences, social networks, self perception and their perception of the backpacker scene. The results were evaluated with a focus on identity and representation.

Backpacker Ideology

For the past 30 to 35 years, the backpacker scene has formed a highly dynamic, constantly changing community that has transformed itself from an offspring of the hippie counterculture to a mainstream movement with good profit margins for the tourist industry as its overall 'biggest spending visitors' (Macbeth & Westerhausen, 2001). In the process, backpacking itself has splintered into various movements, making it hard for the outsider to determine its boundaries from other forms of tourism. However, the code of values and ideals prevalent throughout the community has largely remained the same since its early countercultural stages, and this is what constitutes the inner bond of the scene.

So, the commonly-shared ideology is perhaps the key to understanding backpacker identities. A non-institutionalised community with a high degree of transience and fluctuation, backpackers find it easier to adapt to a general 'code of honour' than to a restrictive set of particular rules or obligations – the latter being exactly what many are actually trying to escape from. In this way, backpackers have a wider scope for individually interpreting and implementing their ideals. At the core of this code of honour lies the endeavour to create travelling experiences, which serve as the bond to other travellers and as the major source of social prestige within the scene, as well as back home. Consequently, travelling experiences are by far the most frequent topic in conversations among backpackers.[2] On this basis, five *'badges of honour'* (Bradt, 1995: 49) can be identified as the 'pillars' of backpacker ideology:

- *To travel on a low budget:* an ideal that in reality is restricted to the three basic necessities of a traveller (accommodation, food, and transport) and is primarily aimed at making the trip last as long as possible.
- *To meet different people* (especially other backpackers, but also locals): an ideal that is seen as the manifestation of the 'global village' idea; it serves as a source of information and forms the strongest inner bond to hold the community together.
- *To be (or to feel) free, independent and open-minded:* an egocentric (and often hedonistic) effort to cast off the restraints, commitments and taboos of one's 'normal' life and have to adapt to the constantly-changing environment of the traveller scene.
- *To organise one's journey individually and independently:* this is designed to challenge one's own flexibility and to dissociate oneself from main-stream, especially package, tourists.
- *To travel for as long as possible:* this ideal is based on the assumption that 'real' travelling experiences cannot be made on short-term holidays; this is important to establish social status within the hidden back-packer hierarchy.

These ideals can be read as the basic symbols with which backpackers construct traveller identities and a sense of community – collectively as well as individually; inward-oriented as well as outward-oriented. They serve to distinguish the backpacker from the (stereo)typical conventional tourist, to pursue a 'better' approach to travelling in general and in partic-ular, to have more 'non-tourist' (i.e. authentic) experiences. The travellers don't necessarily have to be aware of this process, nor do they need to really implement their ideals in practice (Loker, 1993: 3). The feeling of belonging together is sufficient for the community to claim existence and to serve as a source of a collective backpacker identity.

How to be an Anti-Tourist

Why travel 'off the beaten track'?

Cohen (1982: 210) argues that 'solitude ... has become an attraction in a crowded world'– an observation that forms one of the cornerstones of tourist dreams: if solitude becomes a rarity, it generates the promise of luxury. On a lonely beach, I can feel like I 'have it to myself' – an impression that often plays a major role in travellers' tales. This is expressed in the often obsessive efforts of almost every (Western) tourist to take holiday photographs (especially of natural attractions) in such a way that, if possible, no people can be seen on them and in particular, no other tourists.

Consequently, 'getting away from it all', i.e. escaping the stress of the populous centres, is one of the major driving forces of tourism – and of backpacking in particular, as backpackers have 'ennobled' this urge into an ideology. Other people from home are not only associated with stress; they also deprive the experience of its exclusivity in that the strong individualism in Western societies requires the individual to seek exclusive experiences in order to stand out from the masses. Only these can buy them prestige 'on the market of cultural vanities' (Hennig, 1997: 18 – author's translation). The best way to achieve this goal is to visit 'remote places' by travelling 'off the beaten track'. This territorial exclusivity refers only to other tourists and mostly to other Western ones. For example, a major city in the Indian hinterland can qualify as a 'remote place' if it is 'off the beaten (tourist) track' – even if it is popular with Indian tourists (see Sutcliffe, 1997).

This exclusive remoteness is coupled with a passionate quest for paradise: In Western (i.e. Christian) societies, the concepts of remoteness and solitude gain special meaning through being rooted in the Bible. Prophets from Moses to Jesus experienced their spiritual enlightenment at remote, lonesome locations – and always under ascetic conditions:

> In fact it's an idea contained in every traditional religion and culture: that you will not achieve spiritual advancement unless at some point you live without anything. (Tomory, 1998: 52)

So up to the present day, these places are seen as the most re-vitalising and 're-creational' ones; here the individual can regain strength for the tasks that lie ahead – the stressful working routine or the strenuous bus rides when travelling onward. In connection with the need for 'exclusivity' as described above, this means:

> If Nature is curative, performs magical re-creations and other miracles otherwise assigned to Lourdes, God, or gurus, the medicine is weakened by the presence of other humans. To share is to lose power. (Graburn, 1989: 31)

> Paradise – the mythological place of origin, of creation itself (see Genesis 2: 5–25) – serves as the antithesis of modern civilisation (i.e. to its negative

excesses) and, in this way, it is a projection of our own romantic yearning for virgin innocence and originality: 'You walked naked on the beach. There was no rubbish: not a matchstick, not a cigarette [butt], and a freshwater spring at the end of the beach' (Tomory, 1998: 145).

Thus, the touristic 'return' to paradise is a symbolic 'return' to the origins of mankind, in order to make us feel like being without sin (see Cohen, 1982). However, the religious 'centrality' ascribed to paradise has ceased to exist in contemporary perception; today, only geographically peripheral places 'at the edge of the planet' (British respondent) can earn themselves the rating 'paradisical' (Cohen, 1982). This is why Cohen (1982) calls them 'marginal paradises'.

There is also a close connection between the tourist ideal of remote destinations and the concept of the 'insider tip'. An insider tip is always 'off the beaten track'; it conveys the feeling of a blood brotherhood between a few 'chosen ones', and it is only passed on to people to whom one feels connected – or whom one wants to impress. Seldom will backpackers pass insider tips on to conventional tourists, but within the scene they are traded eagerly and such insider information is regarded as highly prestigious. However, it has become tourist common sense that insider tips cannot be found in guidebooks – this would deprive them of their exclusivity – even though such sources always claim to be full of them. So an insider tip can never maintain its secrecy for long, its existence is short lived. In the long run, only places that are located far off the beaten track or in chronic conflict areas are able to preserve this status, making them unattractive for conventional tourism.

Global mobility has brought about another shift in the notion of paradise: it is not exclusively tied to a particular *place*, but can be *imagined* anywhere, unrestricted in capacity. The 'inflation' of paradises (and consequently of insider tips) can quickly become their downfall as tourist destinations are 'normed' like identical clones. Tropical islands fall prey to 'McDonaldisation' (Ritzer & Liska, 1997) and, regardless of their location, tourist advertising always promotes the same parameters: beaches, fine, white sand, palm trees, sun, and crystal-clear water.

This uniformity makes them interchangeable: '*Where* I wanted to go was secondary to *how* I wanted to do it', says an American interviewee. If one paradise falls into disgrace (e.g. through political unrest or its 'invasion' by conventional tourism), those at the forefront of the tourist caravan will move on to the next one. With respect to conflict areas though, backpackers (despite their adventure-oriented ideals) are hardly bigger risk-takers than conventional tourists. So, even traditional backpacker 'paradises' such as Kashmir have become almost totally deserted in recent years owing to civil wars or mere political instability. With no territorial ties left in a globalised mind, particular places have lost their special meaning – and thus their paradisical uniqueness.

Tourists and anti-tourists: A love-hate relationship

The ideals discussed above not only tie backpackers together as a community, but also function as differentiation criteria towards those on the outside. In the construction of ethnicity, the most important and most strongly defended differentiation is often the one against the community that lives closest to one's own. In the case of backpackers, the distinction cannot be made in territorial terms, because as a global community they lack a 'neighbour' to differentiate themselves from. But lifted to a symbolic level, there is proximity, i.e. a similarity of forms. For backpackers, the closest (i.e. most similar) community is that of mainstream tourists, which is why backpacker ideology primarily stands in opposition to mainstream tourism.

Consequently, backpackers reject everything that is assumed to be typically 'touristy'. As 'anti-tourists', they claim to have the more 'authentic' experiences (Loker-Murphy & Pearce, 1995: 825) and to be 'closer to the real people' (*Let's Go*, 1999: online source). Being people who 'know how to get [their] luggage off the carousel' (Wayne, 1990: 448), many backpackers carry the notion that they have an 'inborn' travelling expertise that lifts them above mainstream tourists. Assuming their way of travelling to be the antithesis of conventional tourism – notwithstanding the fact that backpacking has become a form of conventional tourism itself (see Spreitzhofer, 1998) – backpackers strongly oppose being associated with other tourists. Some even avoid visiting first-class tourist sights such as Uluru (Ayers Rock) in Australia – not because they are not interested in them but in order to avoid the tourists themselves (Elsrud, 2001; Uriely *et al.*, 2002). To the passionate budget traveller, the very expression 'backpacker tourism' is a contradiction in terms.[3]

Backpacking as symbolic class conflict

There's an old saying that goes: the difference between travel and tourism is that travellers go places to learn new things and tourists travel to confirm what they already know. (*Let's Go*, 2001: online source)

Travellers don't know where they're going, tourists don't know where they've been. (British interviewee)

Ancient stereotypes such as these survive persistently within the backpacker scene, as they are necessary to express clearly the backpacker's dissociation from other tourists. Other tourists are believed to be naïve, superficial and destructive to the social structures and ecosystems in the host regions. However, this image is nothing new. Ever since Thomas Cook swept the first working-class package tourists into British seaside resorts in the 1840s, 'tourist-bashing' and the debate about the 'real' way to travel have served as the prolonged arm of class conflict, a 'symbolic struggle for social superiority' (Hennig, 1997: 18 – author's translation).

This rejection of 'tourist' settings by backpackers is simply a continuation of this conflict by symbolic means. Consequently, backpackers not only perceive themselves to be the 'better' tourists: most will reject the term 'tourist' altogether, preferring to call themselves 'travellers'[4]: 'The tourist is always the other person' (Crick, 1991: 7). Tony Wheeler, legendary co-founder of the 'backpacker bible' *Lonely Planet* says:

> Tourists stay in Hiltons, travellers don't ... The traveller wants to see the country at ground level, to breathe it, experience it – live it. This usually requires two things the tourist can't provide – more time and less money. (Wheeler, 1992: 35, quoted in Johnsen, 1998)

Wheeler, who has little time and much money, here tries to polarise the difference between travellers and tourists along assumed objective criteria. More frequently, as backpacking is an approach to travelling rather than a categorisation (Pearce, 1990), this distinction is a purely subjective one that defies any technical definition – as we can see in the following two examples:

> It's not a holiday. It's travelling. [That's something] completely different. (Sutcliffe, 1997: 167)

> The one difference I could still latch on to was that tourists went on holidays while travellers did something else. They travelled. (Garland, 1996: 96)

Backpacking as a tourist subculture

Elsrud (2001: 607) points out that in backpacker perception, the tourist takes on the role 'of the mythologised Jones', a Philistine, while the traveller community represents the Bohemian (see Tomory, 2000). If tourist activities seem banal, traveller activities always have a deeper meaning: 'We had fun, sure, but interesting fun, not the simple tourist variety' (Tomory, 1998: 246). At this point, we have to take a glimpse back into history, because here not only the construction of a tourist 'class conflict' but also backpacking's subcultural roots in hippie culture come shining through. The counter culture that hit the roads to the East in the late 60s and early 70s was 'both a symptom and an expression of broader alienative forces ... ' (Cohen, 1973: 94) from Western society, in particular a rebellion against a conformist parent generation: 'Basically, your *parents* were tourists. *Straight* people were tourists. You were a traveller, you had pretensions of another order' (Tomory, 1998: 44). Thus, the distinction between travellers and tourists is a continuation not only of a class conflict, but also of this generational one.

But in contrast to their ideological ancestors, today's backpackers lack an important driving force of the drifter days: a mission. While most hippie travellers were (partly) driven by the urge to change and revolutionise society at home,[5] today's more fun-oriented backpackers do not have such far-flung aspirations. If they do want to change something, then it is about themselves: 'My focus had moved from seeking a perfect society to seeking a perfect state of inner being' (Tomory, 1998: 26). A certain feeling of alienation may still be one of the reasons to go travelling for some, but it is not strong enough to generate energies that reach beyond the self.

The reason for the un-rebellious attitudes of contemporary backpackers is quite simple: While hippiedom has largely preserved its countercultural character, backpacking has gone mainstream (Scheyvens, 2002). Today, the backpacker community incorporates members from all social classes, ages, and political convictions.[6] They come from the centre of society – and most will fully re-integrate after returning home (see Uriely *et al.*, 2002). They may have changed something about themselves, may take up a new job and lifestyle, but they will not start to quarrel with society.

We can see here that the countercultural features of the contemporary backpacker scene do not refer to mainstream society in general but exclusively to its mainstream forms of tourism. Backpacking is merely a stroll into non-conformism, a countercultural 'picnic' – a break from the backpacker's own conformist life.

The struggle against assimilation: Tilting at windmills

To the outsider (and even for many insiders), it is often hard, at times impossible, to draw the boundary between backpacking and other forms of tourism. Over the years, the backpacker infrastructure in many regions has become so sophisticated and institutionalised that it is difficult to draw a clear line where mainstream tourism ends and backpacking begins.[7] Richard, the anti-hero in Alex Garland's backpacker novel *The Beach*, realises that: 'I had ambiguous feelings about the differences between tourists and travellers – the problem being that the more I travelled, the smaller the differences became' (Garland, 1996: 96).

As well as mainstream tourism, the backpacker scene featured 'fixed travelling patterns, established routines and a system of tourist facilities and services ... ' (Cohen, 1973: 95) – already in the early 1970s! But if the boundaries between the two groups are so blurred, how is it that, at any given place where travellers as well as tourists hang out, it is always clear (even to most locals interacting with them) who is a backpacker and who is not? How do they generate this inexplicable talent to distinguish each other at first sight (see Andritzky, 1986: 252)?

An indicator can be traced in Erik Cohen's observation back in the 1970s: the existence of two 'parallel universes' where backpackers (or 'drifters', as he called them) and conventional tourists 'flow along ... segregated institutional channels' (Cohen: 1973: 95) that barely differ in structure. On the bottom line, the interests of backpackers (unspoilt nature and wildlife, outdoor and adventure activities, culture, historic monuments, and generally having a good time) do not differ significantly from those of other tourists. Consequently, a look at the world map reveals that by and large typical tourist and typical backpacker regions are largely congruent.

However, although tourists and backpackers alike might well be travelling to the *same* places, visiting the *same* sights, eating the *same* food, and seeing the *same* national parks, they will be staying in *different* accommodation, visiting *different* restaurants and bars, mingling with *different* people and while the tourist would rather take a taxi or trishaw, the backpacker will walk or rent a bicycle. There are specialised backpacker bus companies, hostels, 'alternative' souvenir shops, tour operators and Internet cafés – often right next to the ones catering for mainstream tourists (see Klein, 1999). These centres of backpacker infrastructure often concentrate a great variety of services in more confined spaces than those of mainstream tourism, being just as 'ghetto-ish' (e.g. the Khao San Road in Bangkok) as all-inclusive hotel complexes.

Even on campgrounds (e.g. in Australia) one can find, neatly separated, the 'backpacker corner' (randomly dotted with tents and their own cars) and the 'tourist corner' (rental camper vans and mobile homes on pitches with a power supply). Through this carefully upheld spatial separation on the micro level, backpackers and other tourists will rarely interact with each other[8] and it is this micro-geographical distinction that can be interpreted as a relic of the ethnic territoriality principle.

However, it must be noted here that these parallel universes are kept apart only by the backpackers and not (or only rarely) by the tourists – they harbour only a one-way opposition. It is very clear that there is no rejection of backpacking by mainstream tourists – at best, they are indifferent to them, while at worst they confront them with admiration and envy. This poses a dilemma for the backpacker scene: When claiming (ethnic) identity, a group's:

... self-ascription stands in a complex relationship to extraneous ascriptions. ... The self-ascription as an ethnic group that is not mirrored in a corresponding extraneous ascription is unstable. (Elwert & Waldmann, 1989: 34 – author's translation)

In Sollors' (1989) terms: to be an 'x' and not a 'y' one not only has to be claimed by the 'x' but also be confirmed by the 'y'. Although backpackers do not claim an ethnic identity in a purposeful manner, there is a striking similarity to certain aspects of ethnicity in their struggle against 'touristification'.

It gets even worse. Since much of the backpacker ideology is merely a purist version of a more general tourist philosophy, mainstream tourism will always strive to follow in the footsteps of its spearhead, the traveller community. In this respect backpackers are explorers, though not the ones they intend to be: As soon as they leave the beaten track to 'explore' new, yet 'undiscovered' places, they pave a new one for mainstream tourism. Involuntarily, they seek out locations for prospective tourist centres and serve as 'scouts' for the tourism industry – a process that can be traced back in consecutive issues of *Lonely Planet* guidebooks (see Cohen, 1982; Riley, 1988).

Set up in Bali, Ko Pha-Ngan, Ko Tao, Borocay, and the hordes are bound to follow. There's no way you can keep it out of the *Lonely Planet*, and once that happens it's countdown to doomsday. (Garland, 1996: 139)

It could be said that the backpacker scene is suffering a collective 'persecution mania'; its only cure is escape – a permanent rearguard action with *'Touristhan'* (Tomory, 2000: 179) hard on their heels: 'The legions of the uncool have the victory, and the old elites are in full retreat' (Tomory, 2000: 136).

This vicious circle poses a great gruelling test for the backpacker community, and backpackers try to solve it by symbolic depictions of difference from conventional tourists in appearance and behaviour. They do this especially in the way they dress (apart from demonstratively carrying the backpack), ideally featuring two characteristics: to look dingy and ethnic. 'Don't waste your precious backpack room taking extra changes of clothes and excessive toiletries' proclaims guidebook publisher *Let's Go* on its website; 'Be simple; be smelly ... I stink, therefore I am. It's life-affirming stuff, stinkiness' (*Let's Go*, 2001: online source). An unkempt appearance is not seen as a necessary evil of travelling, but is good form within the scene. Travellers do this to present themselves as decidedly different from mainstream tourists whom they allege have a clean (Hawaiian) shirt in their suitcase for every single day of their holidays.

More important is the 'ethnic look', i.e. 'dressing up' like the locals: 'I had a little pair of Moroccan slippers and a long shirt, and a headscarf. We looked ethnic. People in the bazaars [of Peshawar, Pakistan] thought we were from Afghanistan' (Tomory, 1998: 166). This kind of 'camouflage', apart from being a playful variation of local dress codes, is used to avoid being perceived as conventional tourists – hardly anything is more annoying, even humiliating to backpackers than locals who treat them like mainstream tourists. At the same time, this 'marked, ritualised "outfit"' (Andritzky, 1986: 251 – author's translation) also serves the purpose of a kind of backpacker 'costume' by which the backpackers themselves can recognise each other when distinguishing their fellow travellers from mainstream tourists (Elsrud, 2001).

The emergence of the 'anti-backpacker'

The vicious circle in the relationship of backpackers to tourists has a further twist: as mentioned earlier, the worldwide backpacker scene has grown to a size that approaches individualised conventional tourism itself. Marshall realises:

> We're not 'travellers'. We're not even backpackers. We're package tourists with differently shaped luggage ... Our guidebooks lead us along a backpacking superhighway where lodgings are always cheap, natives always speak English and restaurants always serve banana pancakes[9] ... (Marshall, 1999: 58)

One of his interviewees adds:

> Travelling across Africa was a total breeze. Everywhere we went there was cheap accommodation, foreigners' food, buses that took you from backpacker centre to backpacker centre. It was idiots' travelling. (Marshall, 1999: 56)

The very infrastructure that backpackers make use of to distinguish themselves from mainstream tourism unmasks the scene as a conformist mass phenomenon: For example, Hooton (1999: 39) observed that the sub-scene of Australian backpackers working in London almost entirely deserts to Spain in summer in order to join the running of the bulls in Pamplona and reassembles for Octoberfest in Munich in late September. In their study, Macbeth and Westerhausen (2001) conclude that; ' ... a trickle of [backpackers] is capable of turning into a veritable flood over a short space of time', attributing this speed to the scene's highly efficient communication network. It is just logical that a new separation of the wheat from the chaff has to take place within the scene; 'The escape of the alternative alternatives [from the pursuing backpacker masses] is inevitable' (Spreitzhofer, 1997: 172; author's translation).

> 'Give Koh Phangan a miss, Rich', a traveller recommends in *The Beach*. 'Hat Rin [Beach] is a long way past its sell-by date. They sell printed flyers for the full-moon parties. Koh Tao. That's where it's at.' (Garland, 1996: 49–50)

At this point, we see a further subdivision of the scene (itself already a subculture), triggering a new process of assimilation once they have been established. This way the spiral of escape keeps spinning and spinning and spinning ...

Consequently, the image that the 'better' backpackers have of mainstream ones is equivalent to their general image of conventional tourism. For many 'real travellers' the scene has lost its innocence – having left the right track and joined the beaten one; they find it hard to keep identifying with the community. To them, the most similar group to distinguish themselves from is not mainstream tourism any more, but mainstream backpackers – these are mainly associated with the stereotype of the young party backpacker. Anti-tourism has given way to anti-backpacking as their major category of distinction, and so they often tend to relish in 'backpacker bashing' more than in tourist bashing (see Sutcliffe, 1997: 11). Asked about the worst people they ever met while travelling, respondents mentioned other backpackers much more frequently than mainstream tourists. A Canadian woman had a crushing verdict: 'Backpackers have no concept of travelling' – probably the most offensive accusation that can be directed against a backpacker. So in some backpacker centres, the term 'backpacker' is already in decline, and the use of '(independent) traveller' is back in vogue. Not even 40 years old, and the scene is already going through a major identity crisis.

Among long-term travellers and those who follow less-institutionalised backpacker tracks, a further shift can be observed from anti-tourist attitudes to what we might vaguely call 'post-tourism' or 'post-backpacking', i.e. a perception of tourism as something beyond its conventional categories. These travellers have a different concept of 'travelling': to them, a tourist is someone on some kind of holiday. A long-term traveller, however, cannot identify with this kind of tourist, having ceased to feel that way; to them, travelling has become 'purely habit' (as a British respondent put it). Consequently, many backpackers tend to call backpacking 'a way of life rather than a way of travelling' (Dutch respondent). The journey is not designed to be an interruption from normality, it *is* normality; and it is not supposed to serve any goals beyond travelling itself. So when travelling becomes a 'way of life', the backpacker becomes a traveller. 'Traveller' in this respect is a kind of professional title rather than an occupational one, the scene is a 'socio-professional group', and the difference between the tourist and the traveller can be seen in that tourism is a temporary state of existence, while travelling is a permanent one.

Conclusion

Anti-tourist attitudes are an important ingredient in the construction of backpacker identities – despite the scene's own increasing resemblance to conventional tourism in recent years. On the surface, the segregation takes place along separate institutional channels and by the demonstrative depiction of an assumed non-tourist appearance and behaviour. But more importantly, the dissociation from mainstream tourism is constructed on a symbolic level with symbolic boundaries largely maintained through the adoption of an ideological, decidedly anti-tourist set of values by the hippie scene. Backpacking as a form of tourism may not differ much from the mainstream, but the backpacker as a type of tourist does constitute a distinct identity (Uriely *et al.*, 2002).

These subcultural traits do not reject society as a whole, but only its established forms of tourism, and serve as a challenge to the backpacker's 'alter ego' – which is indeed the tourist: backpackers do not hold up a mirror to society, but to themselves. Thus, backpacking and mainstream tourism can be seen as just the opposite sides of the same coin.

Anti-tourism, in a nutshell, serves to preserve the backpacker's distinct identity despite a contradicting reality: I think *different*, therefore I am.

Notes

1. I understand the term 'scene' here as it is commonly used in German sociology: as an informal, non-institutionalised social group with undefined boundaries and a high rate of fluctuation. Members of a scene (such as punks, artists, or students) share common leisure or professional interests or a certain, often unconventional lifestyle. They frequently meet in particular places ('hangouts') but it is not necessary for everybody to know each other personally to establish an inner bond.
2. Two-thirds of respondents ranked 'travelling experiences' first out of nine possible topics, and all the rest ranked it second.
3. There is an ironic twist to this term in the particular form of 'backpacker tourism' that can be observed among domestic male package tourists to Goa: 'Goa is a pervert's paradise ... These Indian men come all the way from Bombay. The travel agents there have adverts which say that if you don't get a photo of a topless foreign woman then they'll refund your flight costs' (Marshall, 1999: 56).
4. Some actually do prefer the term 'traveller' to 'backpacker', which also has negative connotations to many, as discussed later in the chapter.

5. However, the question whether or not 'the RTK [Road to Kathmandu', i.e. the Western hippie trail to South Asia] was a social ... movement' (Tomory, 1998: 15) was highly disputed within the counterculture, as Tomory's own experience shows: 'They [hippie friends staying at home] told me I was betraying the struggle. ... "You're getting into this hedonistic head-trip because you can't get a proper orgasm"' (Tomory, 1998: 26).
6. However, the majority are in their twenties.
7. Recognising this difficulty, a Scottish interviewee invented the term 'taxi backpacker' for the 'in-between' tourists who travel with a suitcase and neat clothes, but also with a backpacker commitment.
8. In fact, after travelling largely through quite popular tourist areas in New Zealand and Australia for nine months, I realised that I had had conversations with conventional tourists only twice.
9. Banana pancakes are like a 'national dish' to the backpacker scene. Almost everywhere travellers gather in large numbers (especially in Asia), restaurants and cafés serve this favourite backpacker dish in many different variations (with chocolate sauce, vanilla ice-cream, etc.). The question of where to get the best banana pancakes is a popular issue in backpacker conversations.

Chapter 6

The Whole Point of Backpacking: Anthropological Perspectives on the Characteristics of Backpacking

JANA BINDER

> *Because the whole point of backpacking is you are just there to do what you want. It's your trip, so do it. (Susie)*
>
> *This travel feeling is about seizing opportunities you don't have in your normal life. You can only have them while backpacking: the freedom, the thirst for experiences, your curiosity and all the other things. (Andi)*

Even though the first acknowledgement of the phenomenon of backpacking was formulated by the sociologist and anthropologist Erik Cohen (Cohen, 1973), the most prominent definitions of backpackers today are based on quantitative marketing research (c.f. Pearce, 1990):

> They [backpackers] prefer to stay in budget accommodation, they spend more time travelling around [...] than the average visitor, and they enjoy interacting with people, both locals and other travellers. They are also more likely to independently organise their travels. (Loker-Murphy & Pearce, 1995: 840)

In many ways this definition is an accurate reflection of the current state of backpacking research. However, although quantitative studies may give an overview of the characteristics of backpackers, they do not give an insight into the culture of backpacking or focus on the understanding of these practices. This is where qualitative research is needed. Unfortunately, there are still only a few ethnographic studies on the culture of backpacking (e.g. Maoz, 1999; Welk, 2004; Westerhausen, 2002).

In this chapter, I would like to stress the importance of a qualitative approach to the phenomenon of backpacking as a way of addressing methodological questions, processes and perspectives. Such processes are evaluated using qualitative material based on backpackers' own perspectives. The interviews and participant observations used here are the product of a hermeneutic analysis of qualitative data, which will be described below. These 'thick' perspectives are contrasted with statements from the current discourse of tourism research on the backpacking phenomenon.

The discussion of the contrast presented here should be seen as a starting point for future investigations in the field of backpacking. In my opinion, the aim of any future investigation should not be based on further deconstruction of backpacker experiences, but on the conceptualisation of how these experiences fit into the concepts and requirements of late modern societies. What functions does backpacking have for backpackers today? Is there a kind of common self-perception among backpackers? What relationship does the backpacker experience have to everyday life? If we are interested in the management of backpacking tourism, these qualitative issues are just as important as the quantitative ones. An initial approach to these questions is developed in this chapter.

Qualitative Approaches

Ethnography deals with reconstructing the constructions of reality formed by the members of the group under investigation. Only through these 'part-realities' of the individuals can information about how reality is constructed by society be gathered (Berger & Luckmann, 1969). Therefore ethnography tries to alternate the researcher's perspective with the perspective of the investigated, and asks what is important for the investigated actors and how they experience 'their world'. The research takes the actor's perspective as its starting point. Because it is impossible to immerse oneself in the life world of the people investigated, the material of qualitative approaches first of all targets models of reality construction.

Ethnography incorporates both data gathered through participant observation and material gained through interviews. The latter is seen as 'performance' or 'self-representation' material (Honer, 1993). It can best be evaluated through participant observation in the field. In qualitative approaches, a certain scepticism about such data is inherent. Information on social phenomena is not treated as information about these phenomena, but as information on communication and performance. To increase the validity of research, qualitative approaches choose to believe in the advantages of extended research periods with intensive contacts between researcher and actors, and the deep knowledge acquired by the researcher through active participation in the field (Denzin, 1997; Girtler, 1984). The special role of the researchers, their 'inbetweenness' between their part-reality and that of the people under investigation, allows them to establish a double perspective that is useful for the understanding of cultural processes.

Methods

The qualitative data presented in this chapter were gathered during three field trips that studied backpacking culture in South-East Asia, between March 2000 and August 2002. The fieldwork is the basis for a PhD. with the working title 'Long Time Individual Travellers' Self-representation and their Representation of "the Other"'. During this time I taped in-depth interviews with 19 backpackers, who were travelling for more than six consecutive months through different parts of the world (Table 6.1).

Using a participant observation approach, ten backpackers were followed for several days or weeks on their travels. In addition, more than 120 mailings, 12 online travel diaries and 75 photographs were analysed to gain an insight into the representations of the trips. Observations were recorded in three fieldwork diaries, from which the following excerpts are taken. Notes were also recorded from 45 conversations with experts in the tourism industry and with backpackers I met along the way. My own experience as a backpacker helped me to approach the field, and it framed my analysis with a more 'native' point of view.

The following assumptions do not claim general 'truth' for every backpacker, but they claim to have recognised several models or types of reality that seem to be characteristic of the cultural practice of backpacking. These types were derived following the application of a methodology designed to increase abstraction after multiple coding of qualitative material (grounded theory: Strauss, 1994). The circular relationship between the whole and its parts is known as a hermeneutic or interpretative circle, and consists of a movement back and forth between the particular and the general, as the meaning and significance of specific actions, practices, texts etc. are judged in relation to the whole, and ideas about the whole are corrected and amplified by testing them against the parts. This process is still visible in the following text, which examines the different types of text (particular interview quotes and observation protocols versus general assumptions and analysis) in their relationship to and mutual influence on each other. In bringing the reader as close as possible 'to the field' – taking up Geertz's idea of 'thick description' (Geertz, 1983) – with this ethnographic piece of work, I want to contribute to the general understanding of backpacking culture and to the further development of backpacking theory.

The following sections present some of the ideas and 'types' derived from the material concerning self-representation, as well as backpackers'

Table 6.1 Participant information and data collection methods

Name*	Nation of origin	Age	Length of trip	Data material
Susie	Canada	21	9 months	Interview, participant observation, email, photographs
Andi	Germany	27	12 months	Interview, participant observation, email, online travel diary, photographs
Manolo	Argentina	28	24 months (still travelling)	Interview, participant observation
Garry	Great Britain	24	14 months	Interview, participant observation
Doris	Austria	23	8 months	Interview, participant observation
Jason	Great Britain	24	12 months	Interview, participant observation
Mary	Australia	20	13 months (still travelling)	Interview, participant observation
Angela	Switzerland	21	9 months	Interview, participant observation, online diary
Andrea	New Zealand	29	16 months (still travelling)	Interview, participant observation. online diary
Rita	Netherlands	28	6 months	Interview, participant observation
Markus	Germany	31	11 months	Interview, photographs, email
Erika	Germany	30	11 months	Interview, photographs, email
Marina	Germany	26	12 months	Interview, photographs, participant observation at home
Thilo	Germany	28	6 months	Interview, photographs, participant observation at home
Michael	Great Britain	19	7 months	Interview
Sandrine	France	22	14 months	Interview, e-mail
Sam	Australia	25	13 months (still travelling)	Interview
Manuela	Germany	26	12 months	Interview
Sabine	Germany	27	6 months	Interview

* The interviewees' real names have been changed to preserve anonymity

responses as to why they chose the cultural practice of backpacking and what, in their opinion, were the characteristics of that activity.

The Aims of Backpacking: Observations from the Field

'See the world, see different people, different customs'

Cameron Highlands, Peninsular Malaysia: Susie (a backpacker from Canada) and I are sitting in the lounge area of Daniel's Lodge. Manolo (an Argentinean backpacker) recommends doing some jungle trekking, and explains how to get to an aboriginal village. As Susie is interested in different cultures, we decide to go there. Soon it starts raining and the path isn't well marked. After three hours of walking, we arrive at the village. Wooden houses are scattered around two hills, a few children are playing soccer. It is a village like every other village around. We expected something more remote. Next to the central square a couple of children are playing. Seeing us, they begin to scream and rush towards us, excited by our video cameras with LCD-displays. We stay for about fifteen minutes, laughing at their screaming, which follows every new perspective and child on the displays. On our way back Susie is all excited about the aboriginal village and the way people live there. She philosophises about their deep happiness, even though they are poor or because they are poor. She thinks that experiences with local people, like those we just had, are only possible because we are individual travellers. Backpackers interact and do not disturb, she says.

Experiencing 'Otherness' is the starting point for many tourists, and it is extremely important for the backpackers I interviewed. 'The Other' is seen as a chance to question, confirm or judge the 'self':

> See the world, see different people, different customs. It is always about the same question: how can I be this way, for example Catholic, if I don't know what Buddhism or Islam are? How can I say my country is the best country and my life is the best life, if I haven't seen any other ones? So that is the main reason why we want to see the world.

So says Manolo (27), talking about his reasons for backpacking. Like the other backpackers I talked to, Manolo is eager to represent himself as open minded and ready for experiences with different approaches to and ways of life. However, looking at the statements and representations of experiences with the 'Other' and comparing them with the actual practices, in everyday backpacking a gap often appears. Interaction seems superficial, experiences first of all imagined and the staging of 'Otherness' by the local tourism infrastructure more than obvious. In the tourism literature this has led to the assumption that there are no 'real' interactions to be found in 'alternative' or 'individual' tourism either – only in commodified ones (Spreitzhofer, 1998). Erik Cohen describes these interactions in the following way:

> On sight-seeing trips in native localities they [alternative tourists] may indeed strive to observe the 'authentic' life of 'unspoilt' mountain tribesmen or island fishermen; however, such native people tend to be viewed by them rather like a rare species in a national park: they elicit much interest and excitement as representatives of a meaningful, 'natural' way of life, an inversion of rejected modernity. The travellers cherish the native people as symbols of 'authenticity' and derive reassurance from the encounter that such ways of life still exist somewhere in the world; but they do not, generally relate to the natives as fellow human beings. Hence they become primarily concerned with the 'museumsation' (MacCannell, 1976: 8) of the lifestyles of such people and with the prevention of change, rather than with their well-being. (Cohen, 1989: 132)

Even though I agree with Cohen's analysis, the switching of perspectives from outside the scene right into it reveals that there is more to it: it reveals, in addition to a deconstruction of practices, the metaphorical sense behind the claims for 'Otherness' and 'difference' in the self-representations. Obviously the main misunderstanding between backpackers (and tourists in general) and social scientists (and tourism researchers in particular) lies in the definition of the 'Other'. While social scientists are looking for a morally deep involvement with the host cultures, backpackers see their brief contacts with other backpackers, taxi drivers, hostel owners or people sitting next to them on the buses as sufficient 'Otherness' in contrast to the experiences they usually have at home. Eating new food, experiencing heat and different transport modes, speaking a foreign language or talking to non-native English speakers are experiences that provide enough challenge most of the travelling time. Even though many of the backpackers I travelled with were expecting something 'more different' before they started travelling; 'I saw me sitting in a little village in Thailand, learning the language and helping the villagers to build a bridge or something like that' (Garry, 24) – they soon realise that this doesn't work without giving up the travelling itself in the form of constantly moving on.

Overstating an encounter with aboriginal children is therefore a metaphor for the daily encounter with other and sometimes strange backpackers, local bus ticket sellers or adaptations of banana pancakes that taste different every time. Their trip is experienced as something unique and thrilling and therefore is a practice worth representing as 'different', 'real' or 'exotic'. This suggests the translation of a more diffuse sense of 'Otherness' into stereotypical tourist representations of the 'unspoilt, hospitable, friendly native' along distinctive closed national culture concepts.

'The big family of the travellers and the dreamers'

Poipet, on the border between Thailand and Cambodia: having booked a bus ticket from Khao San Road, Bangkok directly to Siam Reap, we tourists are met by a woman who directs the group to a pick-up truck. Everybody is a backpacker and we feel instantly that we are a group in opposition to the children tugging at our sleeves trying to earn a few Reals by carrying our luggage. There are rumours that the main bridge to Siam Reap has collapsed. Everybody feels insecure and realises that Cambodia is different from Thailand. Smiles and staying close together helps, the feeling that there is somebody around you who is in the same situation and who speaks the same language makes everything easier. During the eight-hour ride on a bumpy dirt road in the monsoon rain, soaked, crossing broken bridges, the Western backpackers become close. After we arrive, all six of us decide to check in at the same hostel. For the next few days we celebrate Jason's birthday, go out for meals, bargain our hostel owner down on the prices for accommodation, motorbikes and tour-guides to Angkor Wat. We sit around the temples telling each other parts of our life stories. At home nobody would have befriended any of the others – the ages or interests or characters would be too different, but here that doesn't matter. Everybody is happy to have people to relate to. After four days we part without having exchanged contact addresses.

As Pearce has already pointed out, 'meeting people' is one of the main characteristics of backpacking (Pearce, 1990). The backpacker infrastructure mainly formed by the *Lonely Planet* guidebook is a guarantee that you will meet up with other people while travelling individually. 'The good thing about backpacking is: if you arrive in a backpacker hostel everybody is talking to everybody – there are no barriers. You instantly talk to everybody everywhere and everybody is giving advice because there is that bond between backpackers' (Doris, 23). Doris has been travelling by herself for more than a month now, and has another seven months to go. She represents the group of backpackers as a community that provides safety. The ease with which one can approach new people is based on the common knowledge that everybody is eager to form groups to share fun, costs, risks and experiences. Because of the homogeneous background and common knowledge of most of the backpackers interviewed (educated middle class from post-industrialised countries), common interests and forms of communication make it easy to get along with each other. Mary (20) describes the similarity of backpackers in the following way:

It's not that you can force yourself into this community of backpackers just because you have a backpack on, but everybody is very similar. They all want to see the world, they all try to stay on their budget, they are all open to new friendships and so that's similar. They are all open to trying new foods and wherever their trip is going to take them, they are just going to be excited.

Even though from the outside backpackers are labelled as hedonistic and superficial (Spreizthofer, 1998), they refer in their self-representations to the concept of 'community' to describe the bond they feel between each other. A sociological definition of 'community' is 'a stable, locally engaged population whose members form a unity because of their economic and social relationships and their identification with the community' (Fuchs-Henritz, 1995: 227). The term is, in relation to backpackers, applicable only in terms of the common identification with backpacking. There is no stable, local group of people, nor do they have economic or lasting social relationships. The many references to backpackers experiencing a 'liminal stage' suggests a reference to Turner's (1973) concept of 'communitas' when trying to describe the group. But as Erik Cohen points out in Chapter 3 of this volume, backpackers neither lose their individuality nor does it come to an 'immersion' with their fellow backpackers.

Ethnological definitions of a social network, in contrast, seem to be more appropriate to backpackers, for example: 'Participants related to each other through at least one social relationship. Social relationships are based on exchange, help or communication' (Hirschberg et al., 1999: 270). However, the use of the term 'community' has an important implication: the wish, the image, the representation of backpackers as a group, with social relationships and a common identification with a way of life. The group represented as a community is in fact an 'imagined community'. The term 'imagined community', developed by Anderson (1991: 5) to describe the character of 'nation' and 'nationalism', is also applicable to backpackers: 'It is imagined because the members of even the smallest nation will never know most of their fellow-members, meet them or even hear of them, yet in the minds of each lives the image of their communion'.

During gatherings in hostel lounges, this imagined community starts to re-establish itself with each story, representation or narration of travel experiences that is passed around. Its characteristics are established by referring to the secure and friendly family character, by building up boundaries towards the local 'Other' and non-travellers at home, who 'just work, consume and stay unhappy', as Doris (23) puts it. Manolo (27) uses the metaphor of the 'good family' to describe the identity of the imagined community:

> Sometimes it is unbelievable that you leave all your things in one room with all the people you don't know and nothing happens, in that part we are a family, a good family. This is probably because the other person, sleeping right beside you, is in the same situation, is missing friends as well, is in fear of being robbed or whatever. I think it's the respect for the other and in some way it should be normal, but what's normal? So in part it is like the big family of the travellers and the dreamers against the politicians and bureaucratic.

But, in contrast to what the concepts of community or communitas suggest, there is no real commitment to anybody or anything inside the backpacker network, which is itself an important aspect of the backpacking lifestyle. 'There are many ways to choose how you want to travel around and that's the whole point of backpacking, that you aren't committed, it's your trip, your decision, the whole point of backpacking is to do whatever you want' (Angela, 21). The backpacker community provides security for the individual travelling on his or her own, while at the same time this social network gives space and opportunities for hybridising and playing with personal identities, as there is a lack of social control.

Meeting fellow travellers is at the same time an important component of their self-representation as cosmopolitans. Especially as meeting locals is mostly experienced as more difficult than previously thought and, even though reduced to small talk on buses and in restaurants, as described above, meeting fellow travellers from 'all over the world' is an acceptable substitute.

An insight into backpacking culture shows that the labels of 'cursory' versus 'intensive' communities are not contradictions but in this case are mutually dependent. The cursory nature of backpacker contacts allows intense relationships to be formed without risk. For future research the backpacker community may provide important hints of emerging informal transnational networks and communities, with their very own structures, rules and implications, which cannot be described any more through traditional categories for groups in terms of ethnicity, place, etc. (see Welk, Chapter 5).

'Become open minded'

Nha Trang, Vietnam: Garry tells me that he feels lonely at the moment. He is missing his friends and family. At the moment he is travelling with

Tom, whom he met in Hanoi. They found out that they have the same route to Bangkok via Cambodia. Even though Tom is a little bit too outgoing and Garry hasn't got the feeling that he can talk to him, he thinks that Tom is fun, somehow. In the evening we meet again with a couple of other people, including Tom, at a bar belonging to a diving school. Marie, her boyfriend and another girl are doing their Padi Open Water dive certificate at the moment. They keep on telling us about how afraid they were in the beginning, how unbelievable it was to experience breathing underwater for the first time, how terrifying the emergency exercises are, and how somebody told them the story that one of the dive masters died last week. Marie fetches a book with underwater photographs of the area from the desk of the diving school and shows us the fish and coral they have already seen. 'That sounds so cool", says Tom. 'Why don't you two try it yourself?' Garry is unsure. 'I don't know, I never even thought about me diving.' Tom goes over to the desk and informs himself about prices and how long it will take. 'There's a special offer of US$190, because it is low season everything is included and it takes four and a half days. We could start tomorrow, what do you think?' Marie's boyfriend encourages them. 'It will be an adventure!' Tom and Garry make their way to the counter and sign up for the diving tomorrow.

Most backpackers I met explained to me that all who backpack on their own are forced to get along with themselves, but from time to time they also need to get along with the people they meet. 'I became more patient and tolerant with other people' (Garry, 24). Garry, who had just started travelling on his own in Asia, was happy to have Tom with him. While travelling they got to know each other better and obviously were very different. Being together for 24 hours every day sometimes made their relationship very difficult, but still they kept on travelling together. Garry's fear of being alone was stronger then the hedonistic wish for the 'no commitment while travelling' that Susie had told me about. In retrospect, this experience was framed as a starting point for personal change and growth.

By meeting people along the way who encourage new ideas such as going on a jungle trek or taking diving courses, individuals find themselves in situations they haven't imagined beforehand. 'I myself have become open minded, more open to new experiences, there are so many things that I've done. If somebody would had said some of those things at home like "in a year I see you doing this" [...] I would have been like "no, no not at all, that's not for me"' (Andrea, 29). Andrea represents herself as a new person because of her travel experiences. Having left her job and relationship after a nervous breakdown, she wants to show how the experiences she has had have revealed her strength, something she never thought she had:

In contrast to mass tourism's offer of a temporary escape from the pressures of an ordered existence, long-term travel instead provides a whole way of life whose demands on body and mind tend to be far more challenging to the individual. As a tourism experience, it offers the opportunity for semi-autonomy, personal growth, continuous learning, adventure and self-testing at an affordable price. (Westerhausen, 2002: ix–x)

In his ethnography of modern travellers, Westerhausen (himself an ex-backpacker) tends to not analyse beyond the backpackers' self-representations: becoming tolerant, learning about countries and cultures, becoming interested in the political, economic and cultural situation of one country, learning about oneself, and reflecting on one's biography.

Shields (1991) shows in his book *Places on the Margin* that the space in which backpacking takes place lacks social control and is therefore experienced as a counter-place to 'normal life'. The representations of these experiences, of course, never involve the standardisation of most of the experiences, but this is at the same time not important. A view from the inside shows that the individual experience is far more important than is acknowledged by the idea that backpacking culture is simply a standardised, commodified culture of closed enclaves (Spreitzhofer, 1998). Further research should reveal why experiences while backpacking seem to be different from similar experiences at home. One hint could be that the time of backpacking is, because of its structure (relative safety, well-developed infrastructure, no social control), a special 'no-risk-situation' in which new situations can be approached with playfulness. During the backpacking phase, a lot of requirements that are important in late modern societies (mobility, flexibility, team experiences, change management, spontaneity) can be experienced, and challenges can be faced without risking failure (Binder, 2003).

'Be less materialistic'

Perhentian Islands, Malaysia: after twenty hours of travelling in an overnight bus to save money for accommodation, in a third class train on a wooden bench and on the slow boat to the island non-stop, we finally arrive at Long Beach. After six months of travelling, Susie knows exactly what to do: check out the *Lonely Planet* 'Budget' section, for a good cheap place to stay. The place we find costs 15 RM per person, which is too expensive for our budget. We try the next one. The roof leaks and we can smell the clammy mattresses. In the middle of the room we have to take care not to touch the huge spider's web hanging between our beds. We both shiver at the sight of the hut – but it is cheap at 7.50 RM each. 'Come on! We have to do it', Susie tries to convince both me and herself. 'It's going to be fun with all the wildlife. And I am poor, anyway. I am running out of money already and I still have Australia left. If I wanted luxury, I'd only come for a week'. The *Lonely Planet* 'Things to do' section recommends doing some diving on the island, so we have a look at the offers of the different diving schools. Susie decides on one of the most expensive offers: a day trip including two dives, turtle and shark watching, barbecue and a party on a little island. While taking her credit card out and signing the bill she tells me that this probably will be a once-in-her-lifetime-experience, so it would be stupid not to take the opportunity.

The idea of renunciation relates to what Pearce (1990) has identified as a preference for budget-style accommodation. One obvious reason for this preference is the lack of money for travelling long-term in more luxury. Before travelling, the backpackers I talked with calculated their finances to see how long they can plan to be away for. These calculations were based on a budget of US$10 a day in so-called 'cheap countries' in Asia (excepting Singapore and Japan), South America or Africa and US$30 for Europe, Canada, USA, Australia and New Zealand, all inclusive (this matches the global nomad survey findings in Chapter 2). To make ends meet they had to keep thinking about their budget or start to work while travelling:

> The biggest part of backpacking is travelling: bus, train, boat, waiting, waiting, waiting, for hours and hours, sweaty and dirty without a shower, bargaining with taxi drivers, searching for cheap hostels, saving money, economising, economising, economising. That is a very important part, too. But that's the way it is, you are travelling on a budget and you have to watch out, otherwise you have to return home earlier.

So says Doris (23), confirming what Susie (21) and many others had told me before. In these comments they frame backpacking as something serious, a kind of labour that is aggravating and not about fun:

> I reckon, most of my friends would rather work than travel with me – they have no idea what it is like, when they tell me, 'Lucky you one year travelling, I wish I could come with you!' They think of it like a holiday. (Markus, 31)

Behind the pure economic reasons that make backpacking seem like a pilgrimage at times, ideological ones do shine through. These are deeply interlinked with the desire for personal development, and date back to the image and ideology of the drifters described by Erik Cohen (Cohen, 1973). 'You have flip-flops for the day, shoes at night and everything you need is in that backpack, so that's really, really cool, you learn to be less materialistic'

(Susie, 21). In the discourse of backpacking, 'normal life' goes hand in hand with materialism, consumerism and superficiality. While backpacking, these things are gone, and the individual is confronted with him or herself again, finally ready to start anew. In this way, materialism is stripped down or cast aside in the process of self-discovery.

New Age philosophies and esoteric versions of critiques of capitalism are very popular among backpackers, like Anton (28):

> While backpacking you are reconciled with yourself, because everything you have is that backpack and what is inside. You are reduced to yourself. Everything around me is the minimum of what I need. I can't be distracted by my CD collection any more nor by my books or anything else. I have to cope with my pure self.

The backpack itself is stylised as an icon, a symbol of this reduction and anti-capitalist renunciation. Poverty is represented as positive reduction, as coming back to the essentials of life. The experience of so-called poverty becomes a valuable commodity for the backpacker – a form of cultural capital (Bourdieu, 1984). Additionally, backpackers – with their relatively low economic capital – see themselves closer to the local people of 'Third World' countries. The anthropologist John Hutnyk, who carried out research among backpackers and volunteer charity workers in Calcutta, criticises this attitude:

> The hypocrisy with which some travellers renounce materialism while looking for the cheapest guest-house room or dorm for their ashram stay is relevant here. It would be an error to think that the global low-budget 'banana-pancake-trail' is not an important component of the ideology as well as the economy of touristic consumption. (Hutnyk, 1996: 10)

For Hutnyk, the backpackers' representations of themselves and the locals as the 'good poor' help to produce and stabilise the constructions of cultural difference and the roles that the different countries play in the world order (Hutnyk, 1996: 9). I think this criticism is correct as far as it goes. As can be seen in the observations described above, 'being poor' can be suspended very easily at nearly all stages of a journey with the argument of 'this is so exceptional' or 'this is why I came here' and a valid credit card. However, backpacking the way I experienced it produces a situation where things normally 'taken for granted' back home such as water, electricity, bathrooms or clean sheets are not available. These experiences are new to most of the backpackers and are therefore starting points for thinking about the 'normal' patterns of life. Even though it may not change these patterns, the interesting question for future research is to get a deeper insight into the relationship between the economic and cultural capital mentioned in the context of backpacking: how low economic capital can produce high cultural capital, and how this high cultural capital may be transformed into high economic capital after a backpacking trip. Some initial indications of this have been given by Desforges (1998) and his observations on the jobs people do after their return from backpacking, but there is still very little research on how these relationships work for the hosts.

'The moment I am a backpacker I feel different'

Rural Area, North West of Chiang Mai, Thailand: after the first day and night of Hill Tribe Trekking in a 'non-tourist area', our guide calls out that breakfast is ready. Everybody complains about their body aching after a night on a wooden floor and one day of trekking. After breakfast, Rita and Angela are going to the creek near the village to brush their teeth. While they are crouching next to the water, trying to make sure that their shoes don't get too wet, five elephants come towards them. They are the first elephants they've seen in their natural surroundings. Rita poses with her toothbrush in her mouth and Angela takes a picture of her. 'Nobody will believe it otherwise. Me, little Rita from X, first of all washing myself in a muddy creek and then brushing her teeth together with elephants, this is so crazy, I can't wait to tell them at home and show them the picture'. After we have packed our backpacks and fed the elephants with the left-overs of the breakfast, we have to mount them. Angela, who is my buddy for the ride, is all excited. 'Can you believe it? Can you believe what we are doing? We are going to ride on real elephants! Everybody else at home is going to the office now and I am riding through paddy fields on an elephant! If they could only see me. This is so crazy'. Three days later we come back to the hostel. The next group is already waiting for our guide to explain the tour to them. He will be going along the same track again tomorrow morning.

The feeling of doing something unique is one of the main reasons for Andi (28) to backpack: 'The moment I am a backpacker I feel different and somehow better than the rest'. Backpacking for him raises self-esteem and allows him to differentiate between himself, other tourists and the non-travellers back home. Every backpacker I have talked to so far has emphasised the appreciation he or she gets for having undertaken such a trip; 'Coming home was great. I felt special. Everybody wanted us at his party – the world travellers. We were like stars for them. And everywhere we showed up a crowd gathered around us to listen to our stories' (Andrea, 29). Back home she felt that their experiences became special no matter how ordinary they were for other backpackers travelling at the same time. Many of the backpackers I have visited and talked to after their travels have maintained this distinction by decorating their flats with photographs and souvenirs from their trips and reviving the feeling of being a 'star' with periodical slide shows. Distinction is a concept developed principally by the sociologist Pierre Bourdieu (1984). It focuses on the wish to stand out from others and to raise one's own lifestyle above that of the masses. This can be achieved in different ways. Each social group has different practices and objects as markers for distinction and they constantly change because distinctiveness can only be something that is rare. This explains, for example, the change in 'valued' destinations. Australia and Thailand, which were once markers for distinctiveness, have become mainstream now, while countries like Cambodia or Myanmar are the new stars.

But the wish for distinction among backpackers is more complex, as there are, for example, still a significant number of backpackers travelling through Australia and Thailand. The important thing for the backpackers I interviewed is not to have done something that nobody else has done before, but to represent themselves as somebody who has personally experienced as much as possible:

> Everybody was trying to talk me out of Australia because everybody is doing Australia, but what's that got to do with it? I want to experience Australia, I want to see it, so I have to go there, no matter if hundreds of other backpackers are there as well. Same with Thailand. It's bad and I cut it short and went to Laos and Cambodia instead, but I have seen it now, and that's it. (Jason, 24)

The distinction is made through the number of experiences one has and is able to talk about after the trip. 'I won't remember anything bad. Everything will be turned into a story and stories are what you take home with you most, so it works out in the end' (Susie, 21).

The sociologist Peter Gross, in his book *The Multioptional Society* (1994), analyses the modern wish to overcome the divergence between what is possible and what one has already done. In his opinion, every person in Western (post-)industrialised societies has to cope with the expectation that he or she should turn every possible experience into something already experienced. Backpacking fits into that idea. The backpackers represented here were constantly accumulating as many experiences as possible. The tourism infrastructure reacts to this and tours are organised that provide as many experiences as possible in a short time so that the backpacker can move on quickly to collecting more experiences somewhere else. Including elephant riding and bamboo rafting in the Hill Tribe treks is one example of this development – and a very successful one (Cohen, 2001: 16).

But these distinctive experiences include not only the classic 'adventures'. Backpackers' experiences are in most cases not risky in the sense of being life-threatening. Everyday travelling provides enough material for distinction back home: 'Trying different food, taking buses to places you have no idea where they are, trying to make connections between buses, everything turns out to be an adventure' (Susie, 21). The desire for adventure is closely linked to the issues of spontaneity, freedom and the unknown in general. Everything 'unknown' and 'new' or 'open' is part of the distinctive experience and is therefore an adventure. Activities that are routines at home (such as riding a bus, eating or sleeping) become part of 'not knowing what it will be like in a new place', 'who you will meet' and 'where it will end'. Experiences are individually defined and not measured by what is considered generally possible. Therefore, they become a unique experience for the individual, with the potential for distinction.

As mentioned above, distinction is always dependent on the social group surrounding the individual. According to Schulze's (1992) analysis of (post-)modern societies, potential backpackers tend to come from backgrounds with a high potential for self-realisation. They have in general more resources than are actually needed for living, and use these resources to develop a personal distinctive style like being somebody who has travelled and has experienced the world – however, not without losing sight of models and orientations given by friends, family, colleagues etc. (Schulze, 1992). However, the question of further research should not end with the criticism of an 'illegal' claim to distinction because the encounters are artificial and commodified, but should concentrate on the functions this distinction has to fulfil.

Conclusion

This chapter has tried to depict some of the reasons for, and the functions of backpacking for backpackers. It has focused on five types of reason that were found in the data of every participant of the sample. These can be paraphrased as: experience of the 'Other', community experience, self development, renunciation and distinction. Through the qualitative approach to the data it was possible to open up the complexity between self-representation, practice and theoretical conclusions drawn so far. From there on, new perspectives and questions for future backpacker research were developed:

- differences between transcultural experience and culturally-closed representations of the 'Other';
- the subjective 'Other': crossing personal borders in tourism practice;

- communities with new implications in a globalised world;
- differences between experiences at home and experiences while backpacking, subjective and structural implications in the context of late modern societies;
- relations between cultural and economic capital gained through backpacking;
- distinction in late modern societies: how it can be achieved, and which functions it fulfils.

This chapter has shown the complexity and various layers behind the characteristics of backpackers and their practices of backpacking. The most important layers are actual travel practices and their representations – a difference that cannot be identified in research based only on question-naires and interviews, as they cover only the layer of representation as exemplified in this chapter. Erik Cohen argues in Chapter 3 of this volume that among the future aspects of research on backpacking should be its dynamic and diverse nature, as well as the difference between the image and the practice of backpacking. Such research can only be conducted with a certain level of involvement, which can be achieved through participant observation. In conclusion therefore, I would like to re-emphasise the importance of long-term qualitative research – not just for acknowledging the existence of a phenomenon, but also in terms of understanding the way it works. This kind of approach allows the processes to be understood more clearly and can indicate, where and if necessary, how the processes might be managed in the long term.

Chapter 7

The Conquerors and the Settlers: Two Groups of Young Israeli Backpackers in India

DARYA MAOZ

Introduction

This study focuses on Israeli backpacking to India. Every year, out of a population of five million Jewish Israeli citizens, 50,000 Jewish Israelis travel to India as backpackers. Most of them are in their twenties, just out of the army; but increasing numbers of older people are joining them. The young ones have been investigated in recent years by Israeli researchers (Noy & Cohen, forthcoming). My pioneering study, however, dealt also with an older age group: young adults around the age of 30 who tend to be at an important transitional stage in their lives – between the end of prolonged youth and the beginning of adulthood (Maoz, 1999).

This chapter examines the prolonged backpacking journey of these Israeli young adults, and compares it to journeys made by Israelis in their early twenties immediately after military service. It is based on in-depth interviews with 44 backpackers (22 of each age group), as well as on field-work that included participant observation. I backpacked in India twice (in 1998 and 2001), travelling with the Israeli backpackers. I lived with the backpackers in guesthouses, ate with them in their favourite restaurants, sat with them in coffee houses, gathering places and enclaves, participated in their everyday routines and in addition held dozens of informal conversations with them. My findings were also compared to the conclusions of Mevorach's (1997)[1] study of young Israeli travellers just out of the army.

While I was there, I overheard a conversation between a local Indian and an Israeli backpacker. The Indian asked the Israeli, 'how many are you?' The Israeli answered, 'five million'. The Indian thought for a minute and then asked the Israeli '... and how many in Israel?' This kind of conversation represents the character of the young Israeli backpacker in India – they are loud and they behave as they please while often disrespecting the locals. In their attitude toward the locals they demonstrate a patronising approach towards the 'Other'. This attitude emerged from the 44 interviews I conducted with the backpackers, from their observed behaviour and above all from the nicknames they had given themselves – the *'conquerors'* and the *'settlers'*.

Both expressions are taken from Israeli political and military jargon. The first is an active military term that refers to the conquest of objectives by force and physical exertion. It is used to describe the younger Israeli travellers, just released from the army. The second term refers to Israelis who settle in the territories of the West Bank and Gaza and stake a claim there. In the Israeli backpackers' jargon in India, it refers to young adult travellers. The use of these terms implies that both groups of Israeli travellers tend to conduct their tourism as a neo-colonialist activity of conquest (Mowforth & Munt, 1998; Said, 1978; Stockwell, 1993).

The Israeli backpackers are usually a distinctive group among travellers in India. Another researcher who conducted fieldwork in South Asia tagged them as aggressive, impatient, strong-minded and in-group oriented, but nevertheless as a group that cannot be overlooked (Hottola, 1999: 77). This chapter tries to explain the distinct character of their journey and attitude towards the locals and will show how the backpackers change with age. I will do this by examining four factors that influence the character of the Israelis' journeys – age, stage of life, destination image and the degree of alienation from Israeli society. These are examined for the two different journeys – that of the young ones, just released from the army and that of the young adults. But first I will describe in detail the character of the two different journeys.

The 'Conquerors'

The conquerors' journeys are mostly a direct continuation of the Israeli army experience: energetic, adventurous, hectic and strenuous, conducted in a closed Israeli environmental bubble, cut off from the local environment. The term 'conquerors' (*ha-kovshim*) refers to those who in their journeys extend the intensive activity they practised in the army. They engage in strenuous treks which last days or weeks, while moving in rapid and constant transit between countries. They are also called 'the trekkers' (*ha-metarkim*). Their self-image is one of people who are physically and mentally capable of conducting hard treks. Yoav (aged 23): '... I emerged from the army with much more fitness and ability to do tough things ... and mentally you know you can do it, you can stand strenuous physical challenges ... '.

The term 'conquerors' is taken from Israeli political–social jargon and refers metaphorically to an act of conquering an objective in military style, in this case the 'conquest' is on foot. The concept of 'conquering the land on foot' was common in Israel in its early years and still is, stemming from the belief that the land of Palestine belongs to the Israeli people (Katz, 1985), and it led to a rise in the importance and centrality of hikes and treks in Israel. The nickname 'conquerors' thus hints at their will to rule the land. Other backpackers – usually engaged in 'doing nothing' – nicknamed those travellers in a mocking way. Instead of relaxing and resting after the long years of army service, they are effectively extending them.

The conquerors are mostly engaged in buying and discussing travel equipment as well as debating the difficulty of the treks. Their conversations also revolve around the army – their experiences and memories from it – and include slang borrowed from it. One of the central phrases used by those backpackers is *pazam*,[2] which refers to one's period of service and seniority, and in the journey to the period of travelling. Their self-prestige and status is determined by the length of their travel and the duration and difficulty of their treks (these criteria are also adopted by some other non-Israeli travellers, c.f. Riley, 1988: 321; Teas, 1988: 36; Welk, Chapter 5 of this volume).

Those young travellers nicknamed 'the conquerors' tend to be connected to other Israeli backpackers, with whom they jointly experience the treks and other activities. They describe the influence of the local culture as negligible and the encounter with the locals as awkward and even repulsive and admitted to having behaved patronisingly. Moran (22): 'I only met them in trains ... I remember one experience, it looked like a slave-train, all were stinky and hairy, it looks awful, I didn't talk to them, of course ... '. Reshef (24): 'No, I didn't feel the need to befriend them ... they see you as a wallet with two legs ... ' Most of those travellers don't seek involvement with the local residents and culture, instead tending to be inward-oriented (Cohen, 1973). Similar conclusions about Israeli backpackers were drawn by Hottola (1999) and Mevorach (1997). This attitude contradicts findings about European travellers, who, on the one hand, try to stay away from the people they escaped from, i.e. travellers from their homeland (Hottola, 1999; Welk, Chapter 5 of this volume) and on the other hand, try to meet the locals and experience the 'Other' (see Binder, Chapter 6 of this volume; Hottola, 1999; Loker-Murphy, 1996).

Many young Israeli travellers try to 'educate' the locals by introducing the Hebrew language into India: Hebrew is spoken by some Indian service providers, and it appears on store signs, on rickshaws, on menus in favourite restaurants of the Israeli backpackers, and in the songs played in them. They conquer the land not only with their feet, but by other means. They bring Israel with them: the language, the food (hummus, pita) and even the Jewish holidays, which they celebrate in Habad houses – Jewish synagogues spread all over India (see also Maoz, 2002). Their enclaves (see Cohen, Chapter 3 of this volume) and environmental bubbles are very solid and closed, and no one, especially no local, can invade. The locals are there for decor and service only and they are mostly used as porters and errand servants.

The young Israeli backpackers regard their adventurous experiences as the whole point of their trip (Mevorach, 1997). Most of them don't see the trip as an opportunity for reflexivity and a quest for identity, as often happens in a liminal stage (Cohen, 1984; Turner, 1987), although it is often conducted at a junction in life as a kind of *rite de passage*. Rather, the trip is often the first opportunity in their lives to test their limits and abilities, to reach independence and to be exposed to new experiences and challenges (Vogt, 1976) while detached from their families, and as such it is a very important step towards young adulthood. Eran (24) says, 'Some kind of phase was seemingly over, all this issue of childhood, and now, after it [the journey] was over I learned to be more independent and take care of myself'.

The 'Settlers'

In the jargon of Israeli travellers in India, the young adult travellers are called *ha-mitnahalim* – 'the settlers'. This expression is borrowed from Israeli political-military jargon for Israelis who settle in the territories that were conquered in the 1967 war. The root of the expression, *nahala* ('patrimony'), implies long-term settlement with no intention of leaving, and within the Israeli context it is clear that such settlement occurs in places that do not necessarily belong to the settlers, but that they have acquired for themselves in a resolute endeavour within a foreign population.

Similar to the settlers in Israel, the young adult backpackers had settled in a foreign country among a local, Indian population, on land that did not belong to them, their settlement being intended for the long term, though not for permanency. But, unlike the younger 'conquerors', the young adults mostly showed an attitude of respect and esteem toward the 'Others' among whom they had settled, by trying to learn from them and adopt their way of life. Most of them did not regard the local inhabitants as inferior, but as people from whom there was something to learn, especially in regard to one's approach to life.

In contrast to the harsh colonialist mentality of the 'conquerors' who saw the natives as primitive and inferior, and even strove to educate them

(Ashcroft *et al.*, 1998), the behaviour of the 'settlers' manifests milder patterns of neo-colonialism that display romantic aspects. They admire and even idealise the Indian, as often happens in colonial discourses (Thomas, 1994) and by going native in many aspects they try to imitate the natives – a central aspect of orientalism (Edwards, 1996; Herz, 1999; Laxon, 1991). The central issues that they adopt from the local culture are relaxation and spirituality – two main characteristics that they ascribe to the Indians. They learn about these by attending various courses such as meditation, Yoga and Reiki, by joining ashrams and by having conversations with the locals. They tend to be quite involved with the local reality – buying things in the market, eating East Asian food, wearing Indian clothes, and using some Hindi words, of which the most common is the word *Shanti*, meaning 'peace and serenity'.

The socialising of the settlers with other Israeli tourists is limited, occurring in short episodes and with single travellers rather than groups of travellers. The 'settler' in India is similar to the type of tourist that Cohen (1972) called the 'drifter' and Vogt (1976) called the 'wanderer', i.e. the most individualist and least established type, who ' ... tends to make it wholly on his own [sic], living with the people ... tries to live the way the people he visits ... has no fixed itinerary or timetable and no well-defined goals of travel' (Cohen, 1972: 168).

Modern drifters, however, make use of an alternative network to the network of services for conventional tourism, that has its own restaurants, hotels, meeting places, enclaves, guidebooks, and so on (Cohen, 1973 and Chapter 3 of this volume; Riley, 1988; Teas, 1988; Vogt, 1976), and they are less adventurous than the 'original drifter' (Cohen, 1973), who hardly exists nowadays (Cohen, Chapter 3 of this volume). The main characteristic of the 'settler' as distinct from Cohen's 'drifter' is that of staying in one place and trying to live a very routine daily life there. This is also a typical aspect of moratorium (Erikson, 1959), namely, the putting off of responsibilities and obligations.

In every interview I conducted, the question arose of how the subjects occupied themselves during the journey. The answer that kept repeating itself surprised me: most of the subjects said that they were not 'doing' anything in India but, instead, were concentrating on 'being' (see Wang, 1999). As backpackers they spent their time very differently than they had on other trips. My fieldwork confirmed their descriptions. They tended to settle for weeks or months in one small village and to live daily, routine, 'regular' lives that mainly involved extended repose, buying things in the market, cooking, smoking, eating, talking and sleeping, with spirituality transcending all the rest. Throughout the span of the journey, which lasted six months to a year (and which had been pre-planned from the financial standpoint), not one of the subjects worked.

Their active pursuit was to take an interest in Eastern spiritual doctrines, sometimes to participate in a *vipsana*,[3] meditation, Yoga, etc., but again, not very extensively. Most of them were in a state of 'shanti'. Gal (31), for example, gave this reply to the question 'What did you do in India?' ... 'What did I do for three months? I drank chai'. Ronen (29) answered a similar question: 'What did I do all the time? Meet people, wander around, go on walking tours. Every meal takes half a day'. Like many young backpackers (Cohen, 1973; Teas, 1988; Vogt, 1976), they too used drugs during the journey, but that was only part of the experience and not its main aspect.

Yet, despite an inactive daily life, these travellers were not superficial like the tourists Boorstin described (1961: 94), as they were engaged, according to their reports, in a serious and profound inward journey, which they described as the real purpose of the trip. The interviewees reported a desire to 'find themselves' during the journey.

In the interviews, the backpackers attributed the spiritual process they had undergone mainly to the place and the people.[4] They perceived India as an ideal venue for a profound spiritual journey, as a spiritual setting. To achieve the spiritual journey that was really the point of their trip; the young adult backpackers strove to familiarise themselves with the local culture by experiencing it directly and interacting with the inhabitants.

The following section examines the four factors identified as influencing the character of these two groups' journeys and which make them so different – age, life stage, destination image and the degree of alienation from the Israeli society. I will also show how they interrelate with each other.

The Conquerors' Journey

Age and stage of life

Most of the young travellers are at a stage of moratorium. They have just been released from military service, which extends the years of moratorium and postpones the process of crystallising self-identity. Military service is characterised by different aspects of moratorium, such as the deferment of many elements that typify the passage to adulthood – including decisions on issues of career or family, intimate relationships and leaving their parents' home. The soldier is indeed physically distant from his or her family but is still dependent on it economically and emotionally, since he or she has not had the opportunity to leave it and begin a truly independent life, thus delaying an important aspect of maturation; namely, separation from parents. The 'independence' that the soldier acquires during military service is limited (Lieblich, 1989).

The trip, then, is their opportunity to be away from their family for the first time and to cope independently with new challenges and then go through and conclude the moratorium stage of young adulthood. It is their private *rite de passage* (van Gennep, 1960) – a path to maturity between the early passage to adulthood (17–22) and the entry into the adult world (22–28) (Levinson, 1978: 23; Levinson *et al.*, 1978).

The issues that occupy the young travellers at this age are usually different from those that arise in older age, as they face decisions of a different kind. Only 1.5% of them associated the period with having to start working, 2.3% associated it with launching a family or parenthood, and 6.9% with struggle about direction in life (Mevorach, 1997). They reported that they did not make the journey in order to 'find themselves,' and that if such a thing had happened, it was unintended. They also did not define the journey's significance in terms of identity or soul-searching. These findings accord with the age of the young people and their stage of life. They had just been discharged from the army, were not yet concerned about the future, and did not feel they had to make fateful decisions.

The timing of the trip – just after the exertion and intensive activity that they knew during army service – is reflected in the character of the journey. Their journey bore a direct relation to the military service they had completed shortly before, taking the form of intensive, adventurous, and strenuous activity, with a focus on doing.

They were still at the stage where the concept of the *hevreh* (an Israeli slang term describing a tightly-knit group of friends) was of central significance. After being accustomed during the army and high school years to a collective and cohesive network of social ties (Katriel, 1999), in order to enjoy the journey they needed to be with a group of people who were similar to them. The army experience was also reflected in their register[5] (Coupland & Jaworski, 1997; Dann, 1996b), which consists of borrowed terms, in the character of their journey, and above all, in the military culture affecting their attitude toward the 'Other'.

Degree of alienation from Israeli society

The backpackers who were just out of the army expressed almost no alienation (unlike the 'original drifter', see Cohen, 1973; 1979) from Israeli society, and saw Israel as the only appropriate place to live, though this attitude moderated after the journey. Mevorach, (1997: 183) quotes a young traveller as saying '... in the journey I've crystallised my stand that the place for me is the country (Israel), this is my place and this is where I want to live'.

Many of them emphasised the special personal relations in Israel: the caring, depth, support, and commitment. Others described their attitude toward Israel before the trip as an idealistic one of believing in the power, uniqueness, and justness of the state and the army. Some 76.3% of the young people said the chances that they would leave Israel were small to non-existent (Mevorach, 1997).

The timing of the journey and the stage of life at which it was conducted are closely related to the extent of alienation that the travellers felt toward Israeli society. The young backpackers were just out of the army and still influenced by its ethos and values (Arkin & Dobrofsky, 1978). Their lives so far had been moulded by agents of socialisation (army, school and family) that instil patriotism and love of the country and society. Their journey was to a large degree an extension of the military-Israeli-collective experience.

Destination image

Postmodern tourism is based on consumption of images, many of which are far from reality (Bruner, 1989; 1996; Dann, 1996b; 1998; MacCannell, 1976; Urry, 1990). Destination image has been found to have a powerful influence on destination choice and tourists' behaviour (see Gallarza *et al.*, 2002). The images of the locals in India that the Israeli young travellers carried bear an oriental character, which reflected in their journey and their attitude towards the Indians. The young travellers borrow the image of the Indians from the image they carry of the Palestinian Arabs and the environment in which they live. Sivan (22) says: 'I had a shock in Delhi. This is how I imagine Gaza. Cows and heat and humidity 100%. Very stinking. It was horrible'.

The Israeli young travellers tend to portray the locals as primitive, backward, dirty and stinking. They see them as lazy, passive and accepting their faith. These kinds of images have often been held by Westerners towards the 'Other' (Comaroff, 1992; Elsrud, 1998; Said, 1978), and by Jewish Israelis towards the Arabs (Even-Zohar, 1981; Eyal, 1996). This is another factor that influences the conquerers' trip, which is secluded and involves little contact with the locals. It also explains the patronising attitude towards the locals and the very nickname that the young Israelis adopted for themselves – the conquerors. The nature of the image has also to do with their age, as they still bear the effects of Israeli socialisation agents and feel deep patriotism for their country.

The Settlers' Journey

Age and stage of life

The transition stage at around the age of 30 is gradually becoming more and more significant in human life. The decisions that the individual is expected to make in this phase will greatly affect the rest of his or her life, since they involve the main elements of human existence – marriage, family and profession (Levinson *et al.*, 1978; Levinson, 1978). In this phase, modern individuals have a kind of last opportunity to re-evaluate their choices, alter them if necessary and build a more satisfactory life for themselves (Levinson *et al.*, 1978). Some people pass through this stage in a smooth and continuous way, but others experience it as an 'age 30' crisis, which may be severe and difficult.

At the age of 30, the 'social timetable' (Neugarten, 1968, 1979) of Israeli society and its expectations of the individual are similar to those in the Western societies in general – to marry, enter the labour market, and establish a family. The average age for marriage in Israel is 24.7 for women and 27.3 for men (Israeli Bureau of Statistics, 2000). In the upper-middle social class, to which this study's subjects belong, the average marriage age is in fact slightly higher. At around the age of 30, people feel they have reached the last moment when they can remain single and career-less without delaying the 'sociological clock'.

The journey is used by most of them as an independent *rite de passage* that will lead them to the next stage of adulthood and reflects their need for self-examination, soul-searching, examination of their past decisions, and making decisions about the future (Levinson *et al.*, 1978). This liminal period, in which they were cut off from their usual physical environment, was an ideal time for them to undertake reflective self-analysis of their current and previous lives (Jung, 1956; Stein & Stein, 1987; Turner, 1987). Also appropriate was the form of tourism they were engaged in (the drifting journey) since it is less organised and institutionalised and lends itself to experiences, transformations and self-discovery (Curtis & Pajaczkowaska, 1994).

Their touristic experience was mainly existential (Wang, 1999), focusing on their feelings on 'being' during the journey (Gottlieb, 1982; Wang, 1999), and on 'hot authenticity' (Selwyn, 1996: 21–25), i.e. the search for the authentic self.

Prior to the journey, unlike the young travellers, the young adults functioned for years without a break or moratorium in a rigid and demanding society, and by the age at which I met them they were already exhausted or, in other words, burnt out.

The subjects perceived themselves as conformists who had conducted their lives on a difficult course in keeping with society's and the family's expectations of them, whilst never rebelling. They had combined work, sometimes at two or three different places, with competitive studies and for a decade since army service had never taken a time-out, a moratorium. This reality had pressured and exhausted them and now caused them, for the first time at the age of 30, to want to flee:

> I couldn't go on. How long can you keep running within the track, it's like an obstacle course, but you keep running till you're exhausted. I got to a point where I couldn't continue any more. (Ido, 32)

By around the age of 30 they took their first moratorium. Their exhaustion was reflected in the character of their journey, as was their fear of the future. In their journey they mainly rested – regained and built up strength for continuing with their lives. The settlers, as their name suggests, just settled down in a location in India for weeks or months and did nothing, but concentrated on being – searching their inner self. For that purpose they turned to Eastern spiritual philosophies, and engaged in different courses.

Degree of alienation from Israeli society

The timing of the journey and the stage of life at which it was conducted are closely related to the extent of alienation that the travellers felt towards Israeli society. The younger backpackers were just out of the army and still influenced by its ethos and values. Their lives so far had been moulded by agents of socialisation and their journey was, to a large degree, an extension of the military-Israeli-collective experience. The young adults, however, had grown mentally distant from their military service. They were at a stage of life where they had to make crucial decisions about their future, and they were impelled to look more closely at the geographic and societal realities of their lives:

> The disappointment ... Not only over the family circle, but also over the national home ... there's a feeling of huge alienation between people. The solidarity and collectivity that Israel had in the early years are gone. Today it's money, appearances, and the rat race. (Yoel, 33)

The sense of alienation from society is not unique to the Israeli young person; according to MacCannell (1973; 1999) it exists in every tourist to one extent or another. Yet when one examines other studies, it does not appear to be central among young backpackers in general, who are rarely alienated from their society (see Cohen, Chapter 3 and Binder, Chapter 6 of this volume), whereas it is more pronounced among older Israeli backpackers. The Israeli young adults report a sense of estrangement from

Israeli society, from its institutions and norms. They have feelings of claustrophobia and stress stemming from prolonged periods of living up to society's expectations and demands.

Their cohort, born around the time of the Six Day War, displays many attributes of Generation X (Brinkley, 1994; Ortner, 1998; Rahav, 1995), including alienation from society, as well as disappointment at the fact that Israeli society has changed. As they see it, initially the country was more idealistic and moral, the society was tight knit and had a vision, whereas the wars and the occupation, the Westernisation and the abandonment of collective values and glorification of individualist ones, have 'spoiled' the country. Interestingly, it is precisely the rise of values emphasising individual desires that, paradoxically, made this backpacking journey possible for them.

The sense of alienation from Israeli society caused the young adult backpackers to keep a distance from other Israeli backpackers and to travel independently, while attempting to get involved with the local population. While the younger travellers experience the recreational mode of tourism (Cohen, 1979), i.e. functional tourism for purposes of entertainment (not stemming from alienation, but from a need for freedom and recreation), the older ones were involved in an experimental mode of tourism. This is characteristic of people who do not adhere any more to the spiritual centre of their own society and engage in a quest for an alternative centre (Cohen, 1979).

Destination image

While the young travellers perceived the locals as inferior (primitive and backward), and therefore treated them as unimportant and only as decor, the older backpackers perceived the Indians as spiritual people that are worthy of imitating and learning from. As with other Western tourists, they too are worried about the materialism and alienation of their own society (MacCannell, 1973, 1976; Mansfeld, 1992) and admire and envy the 'Other' for their 'natural spirituality', harmony with nature (Laxon, 1991; Thomas, 1994) and even wholeness (Schechner, 1977). As Galia (29) stated: 'The Indians, with all their jiffa [dirtiness] have more tranquillity than we do, or will ever have ... they are at one with nature, live simple but joyful lives'. These too are orientalistic images and projections of their Western consciousness, based on the concept of binary relations between the East and the West (Ateljevic & Doorne, Chapter 4; JanMohamed, 1985; Said, 1978), but which can result in a more respectful attitude toward the locals.

India is seen as a sacred and spiritual place – an ideal location in which to conduct the search for identity, and exactly what is required at their stage in life. Nili (33): 'I wanted an inner journey more than an outward one. People are spiritual, it does something to the atmosphere of the place ... '. But the Israeli travellers were not the only ones who perceived India as an ideal place for inner quest. Jung (1963: 257) wrote: 'India affected me like a dream, for I was and remained in search of myself ...'. Their alienation from the Israeli society led them to look for an alternative way of life – calmer; more relaxed; attached to feelings rather than acts; and 'being' rather than 'doing'. The images that they carried about India helped them to achieve this.

Conclusions

Two distinctive patterns of backpacking by young Israeli backpackers emerged from the research, which can be tagged as 'aggressive' versus 'romantic' modes of neo-colonialism. The first pattern is represented in a journey that is secluded from the environment, detached from the locals, is characterised by patronising behaviour, while keeping a firm environmental bubble of 'Israeliness'. The travellers who fit this pattern are usually younger, just released from the army and are nicknamed 'the conquerors'. The mode of colonialism that characterises their journey is aggressive and harsh. The second type is less secluded, more open to the environment, less hectic and characterised by settling in one place and trying to 'go native'. Those are mostly older travellers, in their thirties, who are nicknamed 'the settlers'. They hold romantic and naïve images about the host population and try to imitate them by going native.

The different character of their journeys can be attributed to four major factors – age, stage of life, degree of alienation from their society, and the nature of the image they hold of the locals. Those at a young age and an early stage of life have fewer decisions to make and in Israeli society they also feel close to the army and its atmosphere, with hardly any alienation from the society. Instead there are feelings of patriotism and disrespect toward the 'Other', often perceived as inferior.

Older age in Israeli society means increasing distance from the agents of socialisation, especially the army. They have to deal with more problems and questions regarding the future: they feel less comfortable with society and in turn are looking for an alternative spiritual centre (Cohen, 1979). The attitude towards the 'Other' at this age has an orientalistic nature, but it is nevertheless more open and accepting. These findings match Ganguli's conclusion that images of a destination and its inhabitants tend to soften and become more positive with age (Ganguli, 1975).

A journey of the kind described here has a ritual quality and as such reinforces the values of the society and its solidarity (Bocock, 1974; MacCannell, 1973). When we analyse our findings we can see them as reflections of issues that characterise Israeli society. They can reflect, for example, the tension in Israeli society between, on the one hand, a culture of militarism, separateness, forcefulness and a supercilious attitude toward the 'Other' and, on the other hand, the growing tendency in recent years toward spirituality, including recognition of the 'Other', while still holding orientalistic images of 'them'.

A further tension manifested in this work lies between collectivism, which characterised the Zionist Israeli society in its beginnings, and individualism, a growing trend in contemporary post-Zionist society (Almog, 1992, 1997; Roniger & Feige, 1992). On one hand, in their journey the young backpackers continue the collective military culture; on the other hand, this tendency mellows with age and becomes more open and individualistic.

The dialectical relationships between the two attitudes are complex, since each incorporates the other. The 'settlers', as their nickname suggests, exhibit several traits of the conquering mentality of the younger people, while the 'conquerors' exhibit certain attributes similar to those of the 'settlers' and, despite the military character of their journey, some import into Israel a culture of spirituality, liberality, and openness towards the 'Other'. They also undergo a process of disillusionment during the journey, and after returning show more alienation from and less patriotism toward Israel (Mevorach, 1997). Israeli travellers of all ages who are 'products of India' introduce many 'spiritual' elements into Israel, which infuse the society's cultural essence and alter it.

People tend to travel at junctures in life to seek personal change and growth, to seek answers to questions about their identities and to find things that are missing in their lives (Crompton, 1979; Desforges, 2000; Hastings, 1998; Hills, 1965; Riley, 1988). A phenomenon of inversion supposedly occurs during these journeys (Gottlieb, 1982; Graburn, 1983), and this enables them to construct their identity and seek new ways of life. Nevertheless, not only inversion, but also continuity occurs in these journeys, as they do not stand in a binary opposition to their normal life, as some have suggested (e.g. Urry, 1990). These journeys represent the travellers' attitudes and values stemming, not only from their age and phase in life (as well as gender, status and other aspects that have not been dealt with here), but also from the society they come from, its main characteristics, tensions and tendencies. This relates closely to the concept of 'suspension', which is discussed in more detail in Chapter 15. Upon their return, the travellers may also affect their own society by bringing new attitudes and lifestyles back from their journeys.

Notes

1. Mevorach (1997) studied the backpacking of young Israelis just released from military service. He used questionnaires and semi-structured interviews with 1005 men and women, and focused on the psychological and psycho-social aspects of the phenomenon.
2. In Hebrew – an abbreviation for a minimal period of time.
3. A course of eleven days of a certain kind of meditation done in complete silence.
4. Although one might see any travel destination as an opportunity for a spiritual quest. For example, the writer Jack Kerouac tried to find spirituality when travelling across the USA (see Wilson & Richards, Chapter 8 of this volume).
5. Unlike Murphy's (2001) finding regarding the lack of a unique set of words or phrases used by the backpacking subculture.

Chapter 8

Backpacker Icons: Influential Literary 'Nomads' in the Formation of Backpacker Identities

JULIE WILSON AND GREG RICHARDS

Introduction

Growing numbers of people are adopting the travelstyle of a backpacker for reasons ranging from existential concerns to straightforward feeding of personal curiosity and hedonistic desires. The personal influences that underpin this growth in backpacking as a life experience or a distinct travelstyle are less well known.

The research on the social construction of backpacking presented in Chapter 2 indicated that aspects of popular culture (for example, Jack Kerouac's novel *On the Road*) can act as cultural icons and role models for the backpacker phenomenon. Representations of backpacking in the cinematic and literary worlds are plentiful, not just in overt terms of central 'backpacker' characters, but also influential authors and travel journalists who may inspire the potential backpacker with their narratives and images of far-flung places. Such cultural icons arguably play a role in shaping identities through the images they inspire. The writings of literary nomads such as Bruce Chatwin, Jack Kerouac and Hunter S. Thompson, for example, can influence backpackers not just in terms of their choice of travel destinations, but also in terms of travelstyles, self-representations and aspirations. This chapter aims to understand some of the influences of travel writing on backpacker subculture(s) and travelstyles by examining literary backpacker icons – renowned authors and travel writers.

Analysis of backpacker icons is particularly interesting from an industry perspective, as backpackers may not be as strongly influenced by 'conventional' image formation agents (Gartner, 1993) and may see themselves as fulfilling or occupying a consumptive role different from that of other tourists (Murphy, 2001). Indeed, backpackers often position themselves in opposition to more 'conventional' tourists, who may be likened to the conventional society that has rejected (or been rejected by) sub- or countercultural icons.

In many ways, backpackers can be characterised as 'neo-tribes' (Mafessoli, 1995) or as social groups that temporarily bond together in the midst of social uncertainty and disembeddedness. As Rojek (1997) points out, neo-tribal collectivities are organised around cultural products and particularly around icons of popular culture. By analysing the icons that backpackers identify with, we hope to trace the systems of meaning that bring the backpacker 'neo-tribe' together.

Our analysis pays particular attention to certain characteristics often attached to backpacker experience, such as drifter, heroic figure, hedonist and loner. Examining some of the wider influences on backpacker identities may indicate some of the inspirations for undertaking a backpacker experience. Among the popular backpacking icons examined are Ernest Hemingway, Jack Kerouac, Hunter S. Thompson, Bruce Chatwin, Paul Theroux, Michael Palin and Bill Bryson.

Cultures, Subcultures and Identity

Urry (1990) argues that we are moving towards a 'culture of tourism', which is arguably just one subculture within a wider 'culture of mobility' (Clifford, 1997). In the (post)modern tourism culture, there are some clearly identifiable subcultures – groups of tourists who distinguish themselves from others through shared values and behaviour. In order to be able to analyse the form and function of backpacker culture further, we first need to consider the nature and function of culture itself.

Countless definitions exist for the word 'culture' but in the context of this study we adopt a relatively narrow definition of culture as a system of ideas. Schein (1985) sees culture as the way in which a group of people solves problems and reconciles dilemmas. Culture includes for him the assumptions that govern behaviour. Another widely-quoted definition of culture is that of Hofstede (1991: 5) 'The collective programming of the mind which distinguishes the members of one group or category of people from another'. In this context, culture can be seen as the collection of 'norms', 'values', 'expectations' and 'goals' that distinguish a group. A number of important features are implicit in Hofstede's approach to culture. Culture is firstly a shared system of meanings, determining what people pay attention to and what assumptions they make about the world. In order to understand each other, we have to have a shared system of meaning. Culture is also relative; there are no cultural absolutes – each culture has its own world view. Culture is essentially learned, and can be seen as deriving from the social environment rather than the individual and, therefore, culture is about groups. Backpackers are arguably a clearly identifiable subcultural group within the modern tourism landscape.

In examining the culture of backpackers in this chapter, we attempt to break their culture down, in order to identify some of its basic building blocks. One model that analyses the different elements of culture is Schein's (1985) analysis of the different 'layers' of culture. According to this, the basic elements of a culture include assumptions, norms, rituals, heroines / heroes and symbols.

Assumptions are self-evident truths that form the most basic level of a culture and are never questioned. In the subsequent layer, *norms* establish the group's rules about suitable and unsuitable behaviour and what is 'good' or 'bad' in cultural terms. *Rituals* are collective activities not directed to a particular goal, but necessary for the maintenance of a culture. In the next layer of the cultural 'onion', *heroines and heroes* are people (real or imaginary) who represent characteristics that are important to a culture. For example, in travel cultures, many journeys follow in the footsteps of famous travellers. Finally, *symbols* are words, gestures, images or objects that have a meaning recognised only by members of the culture. Many authors have commented on the *Lonely Planet* guides as a symbol of the backpacker (e.g. Sutcliffe, 1997). New symbols are easy to develop and old ones can disappear or be copied. Symbols, as the outermost layer, are the most visible elements of a culture.

Taken together, these different elements of a culture form the raw materials for identity formation. However, in terms of identity, it is often easier to say clearly what one is not than what one is. It may follow that ' ... in times of uncertain identity (such as the present), definition may be achieved most effectively by naming clear outsides rather than by attempting to reduce always-diverse and hybrid insides to a stable unity' (Clifford, 1997: 65). In other words, a culture or subculture may find it easier to identify itself in terms of what its members are not. Particularly in terms of subcultures, the identification of the group often rests on a rejection of and opposition to the dominant culture. One might therefore expect to find elements of this opposition in any 'backpacker culture' and the cultural elements used to establish its identity. As Urry (1994: 91) argued: 'identity almost everywhere has to be produced partly out of the images constructed or reproduced for tourists' and one would expect this link to be strong for backpackers actively seeking travel experiences.

Therefore, we concentrate on the elements of the backpacker culture that are most visible – iconic heroines, heroes and symbols. By analysing these 'outer layers' of the backpacker culture, we aim to uncover some of the deeper meanings – the assumptions, norms, values and rituals that underpin the subculture.

Why Look at Travel Writers as Icons?

Dann (1999) argued that an important, though often neglected, vehicle of tourist socialisation is the medium of travel writing, since it tends to adopt a critical stance toward the overall phenomenon that it is treating. He also noted, though, that there have been no comprehensive inquiries as to how travel writers deal with the autobiographical conflict (which exists within themselves) between the roles of 'traveller' and 'tourist'. Moreover, he argues that there is no exploration of the paradox that the richer the portrayal of (undiscovered) places of travel within travel writing, the more likely it is that they will become transformed into (discovered) tourist destinations.

Pratt (1992) argues that, for the most part, (academic) study of travel writing has tended to be either naïvely celebratory or dismissive, although he does see a clear connection between travel writing and the forms of knowledge and expression that interact with it, asking how travel writing has 'produced the rest of the world' (Pratt, 1992: 5).

Along similar lines, Clifford (1997) maintains that the travel writer's transient and literary approach, sharply rejected in the disciplining of field-work, has continued to tempt and contaminate the scientific practices of cultural description. Anthropologists are (typically) people who leave and write. However, travel and travel discourse should not be reduced to the relatively recent tradition of literary travel: a narrowed conception that emerged in the late nineteenth and early twentieth centuries. This notion of 'travel' was articulated against 'an emerging ethnography ... on the one hand, and against tourism (a practice defined as incapable of producing serious knowledge) on the other' (Clifford, 1997: 65).

Clifford also argues that there has been an emergence of 'sophisticated travel', catering to the independent traveller. This literary tradition of sophisticated travel, whose disappearance has been lamented by critics such as Daniel Boorstin and Paul Fussell, has been reinvented by a long list of contemporary writers – Paul Theroux, Shirley Hazzard, Bruce Chatwin, Jan Morris and Ronald Wright among others.

Dann (1999) looked at how travel writing manages this distinction between traveller and tourist. He argued that travel writing has continued popularity as a promotional medium and that by writing out the tourist via the universal categories of space and time, writers can 'appeal to the anti-tourist who resides in every tourist' (Dann, 1999: 159). He noted that the metaphor of a journey to the timeless periphery might also strike a chord in many readers, as it refers to life itself as a form of travel. The form of the novel, often based on the idea of a hero setting out, experiencing trials and adventure, and returning home victorious and changed (Dann, 1999), mirrors the quest of the traveller. This homology of literature and travel, allied to reading as a major source of information about the destination, provides a strong link between reading, writing and travel. Therefore, we would argue that the close identification of travellers with what they read means that travel writing may provide interesting information about the meanings attached to travel.

Methodology

The range of books read by travellers is vast: more than 200 titles were being read 'on the road' by the 160 respondents to the social construction study presented in Chapter 2, for example. In order to find out what back-packers might consider to be influential sources among these, the *Lonely Planet* website's 'Thorn Tree' discussion group was used to elicit a shortlist of popular backpacking icons for closer examination. The Thorn Tree is the discussion section of the site, which had over 80,000 registered users in 2002, illustrating the importance of information exchange among travellers.

An informal request for information was placed on the Thorn Tree site in November 2001:

> So come on then, who are the greatest 'backpacker icons' of all time? What characters from films and novels inspired your backpacking expe-rience? Post a reply giving your top three icons and we'll see who tops the International League Table of influential nomads...

This request generated 32 responses, most of which identified multiple literary or film icons as influential nomads. Most of the icons mentioned were authors, book titles or characters, perhaps underlining the portability of books for travellers. The writers most frequently mentioned were Hemingway, Kerouac, Hunter S. Thompson, Chatwin, Theroux, Bryson and Palin. Other authors listed included Wilfred Thesiger, Robert Byron, Edward Browne, George Curzon, Lady Anne Blunt, William Dalrymple, T.E. Lawrence, Sir Richard Burton and Laurens van der Post. The popu-larity of Hemingway, Kerouac, Chatwin, Theroux, Bryson and Palin among backpackers was underlined by their subsequent listing as 'fave travel writers' in response to an independent posting on the Thorn Tree site two months later.

The male dominance of the selections is perhaps not surprising, given the nature of the Internet, which also explains the predominance of English language sources. But this may also reflect travel writing as a whole: '... Travel writing has been mainly a male preserve, certainly one associated with exploration, scientific discovery and imperial quest' (Dann, 1999: 170). Women who responded were much more likely to mention female authors: 'Lady Mary Wortley Montague and other Victorian and Edwardian travelling ladies. Gutsy and inspiring in an era when it was entirely "unfit" and "unbecoming" for a "lady" to be travelling' (ryb,[1] 19 November).

The influence of books was more obvious than other forms of popular culture, but there were clear examples of travel stimulated by film: '... but I was influenced to leave my home for places unknown because of repetitive viewings of *The King and I* starring Yul Brynner. Something about "Anna" moving away with only a piece of paper to fall back on ... there's an adventurous soul' (nightsnwhitesatn, 23 November). More esoteric movies were also found to be inspirational: 'Harry Dean Stanton in *Paris, Texas,* the film *Alice in den Städten* (Wim Wenders), the Japanese couple in *Mystery Train (Jarmusch)*' (Anon., 20 November)

In demarcating travel writers for the purpose of analysis, characteristics such as language, educational background, age, period of writing and target audience could be used (Dann, 1999), as well as the mode of transport employed by the writer on their travels. Beyond this, authors and their writings can be demarcated in generational terms, in geographical terms, in popularity terms, in terms of whether writing is their main occupation and in terms of the cultural movements they represent, or embody.

Table 8.1 shows the authors selected for analysis in this chapter, in the broad context of the orientation of their writing. These authors fall roughly into four generations: Hemingway as the 'founding father', then the 'Beat Generation', the 'sophisticated travellers', and contemporary 'travel celebrities'. We will analyse the authors from each of these groups, beginning

Table 8.1 Literary backpacker icons analysed

		Writers who travel
Ernest Hemingway	'Founding Father'	
Jack Kerouac Hunter S. Thompson	'Beat Generation'	↑
Bruce Chatwin Paul Theroux	'Sophisticated Travellers'	↕
Michael Palin Bill Bryson	'Travel Celebrities'	↓ Travel writers

with Ernest Hemingway, as his work arguably influenced those of later generations very strongly. From the Beat Generation, we focus on the work of Kerouac and Thompson, two of the most important figures writing about travelling in the 1950s and 1960s. The 'sophisticated travellers' Bruce Chatwin and Paul Theroux produced major works in the 1970s and 1980s, generating a new style of travel writing that was more historically situated and detached from contemporary culture than the Beat Generation. From the contemporary generation of travel 'celebrities' we examine the work of Michael Palin (whose more literary style echoes his admiration for Hemingway) and Bill Bryson, who travels and writes in an altogether lighter vein.

Not only can a development of different styles of travel writing be traced over successive 'generations', but the focus of this writing has arguably changed as well. Hall and Kinnaird (1994) make a distinction between 'travellers who write' and 'travel writers'. Arguably, the early generations of writers travelled in order to write, whereas for the later generations travel is an end in itself, which later becomes the subject of their writing. However, the distinction between writers who travel (for whom the goal is the written word) and travellers who write (for whom the central purpose is the journey) is becoming blurred. This blurring increases '... as travel for writers has become more ubiquitous' (Hall & Kinnaird, 1994: 191–192) and as travellers increasingly need to finance their trips (Dann, 1999).

In order to trace the development of these backpacker icons and the relationships between them, the following brief analysis of key texts deals with each of the generations in turn.

Hemingway: The Great Adventurer?

It could be argued that in all the writers, one could identify Hemingway as an antecedent influence. As an indication of Hemingway's appeal to backpackers, it is worth stating that the *Lonely Planet* guides make frequent references to 'Hemingway's haunts'. This is particularly the case for destinations such as Cuba (with Havana being strewn with 'Hemingway's hangouts'), Spain (enough bullfighting 'to make Papa Hemingway blush'), Florida (with Key West coined as 'the legendary land of Hemingway') and Chicago (his birth place), where the Ernest Hemingway museum contains extensive memorabilia.

Hemingway started his career as a newspaper writer before joining the US army and later resuming as a reporter and writer. He was known for drawing on his personal experiences when writing, for example; he used his experiences as a reporter in the Spanish civil war as the background for

For Whom the Bell Tolls (1940). A great sportsman himself, Hemingway liked to portray soldiers, hunters and bullfighters – tough people who take a very modern approach to living – everything in its place and a natural order to things, with challenge and adventure making the man.

Hemingway's writing has been highly influential in terms of the number of writers who have since emulated his writing and travelstyles. For example, Michael Palin's admiration for Hemingway induced him to retrace some of the writer's footsteps, and his search for authentic, heroic experiences, usually to be found in traditional, simpler ways of life:

> Struggles, peasant pride, redemption through physical pain, the confrontation with nature that strips away sham and compromise. This is what comfortable, bourgeois ... Ernest saw in Spain and it drew him like a magnet. (Palin, 1999: 72)

Nature was seen by Hemingway as a fitting adversary and a friend – at least as long as the game lasts: 'fish ... I love you and respect you very much. But I will kill you dead before this day ends' (Hemingway, 1993: 45). For several of Hemingway's characters, close to nature and embedded in the richness of everyday experience, travel is a dream. People who travel without dreaming, on the other hand, are the modern tourists for Hemingway, who are to be pitied for their stupidity. When the Old Man finally lands his fish on the beach in *The Old Man and the Sea,* the ravaged skeleton becomes a tourist curiosity. In their ignorance, the gawping visitors don't know that the fish is a marlin: 'I didn't know sharks had such handsome, beautifully formed tails' (Hemingway, 1993: 109).

The simple, adventurous life described by Hemingway is so attractive to contemporary readers that many travel to recreate the Hemingway experience. Palin encounters Hemingway aficionados in Key West, eagerly following the supposed lifestyle of their hero, although brushing aside any questions about what books of Hemingway's they might have read (Palin, 1999).

Hemingway's influences are evident in the work of all of the other writers we have examined: both implicitly (in terms of common characteristics) and explicitly (through an inheritance of Hemingway's travel and literary styles).

Jack Kerouac and Hunter S. Thompson: On the Road with the Beat Generation

Jack Kerouac

In the late 1940s, Jack Kerouac famously helped to found the beat movement with fellow contemporary authors, Allen Ginsberg and William

Burroughs. After serving in World War II, Kerouac travelled around the USA and wrote many books about his adventures and experiences. *On the Road*, first published in 1957, is the classic testament of the Beat Generation. Typed in three weeks onto twelve-foot-long rolls of paper, the book was based on nearly a decade of travelling across the US, collecting material and character sketches. According to Miller (2002), Kerouac '... lived to wash in the truth of experience, trying to find the people and moments that would bring him ever closer to that world-waking enlightenment'.

Alienation is a recurrent theme in *On the Road*. Kerouac writes:

Suddenly I found myself on Times Square. I had traveled eight thousand miles around the American continent and I was back on Times Square; and right in the middle of rush hour, too, seeing with my innocent road-eyes the absolute madness and fantastic hoorair of New York with its millions and millions hustling forever for a buck amongst themselves, the mad dream – grabbing, taking, giving, sighing, dying, just so they could be buried in those awful cemetery cities beyond Long Island City. (Kerouac, 2000/1957: 96)

Kerouac's novels often express the crazier, unhinged aspects of his self-identity: ' the sensation of death kicking at my heels to move on, with a phantom dogging its own heels, and myself hurrying to a plank where all the angels dove off and flew into the holy void' (Kerouac, 2000/1957: 157).

On the other hand, Kerouac's books often emphasised his need for understanding the context of his travel, expressed as a quest for learning, for spirituality and at a more existential level. For example '... this book is to prove that no matter how you travel, how "successful" your tour, or fore-shortened, you always learn something and learn to change your thoughts' (Kerouac, 1982/1966: Chapter 14).

Kerouac's accounts of his adventures not only gave the Beat Generation a 'bible' of sorts (*On the Road*), but also inspired the writing and travelling of many of his contemporaries and successors.

Hunter S. Thompson

Hunter S. Thompson was born in Kentucky in 1931 and like Hemingway was an avid sportsman from childhood onwards – although his limited abilities led him to become a sports writer and reinforce his passion for sport. Arguably, Thompson was the founding father of gonzo[2] journalism; writing fiction, reporting facts, philosophies, critiques, theories and cutting straight to the heart of American culture. Thompson's (mis)adventures have firmly established him as the anti-hero of many countercultures, as the following suggests:

Hunter S. Thompson is known for his own particular warped vision of the truth, a fascination with weaponry and the pharmaceutical habits of a crack whore let loose in an opium den with a Platinum American Express card ... He is a Gen-X idol. (Malisow, 1998)

Thompson's classic *Fear and Loathing in Las Vegas* was subtitled *A Savage Journey to the Heart of the American Dream*, a reference to what he saw as America's slide into conformity after the radicalism of the 1960s. This account of gonzo excess is just a snapshot of one phase in Thompson's own journey towards respectability. A much more revealing account of Thompson's own attitudes to travel are provided by his correspondence. *The Fear and Loathing Letters* present a full record of Thompson's correspondence from 1958 onwards (Thompson, 1998; 2000).

In the 1950s, Thompson indulged his fantasies of escape through reading Kerouac's *On the Road* but found Kerouac's other books to be 'withered appendages' in comparison (Thompson, 1998: 140). Like Kerouac and the rest of the Beat Generation, Thompson felt himself to be on the margins of modern society. Unlike Kerouac, however, his marginality was more spiritual and cultural rather than geographic. He felt a need to escape the cultural centre of the modern world: New York:

> I think I need beaches and blackness and moonlit nakedness. New York is a huge tomb, full of writhing, hungry death. All this talk about San Francisco gives one pause: there is also talk of Italy, St Thomas and Tahiti, and other refuges for the poor in spirit. (Thompson, 1998: 108)

Thompson's original motivation for hitting the road was therefore a 'push' motive, which like Kerouac, led him to restless, incessant travel:

> This past year has been a holocaust. Counting on my fingers, I see that I spent six months in Puerto Rico, one in the Virgin Islands, one in Bermuda, two in New York, one in San Francisco, and two in Big Sur – in that order. This makes Kerouac look like a piker. In the entire 12 months I have written three decent short stories, one brochure (by long odds the most profitable – $25 a day), a weird collection of journalism, and countless letters. The rest of the time I worried about either movement, money or police. (*The Proud Highway*, Thompson, 1998: 244)

However, over the years, Thompson not only recognised what he was escaping from, but also what he was seeking on the road. New York was not just lacking in spiritual meaning for Thompson; it also failed to accord him the worldly status he felt he deserved: 'The truth is of course that I want to get even with this town for not recognising my genius and paying me accordingly' (Thompson, 1998: 314). But in addition to the push factor of a lack of cash, there was also the pull of adventure in that he was '... becoming more and more certain that this South American adventure is my very last chance to do something big and bad, come to grips with the basic wilderness' (Thompson, 1998: 317).

Some elements of Thompson's South American adventure were slightly less aggressively adventurous than Hemingway might have liked, however:

> I want to walk on a morning road in Brazil and stop at a good place for a cold beer. I don't even want to understand what they say. Just grin at them and drink, then walk on ... way in the distance I see a clear spot, a splash of sunlit green and a sign saying 'cerveza'. (Thompson, 1998: 318)

The cheapness of South America was for Thompson a major draw, just as the affordability of Spain had been an advantage for Hemingway. He professes: 'I am down to 10 US dollars but have developed a theory which will go down as Thompson's Law of Travel Economics. To wit: full speed ahead and damn the cost: it will all come out in the wash' (Thompson, 1998: 338). However, Thompson's devil-may-care attitude to money contrasted with his constant worries about it. Although he seldom had much money in his early travels, the ability to consume to excess became an important theme in his writing, which reached its climax in *Fear and Loathing in Las Vegas*.

Sophisticated Travellers? Bruce Chatwin and Paul Theroux

Bruce Chatwin

Chatwin's travel writing career apparently began when he threw in his job as a director at Sotheby's in order to live with and study nomadic tribes in the Sudan. He had offered the excuse that his doctor said that he needed to view distant horizons in order to correct an eye defect (a self-confessed psychosomatic illness). Chatwin, the 'restless and randy traveller' (Miles, 2000), later left his steady job writing for the *Sunday Times* with a telegram stating, 'Have gone to Patagonia'. He died in 1989, of what was described at the time as a rare Chinese disease (later acknowledged to be AIDS).

Chatwin's books exhibit a preference for relating strange, unusual and even ridiculous experiences, occurring outside their cultural context, over detailing the day-to-day / routinely authentic practices he encountered. In *What am I Doing Here?* (Chatwin, 1996/1989), his accounts are often accompanied by rich descriptions of the historical backdrop of the characters or places he experiences. We might also argue that Chatwin displays a greater degree of engagement with his travel (with perhaps the exception of

Hemingway) and communicates more of a sense of risk and relative depth of his experiences than the other authors we have analysed. On Timbuctoo:

> To the passing visitor there are only two questions. 'Where is my next drink coming from?' and 'Why am I here at all?' (*Anatomy of Restlessness*, Chatwin, 1996: 28)

Chatwin famously blurred the boundaries between fiction and non-fiction in his writing. However, according to Chatwin's biography by Nicholas Shakespeare (2001), the fictionalised versions of real people, places and events appearing in Chatwin's books often led to situations where the people written about often recognised themselves and did not always appreciate the distortions of their culture and behaviour:

> I quit my job in the 'art world' and went back to the dry places: alone, travelling light. The names of the tribes I travelled among are unimportant: Rguibat, Quashgai, Taimanni, Turkomen, Bororo, Tuareg – people whose journeys, unlike my own, had neither beginning nor end. (*The Songlines*, Chatwin, 1998: 18)

> I ordered coffee and a double brandy at the bar, and took a second brandy back to the room. Reading Strehlow had made me want to write something. I was not drunk – yet – but had not been so nearly drunk in ages. I got out a yellow pad and began to write. (*The Songlines*, Chatwin, 1998: 71)

Chatwin's 'wealth' of incidental writing is often referred to, perhaps attributable to his obsessive, well-documented attempts to record his experiences in notebooks: 'To lose a passport was the least of one's worries; to lose a notebook was a catastrophe' (*The Songlines*, Chatwin, 1998: 160). Chatwin has been criticised at times for his extravagant notions surrounding the significance of nomadism, but it could be argued that it is these very notions that place Chatwin's work firmly within the boundaries of Clifford's (1997) concept of 'sophisticated travel'. His untimely death has more than likely served to reinforce this by creating a posthumous mystique around the author and his writing.

Paul Theroux

The work of the American travel writer, novelist and journalist Paul Theroux is peppered with anecdotes and fatalistic asides as to the nature of the traveller as different from the tourist: 'Tourists don't know where they've been, I thought. Travellers don't know where they're going" (*The Happy Isles of Oceania*, Theroux, 1992: 18). Theroux's musings on this subject became so famous that they are often repeated or paraphrased by back-packers today, as one of Welk's respondents demonstrates in Chapter 5 of this volume. Like Chatwin, Theroux often makes a point of blending fact with fiction, albeit often with more wit and humour. It could be argued that the travelstyles of these two authors have as much in common as their writing styles. Certainly, their 1985 collaboration *Patagonia Revisited* (Chatwin & Theroux, 1985) bears testament to their mutual admiration, similar outlooks, preferences and travelstyles.

Theroux is known for his highly personal observations on many locales, a theme that is often underpinned with accounts of friendship:

> I've made friends along the way, I may say. In every book I've written there has been someone ... in one case, my book about the Pacific, while travelling around the Pacific I became very friendly with a village in the Trobriand Islands. And I send them things. They write me letters. I try to help them out, and visit them from time to time. It's become much more than a friendship with one person, but a friendship with a whole village. That's a very, very nice part of travel. (Theroux, 1999)

Another strong theme in Theroux's writing surrounds contempt for tourists as agents of negative change for previously unspoilt places, often written out with irony and sarcasm:

> It is almost axiomatic that as soon as a place gets a reputation for being paradise it goes to hell. (*The Happy Isles of Oceania*, Theroux, 1992: 370)

> The fact that few people go there is one of the most persuasive reasons for travelling to a place. (Theroux, 1992: 383)

Perhaps more so than with Chatwin, loneliness and a desire for solitude are also very visible elements in Theroux's writing, be this in his characters or in his (more) biographical accounts:

> A traveller has no power, no influence, no known identity. That is why a traveller needs optimism and heart, because without confidence travel is misery. (Theroux, 1992: 446)

> It is usually expensive and lonely to be principled. (Theroux, 1992: 426)

Rather than conceiving of travel as an escape from boredom and routine, Theroux is conversely fond of highlighting travel experiences (or at least aspects thereof) as vehicles of ennui or tedium. Instead of accentuating the thrills and dangers, he is often sceptical and flippant about the supposed glamour that comes with a nomadic lifestyle (or that which is associated with global travel per se). This is interesting, especially when considered against Clifford's notion of 'sophisticated travel'. Theroux (writing in the *Washington Post*, date unknown) appears to reject profusely any notion that his pursuits in travel are sophisticated in any way: 'Travel is glamorous only in retrospect'.

Travel Celebrities: Michael Palin and Bill Bryson

Michael Palin

Michael Palin, former Monty Python member and film star, became a celebrity travel writer and journalist, making TV programmes about trips around the world (*Around the World in 80 Days*), around the Pacific Rim (*Full Circle*) and from the North to South poles (*Pole to Pole*). Palin is a self-confessed Hemingway fan, having written both a travel book, *Hemingway Adventure* (Palin, 1999), and a novel, *Hemingway's Chair* (Palin, 1995) about Hemingway. Palin himself traces his first encounters with Hemingway to his teenage years in Sheffield and reading Hemingway's books for his A-level exams. These books stimulated his urge to travel because '... The sense of place, the intensity of smell and sound, the sheer physical sensation of being taken somewhere else was fresh and powerful and exhilarating' (Palin, 1999: 1).

The common ground between Palin and Hemingway, according to Palin, is 'a love of adventure'. Hemingway, as 'one of the most uncompromisingly masculine writers of the twentieth century' (Palin, 1999: 7) had plenty of adventure, something that Palin wishes he could recapture. But there is also a larger, deeper regret which Palin feels is to do with 'that old cliché, lost childhood' (Palin, 1999: 15). Following in the footsteps of Hemingway he feels that '... it's ironic that this rush around the world to recapture the spirit of Hemingway should have stirred such an acute memory of days when there was no rush at all' (Palin, 1999: 15).

Palin seems to be reflecting on one of the most important motivations for travel – the feeling of missing something in one's own existence. Very often, travellers seek to fill this gap with the experiences of others. This also strikes Palin about Hemingway's own travel experience:

> I'm struck by the number of times the local Indians feature [in his books]. It's as if Hemingway found something in their way of life that was lacking in his own, something raw and elemental, a direct confrontation with sex and death and pain. (Palin, 1999: 16)

Recognising a fellow traveller, Palin sets out to discover the 'real life adventure' of Hemingway's life, ironically knowing that he can never recapture that adventure, particularly not with a TV crew in tow.

Palin regrets the creation of the Hemingway 'industry', even though he has played a major role in supporting it. He observes; 'Harry's Bar today is merely busy, full of people trying to be Hemingway' (Palin, 1999: 39).

The problem with tourists and Hemingway imitators is that they are experiencing recycled experiences. Palin sees in Hemingway somebody who was stimulated to travel through natural curiosity and 'a mixture of boredom and boastfulness. Having sought new places and new experiences, he used all his reporter's wiles to make it seem that he was the first to discover them' (Palin, 1999: 121). Palin appears to have the same knack in the newer medium of television. Having recreated Phileas Fogg's journey round the world, Palin created new and apparently original challenges of his own, travelling the Pacific Rim and tracing a line of longitude from Pole to Pole. However he laments: 'Actually the South Pole didn't seem that remote ... There's a big American base there called the Scott/Amundsen base, with a sort of hamburger joint underneath the pole!' (Interview with Palin, www.plys.com, 2002).

Bill Bryson

Bill Bryson first attracted attention for *The Lost Continent* (1990), his humorous description of a journey through small town America in search of his lost youth. He followed this up with travelogues on Europe (1993), the UK (1997), the Appalachians (1999) and Australia (2001). In *Neither Here Nor There* (Bryson, 1991), Bryson revisits many of the destinations he had first visited on a tour of Europe in 1972. The book therefore retraces the steps of Bryson the young backpacker, except that the middle-aged author is travelling in considerably more comfort.

One of the themes that pervades much of Bryson's other work is the need to get off the beaten track. He starts his 1991 trip in northern Norway, 'as far north as you can get with public transport' (Bryson, 1991: 26). Given his penchant for out-of-the-way places, it is perhaps surprising that Bryson complains loudly about the discomfort of travel and the fact that people are unfamiliar with American popular culture. Hemingway's embrace of local culture is lost on Bryson, who prefers to work at the level of national stereotypes (Bryson, 1991: 39), particularly where this creates humorous effect.

The French and Italians, for example, are reprimanded for their rudeness and queue jumping (even if Parisians have become politer since the 1970s). Once the foreign is safely stereotyped, there is no need to understand the culture or its members. In at least two places in *Neither Here Nor There*, Bryson insists 'I don't *want* to know what people are talking about' (Bryson, 1991: 168). Although everyday conversation is uninteresting for him, behaviour that strengthens the stereotype can be admired, as with the

Italians 'expending their considerable energies on the pleasurable minutiae of daily life – children, good food, arguing in cafes – which is just how it should be' (Bryson, 1991: 168). But usually, the detail of everyday life in foreign countries is more likely to be a source of fun for Bryson, who achieves comic effect by exaggerating how different people are in everyday situations. The combination of foreign rudeness, strange food (particularly if written in a strange foreign language: Bryson, 1991: 88) and unfamiliarity with American culture conspires to strengthen the stereotypes. But Bryson (1991: 52) justifies this by pointing out that 'Europeans have been living up to their stereotypes for 300 years' ever since the Grand Tour. The blame for stereotyping is thus neatly passed on the stereotyped – the implication being that it is their fault for behaving as expected.

While the people may do as they are expected to, Bryson himself finds travel more pleasurable if it is unplanned: 'travelling is more fun – shit, life is more fun – if you can treat it as a series of impulses' (Bryson, 1991: 161). The unplanned nature of Bryson's travel is hardly on the level of Hunter S. Thompson's thinly disguised chaos, however. Bryson's impulses are more closely related to the casual strolling of the 'flaneur', discovering new corners of each city he visits (Bryson, 1991: 130) but hardly exposing himself to danger or serious uncertainty.

Given the style of Bryson's tourist consumption, he is relatively scathing of other tourists, noting with dismay how their numbers have grown since 1972. But he himself follows the classic pattern of the urban tourist, visiting famous museums and cathedrals. However, rather than high culture, it is popular culture that has the most important effect on Bryson's destination choice. Films in particular are a stimulus for travel, as in the link between *La Dolce Vita* and a visit to Rome (Bryson, 1991: 162).

It is clear, though, that Bryson is not reflexive about the reasons why he travels. He knows what he likes, but not what he is travelling for.

Discussion

Our examination of iconic writers reveals a number of important themes that link them to symbols of the backpacker culture. Taken together these themes reveal something about the deeper layers of the backpacker culture: its assumptions, rituals and heroic figures.

Assumptions and norms

Tourist angst

The term 'tourist angst' was first coined in the 1970s by the British journalist Alan Brien to describe 'a gnawing suspicion that after all ... you are still a tourist like every other tourist' (cited in Fussell, 1980). Since then, a number of researchers have analysed the phenomenon of tourist angst (e.g. Fussell, 1979; 1980; MacCannell, 1989) and in particular, Dann (1999) makes a link between tourist angst and travel writing:

> They [the travel writers] may be responsible not only for the creation of tourist angst, but for inducing in themselves travel writer's angst: the recognition that they have contributed towards the unsustainability of tourism. (Dann, 1999: 182)

Just like the travel writers, backpackers may also be suffering from a form of tourist angst, which may be an empowering act of identification for the backpacker. When detaching oneself from the tourist role, a conspiratorial feeling might be induced by reading literary accounts of travel and making a (probably unrealistic) distinction from one's own behaviour. Having read and digested the critical narratives, one might begin to feel 'licensed' as an anti-tourist, or a bona-fide traveller.

Backpackers now seem to have taken tourist angst a step further by developing 'backpacker angst'. It is particularly revealing that none of our respondents listed books about backpackers among their icons, even though the research in Bangkok (Chapter 2) revealed many backpackers reading Alex Garland (1996) and William Sutcliffe (1997) while travelling. Perhaps some backpackers decline to identify with their writing as the figures portrayed by these writers are not 'real backpackers'. This may also reflect a generational shift taking place in terms of both travel writing and the practice of backpacking itself. Some backpackers lament the changes taking place in backpacking in the same way as 'travellers' lament the growth of tourism. In so doing they are creating an identity linked to forms of backpacking imbued with the values of Hemingway, Kerouac and Chatwin: adventurous, spontaneous and heroic. This is also a rejection of the modern backpacker and the writings of Garland and Sutcliffe. For example, the social construction study (Chapter 2) indicated that most backpackers were happier to identify with Kerouac than they were to identify *The Beach* as a book about 'real backpackers'.

Outsider/Anti-establishment

A clear link between all the iconic writers is their position as outsiders. This is most clearly seen in the rejection of mainstream society by the early generations of writers, but even the travelstyle of Palin (originally a satirist) and Bryson (an American exile) can be positioned well outside the mainstream, even if their writing is well within it. A similar picture emerges in terms of the backpacker. Originally positioned as the loner or the drifter, backpackers are often characterised as holding anti-establishment or ambivalent views toward their own culture (Cohen, 1972; 1973; Riley, 1988; Uriely *et al.*, 2002; Vogt, 1976). The role of backpackers as social outsiders may have applied generally in the 1970s when most of this original theorising took place, but the emergence of backpacker angst indicates that backpackers are now just as likely to place themselves outside the tourist society in general, or the backpacker society in particular (see Welk, Chapter 5).

Authenticity

Authenticity has long been identified as one of the major driving forces for tourism, and recent empirical work has confirmed the concern of back-packers for issues of authenticity (Giesbers, 2002). This concern is also evident among the writers analysed. Hemingway deplored the encroach-ments of modernity, and his concern for the original, the true and the natural in travel experiences is echoed by the other authors to varying degrees. The most radical form is found in Chatwin, whose rejection of the artificiality of modern life leads him to the conclusion that travel is the only truth. Travel therefore becomes the natural mode of existence – the nomadic alternative to modern society. The backpackers, to the extent that they position themselves as 'global nomads' therefore see themselves as leading a more 'authentic' life than other types of tourists.

'Off the beaten track'

The search for authenticity arguably motivates backpackers to travel off the beaten track in search of areas not yet contaminated by tourists or other backpackers. All our travel writers demonstrate a love of out-of-the-way places, such as the most northerly town in Europe (Bryson, 1991). Plus, as already noted, in backpacker-angst situations, there may be a tendency to play down visits to popular places and argue that, unlike tourists, they don't take photographs (Uriely *et al.*, 2002).

The irony of course is that, by searching for unique experiences off the beaten track, backpackers open up the places they visit to other back-packers – and ultimately to other tourists. There is the famous case of a German backpacker who, disillusioned with the commercialisation of Bali, travelled to the then isolated Gilli islands off the coast of Lombok. The start of the tourism industry in these Indonesian islands can apparently be traced directly to this one backpacker (Bras, 2000). This means that back-packers today find it increasingly hard to get off the beaten track, which is producing a search for other forms of extreme experience or 'kicks' (de Cauter, 1995). The bungee jump may be higher than ever before, the destinations of choice more politically unstable and dangerous. In this respect, there may be an unconscious disregard for what they know to be socially responsible, culturally respectful and environmentally friendly, in a determined attempt at 'distinction' (Bourdieu, 1984). This may fuel the well-established discussion about whether backpackers are on the whole 'good' or 'bad' types of travellers.

Rituals

Overindulgence/Excess/Hedonism

One of the strongest themes among our iconic writers is that of overindulgence. In the case of the early writers, this was mainly a hedonistic search for pleasure, while the later writers indulge more consciously in spending that most precious of modern commodities: time.

For the early generations the problem was not time, but money. Hemingway commented often on how cheap things were abroad. Thompson was obsessed with finding the money for rent or cigarettes. Throughout *On the Road*, Sal Paradise asks his Aunt to wire him more funds for his bus tickets. When funds did become available, however, these were usually invested in binges of champagne (Hemingway), whisky (Kerouac) or the complete range of mind-expanding substances (Thompson).

Thompson and Kerouac in particular can be seen as harbingers of the more spoilt post-war generation of backpackers with a ready supply of credit and parents able to bail them out. Even so, complaining about lack of money is a constant theme in Thompson's early writing and a common source of backpacker conversation today (see Fitzgerald, 2000; Welk, Chapter 5 of this volume). This may imply that the sharp contrast between luxury and comfort at home and penury on the road heightens the back-packing experience for many.

Another way of heightening the contrast is to indulge to excess. Drinking is particularly important in this regard, being related to mascu-linity as well as to the search for a different reality. As Cohen (1973) notes, backpackers are often associated with drug culture, but, for the backpacker icons analysed, the drug of choice is more often alcohol. Alcohol is avail-able everywhere and as Hemingway and Hunter S. Thompson constantly emphasise, a lot cheaper abroad, while Chatwin's semi-autobiographical character 'Bruce' in *The Songlines* (Chatwin, 1998/1987) drinks copious amounts of brandy while writing his notebooks.

Impulsiveness

Binging on alcohol is also an expression of impulsiveness, which is clearly evident in the lifestyles and travel behaviours of our writers. Improvisation was an essential element of beat poetry and the jazz music that inspired Kerouac and Thompson. For them, improvisation was an essential source of creativity. Travel was therefore a means to artistic ends, rather than an end in itself. For the later generations, and particularly Bryson, improvisation is transformed into impulsiveness. Bryson is the classic 'flaneur', for whom impulsiveness is to be enjoyed for its own sake.

The irony of the improvisation and impulsiveness of travel writers, however, is their obsessive concern with recording the details of their journeys. For the different generations, the recording of experience marks the developmental continuum from the writer as traveller to the traveller as writer; from the modern authentication of experience to the postmodern exploitation of experience as 'soundbites' in the life story. For Hemingway, the obsessive detail of life is captured in finely-woven prose. For the Beat Generation, words and images were the collage that framed the scenario. For Chatwin, the travel notebook is a priceless, irreplaceable treasure and the visual arts (particularly photography) are an obsession. For Bryson and Palin, every element of experience, however awesome or trivial, is something that serves to mark out the traveller as different from the tourist and therefore is worthy of attention.

Heroines/Heroes

The rituals embodied by the iconic writers often derive from the examples of heroic figures, often captured later in their writings. These heroes (rarely heroines) include other writers, figures from history and sportsmen. The clear links between all the writers featured in this analysis underline the important role of heroes and heroines in stimulating and authenticating travel. Palin describes how he read Hemingway as a boy, and later retraced Hemingway's steps in a book and television series. This is also evident from Chatwin's admiring accounts of other writers: André Malraux and Salman Rushdie, for example.

As well as other writers, historical characters are important sources of inspiration. Chatwin is the prime example of this, weaving Butch Cassidy into his depiction of Patagonia at every turn. Bryson, while showing disdain for the natives of the Appalachians in *A Walk in the Woods* (Bryson, 1997) recounts the heroic tale of Earl V. Shaffer, the first man to hike the Appalachian Trail from end to end in a single summer in 1948. Like many intrepid travellers, Shaffer was also initially disbelieved when he recounted his exploits.

Such heroic figures serve to support the exceptional nature of the travel writers and their exploits, just as backpackers recount stories of their travels to gain themselves heroic status (Giesbers, 2002). The reality of backpacker angst is of course that backpackers have lost their heroic status in the eyes of other tourists. Backpacker angst effectively says to the backpacker: 'you are no better than us, maybe even worse'.

The basic link between these authors remains their symbolic ability to stimulate others to travel. As Palin remarked of Hemingway, it is the art of turning one's own experience into something novel and exciting that whets the appetites of readers. The stimulus to travel is usually something that the reader feels is missing from his/her own life, such as adventure, heroism or impulsiveness. Living vicariously through reading about the adventures of others, the would-be backpacker longs to experience the novelty and danger described in the books. But the novelty, once communicated, has already disappeared – destroyed by its own literary representation. The pursuit of the literary travel experience, just like the search for authenticity, is doomed to fail (Rojek, 1993), and this is literally the case for readers of Chatwin, since some of the places he describes are fictional.

In this respect backpackers are arguably no different from other tourists – they just tend to spend longer searching. Clifford (1997) for example sees travel as an inclusive term, embracing a range of more or less voluntaristic practices of leaving 'home' to go to some 'other' place. This displacement, he argues, takes place for the purpose of gain – material, spiritual or scientific – and it involves obtaining knowledge and/or having an 'experience'. Looking at the relative lack of distinction between our writers and increasingly also between backpackers and other tourists, Clifford is probably right. The practices engaged in by all travellers, and therefore those that are endemic to the culture of travel, are very similar. In this respect, even those who seek to establish differences and distinction through their consumption of 'sophisticated travel' and the writings of Theroux and Chatwin, instead may end up replicating the same practices as those who read Hemingway, Kerouac and the rest. If backpackers, travellers and tourists all seek and fail to find the same things, it becomes increasingly hard to establish identity in terms of what these groups are and, as Clifford (1997) suggests, it is easier to establish identity in terms of 'outsiders' – what we are *not*. As such, the identity of many backpackers is drawn from their not being tourists. Consequently, the backpacker may be trying not just to place him/herself on the edge of mainstream society, but also on the edge of the mainstream tourism culture. Many backpackers, like the iconic writers we have analysed, therefore place themselves on the edge of society, on the edge of tourism and on the edge of travel.

So in fact, we could argue that the culture of the backpacker is based on one of the major problems of modern society – the uncertainty of identity. It is perhaps easier to reject the act of being a tourist, having a stable job, or staying in a luxury hotel, than to find out who you are. By the same token, the popularity of backpacking has now created a situation in which the backpacker becomes the object of denial – 'I am not a backpacker' is a new means of establishing an identity as a sophisticated traveller. Our research provides some empirical underpinning for this idea. A relatively small proportion (28%) of the global nomad survey respondents were willing to identify themselves as 'backpackers' as opposed to 'travellers' or 'tourists', and even in the Khao San Road, the proportion of respondents opting solely for the backpacker label was less than a third (See Chapter 2).

Conclusions

Literary sources can reveal much about the backpacker phenomenon and its constituent elements. The analyses presented in this chapter have raised some interesting ideas as to the referents of the backpacking subculture(s) and in particular, to the most influential traits of the travel writers considered to be 'iconic' in such circles.

In particular the selection of writers from different eras and genres indicates a developmental trajectory in travel writing that mirrors the development of backpacker tourism. Travel writers, just like backpackers, are today less often outsiders, and more often ironic than idealistic travellers. This may signal a shift of backpacking into the mainstream of tourism experiences, accompanied by the rise of 'backpacker bashing'. It is no accident that backpacking has become more popular as an object of research in recent years, just as bestselling novels about backpackers have appeared on the scene (Barr, 2002; 2003; Garland, 1996; Sutcliffe, 1997).

Just as perhaps 'real' backpackers have been swallowed up by mainstream tourism, so have 'real' travel writers. Hemingway has been replaced by Garland, books are being replaced by TV and film, and heroes by celebrities. What remains is a Boorstinesque lament for the way we used to be, on the part of older-generation backpackers who now form an important part of the travelocracy (Tony Wheeler, for example – see Welk, Chapter 5). This lament is eagerly joined by the modern 'tourist', who sees the backpacker's fall from grace as a justification for his or her own style of travel.

What this developmental trajectory also indicates is an increasing differentiation of travel-writing styles. Although the major themes of travel remain intact, the travel practices of writers have changed significantly. The uncompromising modernism of the early generations has been replaced by the radical cynicism of Chatwin and Theroux and finally the postmodern distraction of Bryson. One would expect that the backpacker readers of these different generations would also identify themselves with different types of travel practices, underlining the differentiation of the backpacking experience. Backpacking today is perhaps better seen as a series, or continuum of sub-ideologies of its own, rather than as one part of a general tourist typology. This differentiation is most strongly reinforced by the emergence of 'backpacker angst' and the resulting flight from the label 'backpacker' on the part of many who engage in backpacker practices. Just like the 'off the beaten track' experiences that the backpackers seek, the backpacker as a clearly defined species of tourist is disappearing, just at the moment of its discovery.

Notes

1. Ryb and nightsnwhitestn are web nicknames, or monikers, belonging to the respondents in the exercise.
2. Gonzo journalism is a highly subjective and extremely personal form of reporting. By all accounts, Thompson coined the 'Gonzo' style when, as deadlines approached, and with his article still not completed, he would resort to ripping pages out of his notebook and sending them to editors.

Part 3

In the Footsteps of the Global Nomad

Chapter 9

Backpacking in Scotland: Formal Public Sector Responses to an Informal Phenomenon

CLARE SPEED AND TONY HARRISON

Introduction

This chapter focuses on backpacking in a North-West European context and specifically on Scotland. It presents the characteristics and motivations of backpackers visiting Scotland and analyses the responses of governmental organisations in addressing the needs of a relatively new tourist market for the country. It also evaluates some of the reasons for the paucity of research into and market knowledge of the British backpacking sector (Shipway, 2000).

The first aim of this chapter is to present the characteristics of backpackers in a Northern-hemisphere destination so that, if read in conjunction with the mainly Southern-hemisphere data produced to date, one can begin to produce a broader picture of this tourist category. Second, the chapter aims to evaluate the responses of those organisations normally charged with providing the infrastructure and policy initiatives that are required for an identified tourist market to grow and be sustained long-term within a country. Again, this should be viewed as a broadening of the collective view that has been developed to date.

The chapter is in three parts. First, information is given on backpacking in Scotland. This includes the context of Scottish backpacking (after Speed & Slater, 1999) and the characteristics, motivations, activities and impacts of backpackers are presented from primary research findings of a nation-wide survey carried out in Scotland (after Speed & Harrison, 2000). Second, backpacking is assessed in the context of public policy and public-private sector initiatives in Scotland (Scottish Executive, 2000; VisitScotland, 2002). Third, an evaluation is made of the barriers, conflicts and contradictions that appear to occur between the phenomenon of backpacking and the public sector response to that phenomenon.

Backpacking in Scotland

The Scottish tourism context

Scotland's tourism product suggests an appeal to backpackers: lochs, mountains, wilderness, historic cities, culture and nightlife contained within areas of concentrated population (cities) and areas of depopulation and remoteness (highlands and islands). Strengths of Scotland's tourism product with an appeal to backpackers can be found in the Scottish Tourism Strategy (Scottish Executive, 2000) including:

- Scotland's position as an outstanding rural destination with dramatic scenery, space, light and greenness. Research among target market segments, particularly in Western Europe, shows that getting away from the stress and pace of modern life to the great outdoors is a major motivator for holidays.
- History, heritage and culture, which research shows are key elements of Scotland's appeal. This includes well-known icons such as whisky, tartan and highland dancing/games.

In terms of volume and value, VisitScotland (2000a) figures can be combined with primary research findings (Speed & Harrison, 2000) to provide the comparison in Table 9.1. In Scotland in 1999, more than twelve million tourists took overnight trips and spent £2.5 billion, whereas backpackers contributed an estimated £20 million (Speed & Harrison, 2000); around 1% of the total tourism market.

The Scottish backpacking 'industry'

In the decade from 1990 to 2000, there was an increasing presence of backpacking in the Scottish tourism scene. The primary locations for backpacking activity include the gateway cities of Edinburgh and Glasgow

Table 9.1 Average length of stay and expenditure in Scotland

	Overseas visitors	*Scottish tourists*	*English tourists*	*Wales/ N. Ireland tourists*	*Backpackers*
Average length of stay (nights)	9.6	3.3	5.4	5.0	24.0
Average expenditure per trip (£)	463	82	214	211	669
Average expenditure per night (£)	48	25	40	49	28

Source: VisitScotland (2000a) and Speed & Harrison (2000)

which show evidence of a growing and competitive supply of backpacking services. Table 9.2 indicates the distribution of backpacker accommodation –'primary' locations refer to cities and large towns with major transport links, through to 'quaternary' locations representing isolated areas with little or no normal transport service access. Linked to the cities are some key backpacking routes with clusters of hostels in Oban, the Isle of Skye, Fort William and Inverness in the Highland region, serviced by backpacker bus companies. These mini-buses operate either jump-on-jump-off services at an inclusive price, or two, five and seven day tours linking with accommodation locations. As such the provision of backpacking services is beginning to be characterised by vertical integration.

The backpacking scene in Edinburgh has been dominated by two suppliers. Scotland's Top Hostels operate two hostels in Edinburgh (the larger being the 300-bed Castle Rock Hostel), as well as five other hostels in locations including Oban and Fort William. Started in the late 1980s by an individual entrepreneur, a decade later this independent hostel group set up MacBackpackers buses, linking its hostels with either jump-on, jump-off services or inclusive tours, recognising a gap in the market left by the demise of the pioneer backpacker bus company Go Blue Banana.

The Radical Travel Network (formerly Haggis Backpackers) was similarly set up by independent family owners concentrating more on transport and tours, but providing hostel accommodation in the key cluster locations in the Highlands. The Radical Travel Network has three geo-graphic tour brands (Haggis England, Haggis Scotland and Shamrocker Tours Ireland). Growing corporate interest in the Scottish backpacking scene was evident in the purchase of Radical Travel Network by Kontiki during the winter season 2000–01.

A major supplier of backpacker accommodation throughout Scotland (with approximately 70 hostels) is the Scottish Youth Hostels Association (SYHA), part of the IYHA, also offering discounted tickets and passes on

Table 9.2 Supply of backpacker accommodation by location

Location category	% distribution
Primary	10.9
Secondary	15.9
Tertiary	27.4
Quaternary	45.8

Source: Speed & Slater, 1999

public transport (coach, rail, ferry) and visitor attractions. The growing importance of this market is evident in the movement into Scottish backpacking, first by backpacking suppliers operating elsewhere in the UK, and second by diversification of other accommodation operators into the backpacking sector. An example of the former is the recently-developed St Christopher's Inn in Edinburgh, part of a group of eight hostels nation-wide. An example of the latter is the development of Eurohostel in Glasgow. Eurohostel marks the entry into the backpacker market of a former luxury hotel owner as part of a portfolio of products including luxury serviced apartments. Both of these new developments are distinctive in that they contain no self-catering facilities for guests. Other significant supply developments include a group of around 50 hostels that formed a loosely linked organisation in 1993 called Independent Backpacking Hostels Scotland (IBHS), and produced the leaflet '*Independent Hostel Guide – Budget Accommodation*'. In the Highlands region, 44 hostels have formed a marketing consortium called Highland Hostels. Backpackers can also use public transport, but this tends to be more expensive, less flexible and less frequent than the bespoke backpacker bus services.

Backpacking in Scotland, then, is characterised by fragmented supply: a large number of small independent suppliers, and a small number of larger suppliers. There is evidence of vertical integration, the development of marketing consortia and the entry into the market of larger travel and hospitality concerns. Geographically, backpacking has two main gateway cities and several other accommodation clusters standing out from the otherwise-dispersed backpacker accommodation. Identifiable routes are emerging in response to the supply of transport and tours, for example from the main cities up the West Coast of Scotland and from Inverness to Edinburgh in the East.

The Scottish Backpacker Study

Methodology

According to a previous study (Speed & Slater, 1999) that established a database of 201 backpacker accommodation providers, the supply of backpacker accommodation in Scotland is characterised by an ever-increasing independent hostels sector and a relatively large but static number of Scottish Youth Hostel Association (SYHA) premises. The development of the independent sector over recent years is such that, from supplying only a small fraction of the total bed spaces to the market, it has become the predominant accommodation provider. Results of the Scottish Backpacker Study are based on the responses of 345 visitors ($n = 345$, unless otherwise stated) identified as backpackers by their use of specialist backpacker accommodation and tour services. A total of 2,710 questionnaires had been distributed among backpacker hostels, SYHA establishments and tour buses throughout Scotland, and the response rate was 13%. The primary research methodology was considerably informed by previous studies undertaken in Australia (Pearce, 1990; Loker-Murphy & Pearce, 1995; Loker-Murphy, 1996; Buchanan & Rossetto, 1997).

Results of the study

Country of origin

The country that generated most backpackers was Australia (21.7%), followed closely by Germany (20.6%). All generating countries are shown in Figure 9.1. The USA, Canada and New Zealand were the only other significant single generating countries.

Gender and age (n = 343)

Most of the respondents were female (60.6%), somewhat different from the results of most recent Australian surveys (Buchanan & Rossetto, 1997; Loker-Murphy, 1996; Loker-Murphy & Pearce, 1995), where male respondents dominated. The balance in favour of females was consistently reflected across all major generating countries and regions. As shown in Table 9.3, the 16–24 age category was the largest, followed by the 25–34 age group, which is indicative of the typical backpacker profile as reflected in other surveys (Slaughter, Chapter 10 and Newlands, Chapter 13).

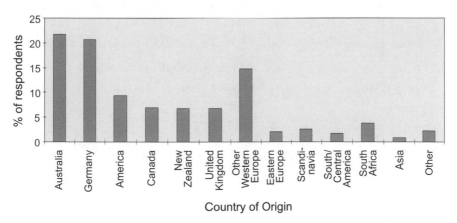

Figure 9.1 Backpacker visitors by country/region of origin (n = 345)

Table 9.3 Age categories of respondents (*n* = 343)

Age	Frequency	Percentage
1–24	184	53.5
25–34	129	37.4
35–44	11	3.2
45–54	10	2.9
55–64	6	1.7
65 +	2	0.6
Non response	3	0.9

Length of stay *(n = 177)*

The average length of stay (based on actual and intended stays) in Scotland for a backpacker was just over three weeks, although this figure differed greatly between generating countries as illustrated in Table 9.4. Of the main generating countries, Australians intended to stay the longest (8.25 weeks) followed by Canadians (5.1 weeks) and New Zealanders (4.3 weeks). Germany, the largest market of the neighbouring countries to Scotland, had an average length of stay of 2.6 weeks. These figures represent a much shorter stay than that shown in Australia, although this is probably a function of the proximity of other destination countries to Scotland and the size anomaly between Australia and Scotland. Indeed, 58.0% of respondents (*n* = 339) indicated that their trip to Scotland was part of a larger trip plan, which itself had an average length of 25.3 weeks. However, more than half (55.1%) of respondents stayed less than the average, while only 18.2% stayed

Table 9.4 Average length of stay: Tourists and backpackers (*n* = 177)

	Average length of stay (nights)	
Country of origin	All tourists in Scotland	Backpackers in Scotland
Australia	11.2	57.8
Germany	10.9	18.2
USA	8.1	14.0
Canada	15.0	35.7
UK	4.6	14.0
All countries	5.3	22.0
Overseas only	9.6	21.0

Table 9.5 Length of stay categories

Length of stay	Frequency	Percentage
Less than 1 week	4	2.3
1 week	34	19.3
2 weeks	59	33.5
3 weeks	47	26.7
4 weeks	18	10.2
5–8 weeks	7	4.0
9–12 weeks	1	0.6
13–20 weeks	4	2.2
21 weeks plus	2	1.2
n	176	100

more than three weeks (Table 9.5). Overall, the majority of backpackers were likely to be on either a two-week or a three-week trip to Scotland.

Size of party (n = 334)

Almost half of the respondents (48.5%) were travelling with a pre-arranged companion on their trip, while a third of respondents (33.5%) were travelling alone. Some backpackers were travelling with family members (13.2%) and a small number (4.8%) had decided to travel with a casual acquaintance they had met in transit.

Employment

Respondents were asked about their likelihood of gaining employment while in Scotland by indicating whether they had already worked or intended to work during their stay: 12.2% of respondents had taken up employment during their time in Scotland, while a further 9.0% indicated an intention to work whilst in Scotland.

In Table 9.6 it is evident that, of the main generating markets, 28.0% of all Australian respondents (21 of 75) had gained or intended gaining employment during their stay. Some 21.7% of New Zealanders, 16.9% of Germans and 12.5% of Americans and Canadians had worked or intended to work during their holiday. It is interesting that several Germans worked during their visit, given that on average they stayed only 2.6 weeks.

Places visited in Scotland

The idea that backpackers travel more widely within a country than a typical tourist (Loker-Murphy & Pearce, 1995; Pearce, 1990) is reinforced in

Table 9.6 Employment intentions during holiday in Scotland

	Have worked during holiday in Scotland (number)	*Intend to work during holiday Scotland (number)*	*Likelihood of employment**
Australia	13	8	21
Germany	6	6	12
New Zealand	4	1	5
America	3	1	4
France	2		2
Ireland	2	1	3
Netherlands	2		2
Poland	2		2
Sweden	2	1	3
Austria	1	2	3
Canada	1	2	3
Spain	1		1
Italy	1	3	4
South Africa	1	2	3
Malaysia	1		1
England		2	2
Israel		1	1
Peru		1	1

*Likelihood of employment = Have worked + Intend to work

Table 9.7. Although Edinburgh was the most visited place, the next most visited places were Inverness (almost as popular as Edinburgh), Fort William and Skye. The two most popular routes were those running between Edinburgh and Skye – either via the West coast (Oban and Fort William) or through the middle of the country (Perth and Inverness). The lower ranking of Glasgow than Edinburgh may be more to do with the relative lack of backpacker services in the city at the time of the study, as both Edinburgh and Glasgow have main line rail and coach links with London. Almost a third of respondents indicated that John O'Groats and the surrounding area were likely to be visited – again illustrating the will-ingness of backpackers to travel to remoter areas of a country.

Table 9.7 Places visited in Scotland (%)

Place	Likely visitation*	Have been	Intend to visit	Not going
Edinburgh	88.1	78.6	9.5	11.9
Glasgow	56.9	38.3	18.6	43.2
Oban	52.2	40.3	11.9	47.8
Fort William	75.6	59.7	15.9	24.3
Skye	72.8	58.3	14.5	27.2
The Isles	13.3	10.4	2.9	86.7
Inverness	85.2	74.5	10.7	14.8
Aberdeen	22.3	13.0	9.3	77.7
Perth	55.4	43.8	11.6	44.6
John O'Groats	31.6	21.2	10.4	68.4
Orkneys/Shetlands	12.2	5.8	6.4	87.8

*Likely visitation = Have been + Intend to visit

Larger trip plans

As mentioned earlier, 58.0% of respondents had indicated that their holiday in Scotland was part of a larger trip plan. Table 9.8 illustrates the likelihood of backpackers going on to visit countries other than Scotland. It shows that the great majority of the backpackers (at least those on a larger trip) had travelled

Table 9.8 Other countries visited/planned to visit during trip (%)

Country	Likely visitation*	Have visited	Plan to visit
England	87.5	77.0	10.5
Wales	55.0	29.0	26.0
Ireland	62.0	32.0	30.0
Other European	62.0	36.5	25.5
Asia	20.5	13.0	7.5
Africa	20.0	5.0	15.0
Australasia	19.5	14.5	5.0
North America	26.0	12.5	14.0
South America	16.5	2.5	14.0

*Likely visitation = Have been + Intend to visit

through England before arriving in Scotland – which is understandable given that the major markets for backpacking in Scotland are from long-haul originating countries such as Australia, New Zealand, USA and Canada.

Another interesting factor emerging from Table 9.8 is that most backpackers envisaged the wider European continent as a major part of their itinerary. This would suggest that, for most backpackers to Scotland, Europe as a whole may be the perceived destination. Viewed from this perspective, the average length of stay in Europe (likely to be around 25 weeks) would be comparable with the average length of stay for backpackers in Australia, which according to the studies surveyed by Slaughter (Chapter 10) is about 18 weeks.

Activities undertaken

Figure 9.2 shows respondents' preferred and actual participation in activities. There was relatively low preference and participation for physical and sporting activities, with only hill walking having a high score. On the other hand, social activities such as 'meeting people', 'meeting locals' and 'enjoying small towns' had the highest preference scores. In fact, the participation rates for 'meeting people' and 'enjoying small towns' was higher than the preference scores for such activities. In the latter case, this

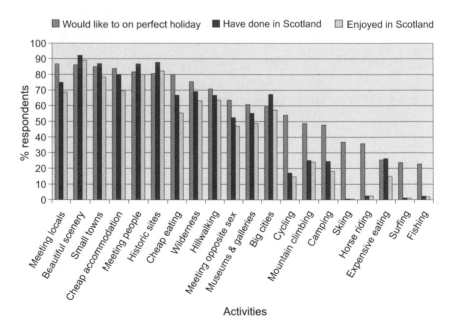

Figure 9.2 Preferred and actual participation in selected activities

again reinforces the idea that backpackers are more likely to seek out more rural settings to enjoy their trip. There was also a high preference for cheap food, although fewer respondents perceived themselves to have eaten cheaply and even fewer to have enjoyed the cheap food they ate. The idea that backpackers do not find food cheap in Scotland is reinforced by the fact that more people participated in 'expensive eating' than they would have liked – and again even fewer enjoyed the experience. So there is perhaps a market opportunity for better targeted and quality food establishments. Continuing the theme of cheap living, there was a high preference and participation in the use of 'cheap accommodation', although from Figure 9.2 it is apparent that there was a gap between participation and satisfaction (enjoyment) with current provision.

When it comes to cultural activities, backpackers exhibit preferences similar to those of the typical tourist. Indeed, more participated in and enjoyed 'visiting historic sites' than had indicated a preference to do so. In addition, there were high preference and participation rates for activities related to the natural environment and the 'enjoyment of beautiful scenery' had the highest participation and enjoyment rate of any category. Again, backpackers' willingness to visit more remote locations within a country was reflected in a high preference for being in the 'wilderness'.

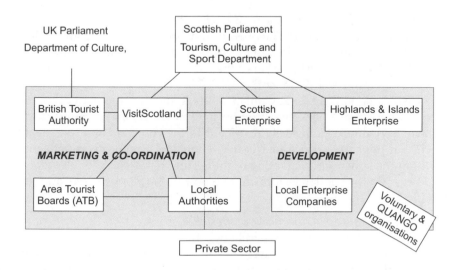

Figure 9.3 Organisation of tourism in Scotland

Source: Authors

Having discussed some of the characteristics of backpacker visitors to Scotland, we will now address some of the policy-related issues, principally in the Scottish context.

Backpacking and Public Policy

Since the inception of the new Scottish Parliament and the production of the National Tourism Strategy (Scottish Executive, 2000), public sector tourism in Scotland has been structured as shown in Figure 9.3. The Scottish Executive is responsible for all tourism policy decisions and has three main agencies for their implementation: VisitScotland, the National Tourist Office (NTO) for Scotland with principal divisions of Marketing and Industry Services; Scottish Enterprise (SE) and Highlands and Islands Enterprise (HIE) the two development agencies for the lowlands and highlands of Scotland, respectively. The British Tourist Authority (BTA), the NTO responsible for marketing Britain overseas, reports to the British Government in London.

Backpacker policy initiatives

Following the work undertaken by the authors in 1999/2000 (Speed & Harrison, 2000), VisitScotland has been addressing the needs of the backpacker market in Scotland via a mixture of activities. This has included: recognition of both an 'official' and an 'other' hostels category in national tourism statistics, the operation of an NTO working group, infrastructure co-ordination through the implementation of an accommodation Quality Assurance scheme, and the commissioning of some research (VisitScotland, 2000b; VisitScotland, 2001).

VisitScotland has two key policy areas in the development of tourism: co-ordination and marketing. Backpacker market-related initiatives to date have been almost exclusively restricted to the co-ordination role, dealing with supplier and service level issues. There has been no apparent activity within the spheres of marketing or marketing research.

Several other policy factors are relevant to the Scottish case, and these will now be outlined briefly.

Changes reflected in national tourism statistics

Since 2000, there has been a change to the United Kingdom Tourism Survey (UKTS) that measures UK domestic tourism, and this has a potential impact on interpretations of who and who is not is a backpacker. The former accommodation category of Youth Hostel/School/University has been modified and now has a separate Hostel accommodation category, which distinguishes between 'official' hostels and others. It should also be noted that there is no similar category in the International Passenger Survey (IPS).

NTO Working Group

The first public policy initiative was the creation of the Hostels & Bothys working group (now the Hostel Overseeing Committee) which concentrated on the supply and quality of hostel accommodation. Created and co-ordinated by VisitScotland, membership of this group includes the Scottish Youth Hostel Association (SYHA), representatives of independent back-packer suppliers (accommodation, transport and tour operators), regional tourist boards and VisitScotland quality assurance officers.

Accommodation Quality Assurance Scheme

As a result of the creation of the working group, the Hostel Grading Scheme and Hostel, Bunkhouse and Bothy Occupancy Survey was initiated in 1999 (VisitScotland, 2000a). Since 1999, Grading Scheme membership has grown to 132 members in 2002 (Current membership May 2002 confirmed by VisitScotland).

Commissioned research

The sole market study undertaken to date on behalf of VisitScotland involved an evaluation of the above grading scheme as perceived by a sample of backpackers (*n* = 86). The main finding from the study was a highly favourable response to the concept of an independently-verified scheme. The sample of 86 respondents may be justified given the focus group methodology, but as such does not constitute a broad market research survey.

The conclusion that the backpacker market specific to Scotland is over-whelmingly in favour of graded accommodation will be questioned later in this chapter in an appraisal of public sector initiatives targeted at the backpacker market in Scotland.

Further work was commissioned in 2000 to consider the growth, devel-opment and future prospects for the hostels market in Scotland. This study summarised the known features of the market and supply, and raised issues for the development of the backpacking sector (VisitScotland, 2000b). It was not, however, based on any responses from backpackers nor from any type of hostel accommodation user; therefore its usefulness as an input into planning and managing the market is restricted.

Barriers to Formality

Scotland, with its newly-established Scottish Parliament and National Tourism Strategy, and growing evidence of a developing backpacker supply sector is a Northern Hemisphere destination that has recognised the backpacking phenomenon. An analysis of public policy statements, commissioned research and the results of the initial Scottish backpacker study reveals a number of barriers to the formal development, organisation and promotion of backpacking in Scotland. These barriers are summarised in Table 9.9 and can be grouped together under three headings: market-related barriers, supplier-related barriers; and policy-related barriers (Figure 9.4). In some cases there is overlap between the three types of barrier.

Table 9.9 Summary of barriers to formality in backpacking in Scotland

Market-related barriers	(1) Characteristics of the backpackers themselves
	(2) Geographical dispersal
	(3) Embryonic stage of market compared with other countries
Supplier-related barriers	(4) Mix of 'informal' and 'formal' accommodation and transport suppliers
	(5) Competitive market – resistance of SMEs to share market research and produce development initiatives
Policy-related barriers	(6) Measurement barriers: • interception problems (point of entry); • measurement in UKTS not IPS (but 92% of market overseas); • quantitative vs qualitative; • one-off survey problems: no measurement of growth; varying methodologies; • lead-time between collection and publication official research.
	(7) Varying approaches between government bodies and independent operators
	(8) Tourism strategy, planning and development affected by external political climate

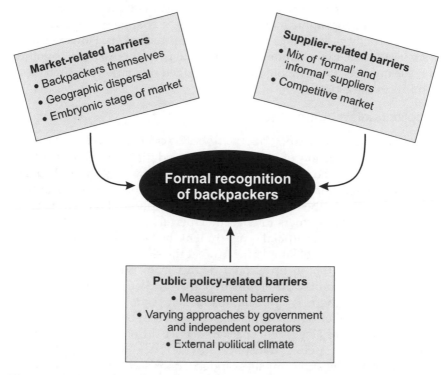

Figure 9.4 Barriers to formal recognition of backpacking in Scotland

Market related barriers

The characteristics of the backpackers themselves

Backpackers have been characterised by informality: their preference for informal facilities, activities, places to stay and means of transport (Pearce, 1990; Speed & Harrison, 2000).

Geographical dispersal

Whilst the geographical dispersal of backpackers throughout Scotland and their associated spending is seen as a positive contribution to national tourism policy objectives (Scottish Executive, 2000), the geographical spread of backpacking, including suppliers, militates against a co-ordinated national policy. It also makes the backpacker market harder to monitor and measure.

Embryonic stage of the market

Quite naturally, public policy makers may be loath to commit resources to analysis of a market that is considered small compared to traditionally-analysed geographic markets. It requires a change of mindset away from the strictly geographical analysis of tourism markets. However, there is some evidence in the national tourism strategy of increasing recognition of niche markets, which should be underpinned by market research (Scottish Executive, 2002).

Supplier related barriers

Mix of 'informal' and 'formal' accommodation and transport supply

The high proportion of informal accommodation suppliers makes it difficult to guarantee a consistent and accurate flow of market data. For example, the total supply of hostel accommodation in Scotland can only be estimated owing to the fluctuating nature of supply, and the resistance of independent hostel owners to what they perceive as the standardisation and bureaucracy of official government bodies. This difficulty in ascertaining the level of supply means that the size of the market may be understated, and this in turn could detract from public policy makers placing emphasis on the development of this market, as noted above.

Furthermore, there is no clear distinction as to what constitutes a backpacker supplier. Whilst it may be obvious that organisations such as MacBackpackers or Haggis Backpackers service the backpacker market, to what extent does public transport provide backpacker services, and bed-and-breakfasts and campsites? Indeed, does accommodation need to have a self-catering element in order for it to be deemed backpacker accommodation? The new trends in hostels (such as Eurohostel) call into question the more traditional characteristics of a 'hostel'. Further research is required to evaluate the use of different accommodation and transport services by backpackers.

Competitive market

Even in its present early stages, the backpacker supply structure is showing signs of integration and concentration. Indeed, there are signs that formal market structures are beginning to emerge. In a country as small as Scotland, the competitive nature of supply can generate a lack of co-operation between industry suppliers, and their willingness to share market research findings is low. In some cases, there are joint marketing initiatives, particularly amongst smaller suppliers. But in the large cities and cluster areas of direct competition, the environment of the larger suppliers is highly competitive. This suggests that the role of market research should be carried out objectively by the NTO.

Policy-related barriers

Measurement issues

One of the major problems with measuring the extent of backpacking in Scotland is how to intercept backpackers. Because many visitors enter Scotland without passing through national border controls, and because backpackers may arrive by many modes of transport into different locations in Scotland, it is difficult for those attempting 'one-off' surveys to intercept an accurate sample of backpackers.

There is also a general lack of official surveys in this area. As mentioned above, changes to the UKTS have produced a separate hostel accommodation category, which distinguishes between 'official' hostels and 'others' (which were previously lumped together as Youth Hostel/School/University) This represents a positive development in the formal measurement and monitoring of backpackers, but it is still not a perfect system.

As domestic backpackers are estimated to be just 8% of the total market in Scotland (Speed & Harrison, 2000) a similar accommodation inclusion in the IPS (International Passenger Survey) is called for in order to reflect the international composition (92%) of the market. However, the use of the term 'hostel' to categorise accommodation does not automatically result in better measurement of backpacker visits. By contrast, the International Visitor Survey (IVS) in Australia does have backpackers as a specified category for which significant analysis is undertaken (Haigh, 1995). For example, the Bureau of Tourism Research was able to estimate that in 1996, the backpacker market represented around 6% of international visitors to Australia, and accounted for $A1.3 billion of direct visitor expenditure in Australia (Buchanan & Rosetto, 1997). Additionally, the Australian government has funded qualitative research that has run alongside the IVS, which (like the UK's IPS) is a purely quantitative measure of tourism demand (Buchanan & Rosetto, 1997).

We have argued that the Scottish backpacker market is at an embryonic stage. In order for it to develop into anything like that of Australia, public policy-making bodies and small tourism businesses alike will require relevant and accurate information in order to formulate successful development strategies. Therefore, some input of criteria more specific to isolating backpackers within the interview process of the IPS would be a step in this direction. Another step would be the commissioning of a UK-wide survey of backpackers at national entry points, so that more analysis could be undertaken, including qualitative analysis of the market.

Alternatives to official surveys are one-off surveys or pieces of commissioned research. Although additional information on the backpacker market is welcome, a number of disadvantages stem from a lack of standardisation. No longitudinal data are generated whereby the growth (or otherwise) of the market can be measured. Different surveys may well utilise different methodologies, which militates against meaningful comparison and data generated by one-off surveys may not be viewed objectively by industry suppliers. An example of this is the difficulty experienced when public policy makers and independent hostels tried to reach agreement on the interpretation of data generated by the Quality Assurance Monitoring Scheme, as well as on the nature and implementation of the scheme (VisitScotland, 2001).

A problem endemic to tourism statistics more generally is the long lead-time between the collection and publication of official research (which in turn applies to statistics relating to backpacking activity). In Scotland, one or two years elapses between the collection of data and its availability for public use (this is also the case in many other countries). In the dynamic and growing backpacker market, where other survey data is not available, timely availability of market research is essential.

Varying approaches of government bodies and independent operators

An invaluable illustration of the problems that can exist between the public and private sector in interpreting the backpacker market and its needs is the implementation of the Hostels Quality Assurance Scheme, which was launched in 1999 (VisitScotland, 2001). The basic premise of such a scheme is that it is objective, consistent and can be used by the public. However, the essential nature of backpacking hostels is often individualistic, informal, varied and difficult to classify using criteria that would readily be applied to other sectors of accommodation. As a result, the appropriateness of the Hostels Quality Assurance Scheme was questioned by a predominantly independent Scottish hostel sector, which suggested that the scheme was unworkable and went against the essential spirit of backpacking. To-date, although the scheme operates with the participation of the large Scottish Youth Hostel Association network, much of the independent sector has not participated since the inception of the network in 1999.

Tourism strategy, planning and development and the external political climate

The policy development of NTOs, as with any public sector body, is affected by changes in priorities and policy at a national level. For example, in Scotland the strategic plan operating between 1994 and 1999 was extended for a year to accommodate the new Scottish Executive, which then launched its tourism strategy in 2000, followed by a further policy document in 2002 (Scottish Executive, 2002). Scottish tourism has therefore been working within three tourism strategies in three years, accompanied by the inevitable restructuring of public sector agencies, in this case, VisitScotland. In such a period of change, it is difficult for NTOs to develop strategic approaches to markets whilst having to accommodate changes to structure, personnel and direction.

The area of policy implementation that has made most progress since its inception prior to the current national tourism strategy is the NTO working group (the Hostels Overseeing Committee). However it can be noted that this group's remit is very much concerned with the co-ordination role of the NTO, dealing with supplier and service-level issues. At present it does not have a market development remit, being situated in the Industry Services division of VisitScotland. Its primary purpose is to develop the quality assurance scheme for hostels. A gap exists for market research, leading to product development, which the quality assurance scheme would then monitor. At present the quality assurance scheme has to operate without a formal marketing research background.

It can be suggested that there is a 'lifecycle' in the approach to the development of new products and markets. The early stages of this lifecycle concentrate on co-ordination and monitoring, with the more 'mature' stages developing a strategic approach within a policy frame-work. Those NTOs that concentrate on the early co-ordination stages, which necessarily involve servicing suppliers' needs, are less likely to be able to develop strategic niche products in line with market demand.

Conclusions

This chapter has attempted to illustrate the barriers to the formal development of the backpacking sector in Scotland. The focus has been on the contradiction between the informal nature of backpacking and the formal processes of monitoring and developing a niche market. By considering the supply structure, the market characteristics of backpackers and public policy initiatives, three forms of barrier emerge: those related to market, supply and policy. Although there are overlaps and links between all three, it can be seen that the primary need in developing a niche market is the availability of formal market data, produced on a systematic and regular basis within a strategic policy framework. Survey evidence of the needs, expectations and levels of satisfaction of backpackers compared with policy initiatives to date illustrate the great distance still to be travelled.

Chapter 10

Profiling the International Backpacker Market in Australia

LEE SLAUGHTER

Introduction

Since the early 1990s, the international backpacker market has been acknowledged as a significant tourist sector in Australia. Although backpackers represented 10% of visitor arrivals to Australia in the year ending 30 June 2002, they accounted for 22% of visitor expenditure, thereby making them a potentially lucrative market (Bureau of Tourism Research, 2002: 7). This market has supported the development of a backpacker 'industry' in Australia, and prompted government and academic interest in the backpacker market.

This chapter begins by tracing the events that led to the recognition of the backpacker market in Australia by industry, academia and the Government. During this process a range of definitions were used to define the term 'backpacker'. The one that is widely accepted in the literature is Pearce's (1990) social definition of a backpacker. Pearce proposed that a tourist should meet five key criteria to be considered a backpacker. He believes that the first of these criteria is a 'basic and necessary determining criterion' while several of the remaining criteria, but not necessarily all of them, also need to be present (Pearce, 1990: 1). The five criteria are:

(1) preference for budget accommodation;
(2) an emphasis on meeting other travellers;
(3) an independently organised and flexible travel schedule;
(4) longer rather than very brief holidays;
(5) an emphasis on informal and participatory holiday activities.

A comparison of the findings of seven independent backpacker studies, conducted over a 10-year period, provides a profile of the socio-demographic and travel characteristics of international backpackers in Australia. While identifying a market segment is important for marketing purposes, monitoring changes in the market over time is equally important. Through timely identification of changes in the backpacker market, more in-depth research can be undertaken to determine why these changes occur, and the extent of their impact. Lessons from the past can then be used to predict and prepare for the future.

Recognition of the Backpacker Market in Australia

Before backpackers had become generally recognised as a market segment in Australia, a range of accommodation establishments and transport operators catered for the independent style of travel that is characteristic of backpackers. For example, the Youth Hostel Association (YHA), which has been active in Australia since 1947 (McCulloch & Murray, 1997), provides hostel-style accommodation for a wide range of tourists, both young and old (despite its name), including independent tourists, school groups, families and special interest groups. Similarly, transport companies, such as McCafferty's Coaches, have been operating in Australia since the late 1960s (McCafferty's, 2002), providing a relatively inexpensive means of transport for a wide range of people, including independent tourists. However, it was not until the 1980s that the term 'backpacker' was coined by the accommodation industry to differentiate them from other subsets of tourists.

The first dedicated backpacker hostel opened in Cairns, Australia, in 1983 (McCulloch, 1991: 11). Named the Backpacker Inn, it differed from YHA hostels in that it was independently owned and operated, did not have the rules that were characteristic of the YHA accommodation chain, and targeted backpackers rather than a range of tourists. By 1990 there were 42 backpacker hostels (as distinguished from YHA hostels) operating in the Cairns area alone (McCulloch, 1991). McCulloch (1991) implies that the introduction of backpacker hostels was instrumental in a 50% decline in the backpacker market share of YHA hostels. As backpacker hostels draw their clientele almost exclusively from the backpacker market, rather than from the wider range of tourists who patronise YHA hostels, the assumption is that many backpackers who stayed in the new backpacker hostels had previously stayed in YHA hostels. Therefore backpackers were in Australia before 1983, although they were not then called backpackers.

The establishment of dedicated backpacker accommodation in the early 1980s was evidence of the accommodation industry's recognition of the potential of the backpacker market. However, it was not until the late 1980s that significant academic research on the backpacker market emerged. The first academic attempt to quantify the size and economic significance of the market was made by Pearce (1990), who estimated the size of the international backpacker market in Australia in 1988 to be 150,000, or 7% of inbound tourists. Pearce (1990) also found that the backpacker market was potentially lucrative, with backpackers' overall expenditure in Australia being twice as much as that of other tourists, although their extended stay meant that their daily expenditure was less.

It was also in the late 1980s and early 1990s that the Australian Government began to show an interest in the backpacker market. In 1990 the Bureau of Tourism Research, Australia's major source of tourism statistics, included backpacker accommodation as an option in its International Visitor Survey. Within a few years this inclusion had provided the basis for many of the statistics on the backpacker market. Pearce's insights into the newly-recognised backpacker market were acknowledged by the Australian government, and reference to his work (Pearce, 1990) is evident throughout government publications.

In the 1993–1994 budget, the federal government set aside $A4 million over a four-year period for the development of the backpacker market (Commonwealth Department of Tourism, 1995). A wide range of initiatives resulted from this funding. Some were intended to provide insights into the structure of the backpacker market (e.g. Australian Tourist Commission, 1995; Buchanan & Rossetto, 1997; Haigh, 1995). Other initiatives included marketing tools such as the Australian Tourist Commission's publication *Australia Unplugged* (Fraser, 1994) and the rating guide for backpacker accommodation in Australia (Office of National Tourism, 1999).

The major publication generated by this programme was the Commonwealth Department of Tourism's (1995) *National Backpacker Tourism Strategy*, which sought to provide a framework for understanding and developing the backpacker market in Australia. This document was the outcome of a consultative forum comprising industry and government representatives. Specifically, it set out to identify key issues and develop appropriate strategies in the areas of marketing, accommodation and investment, research, transport, safety, industry co-ordination, visa issues, and employment and training.

Throughout the *National Backpacker Tourism Strategy* it was emphasised that government, industry and academia needed to work together to ensure that the backpacker market is understood and provided for. However, the government decided not to continue funding after their four year commitment; a decision that may have been influenced by two subsequent changes of government. Currently, government research on the backpacker market is limited to information that can be extrapolated from the quantitative data collected for the International Visitor Survey, with any additional research being funded from a general pool of Federal

Table 10.1 Backpacker tourist arrivals to Australia (1990–1999)

Year	Number of international backpacker arrivals	Annual change (%)
1990	221 490	n.a.
1991	213 336	-3.7
1992	208 264	-2.4
1993	194 432	-6.6
1994	247 056	27.0
1995	272 320	10.2
1996	266 686	-2.1
1997	315 600	18.3
1998	313 900	-0.5
1999	404 300	28.8
2000	not available	n/a
2001	not available	n/a
2002	447 100	n/a
Average compound growth to 1999		7.7%

Source: Bureau of Tourism Research, international visitor surveys 1991–2000

Note: Data for 2000 and 2001 had not been processed by the Department of Immigration and Multicultural and Indigenous Affairs at the time of writing.

Government money that is not dedicated to backpacker research. However, the backpacker market is growing, both in terms of the range and number of facilities provided by industry and in terms of the number of international backpackers visiting Australia, as shown in Table 10.1. Having recognised the existence of the backpacker market in Australia the remainder of this chapter provides a profile of this market.

Research Method

In order to develop a profile of the international backpacker market in Australia, a comparison is made of seven studies conducted between 1989 and 1999. The studies are: *The Backpacker Phenomenon: Preliminary Answers to Basic Questions* (Pearce, 1990), *The Backpacker Phenomenon II: More Answers to Further Questions* (Loker, 1993), *The Billion Dollar Backpackers* (Jarvis, 1994), *Backpackers in Australia* (Haigh, 1995), *With my Swag upon my Shoulder: A Comprehensive Study of International Backpackers in Australia*

(Buchanan & Rossetto, 1997), *The Right Mix – Facilities for International Backpackers in Australia* (Kininmont, 2000), *BTR Niche Market Report Number 1, Backpackers in Australia, 1999* (Thoms, 2002). Note that these are independent studies, rather than a replication of the same research method at set intervals and there are differences between the studies in relation to their research methods, as detailed below. While these differences place some limitations on the comparison, they also highlight similarities in the studies and the need to develop a standardised research method.

One of the difficulties encountered when conducting research on backpackers is defining the term 'backpacker'. This is usually a function of the data-collection technique. Two definitions that are widely accepted in the literature are Pearce's (1990) social definition of backpackers, which was given in the introduction to this chapter, and the government's quantitative definition. While the strength of Pearce's social definition is its 'emphasis on the motivations and philosophies of backpackers' (Haigh, 1995: 4), the weakness is that this can be difficult to quantify. Therefore, some researchers, particularly government organisations, have adopted an accommodation-based definition of backpackers that allows backpacker data to be extrapolated from international visitor exit surveys. To enable the use of data from these surveys, the Australian Bureau of Tourism Research defines an international backpacker as 'an international visitor who spent one or more nights in a backpacker hotel or youth hostel during their stay in Australia' (Bureau of Tourism Research, 2002: 7). In this chapter, no one definition is selected in preference to another. Instead, a comparison is made of the findings of studies that use either definition. The three government-funded studies (Haigh, 1995; Buchanan & Rossetto, 1997; Thoms, 2002) use the accommodation-based definition, while the four independent studies (Pearce, 1990; Loker, 1993; Jarvis, 1994; Kininmont, 2000) use the social definition. Although there are some minor inconsistencies in their findings, the overall similarities suggest that for the purposes of profiling the international backpacker population in Australia, both definitions target the same population. It is acknowledged, however, that the accommodation-based definition can encompass non-backpackers, such as school groups using hostel accommodation. While this will distort the findings to some extent (including those reported in Table 10.1), it is expected that these distortions will apply more to domestic, rather than international, backpackers.

All seven studies claim to be representative of the backpacker market in Australia, although there is some variation in the study areas. The studies conducted by the government are based on exit surveys of tourists Australia-wide. The remaining four studies sourced their data from several states or territories in Australia, which were selected for their popularity as backpacker destinations. Other studies on backpackers in Australia have not been included because they are too destination-specific in their focus, such as *The Northern Territory Backpacker Survey* 1989/90 (NTTC, 1990), *Backpack Travellers Using Commercial Backpacker Accommodation in Queensland* (Wallace, 1991) and *An Analysis of the 'Backpacker' Segment of the Travel Market for Byron Bay* (Taylor, 1994).

The studies that use the accommodation-based definition generally have larger sample sizes than those that use the social definition. The three government studies have sample sizes of approximately 1000 (Haigh, 1995), 1136 (Buchanan & Rossetto, 1997), and 2398 (Thoms, 2002). In contrast, the studies that use the social definition have smaller sample sizes: 596 (Pearce, 1990), 686 (Loker, 1993), 551 (Jarvis, 1994) and 493 (Kininmont, 2000).

The primary data-collection dates for the studies span a 10-year period, giving a basis for monitoring the backpacker market over time. The data were collected in 1989 (Pearce, 1990), between October 1991 and February 1992 (Loker, 1993), between September 1991 and February 1992 (Jarvis, 1994), in 1992 (Haigh, 1995), from June 1995 to July 1996I (Buchanan & Rossetto, 1997), in 1997 (Kininmont, 2000) and in 1999 (Thoms, 2002).

Profile of the International Backpacker Population in Australia

Where possible, data from the studies have been presented in table format. However, owing to the lack of standardisation in questionnaire design, not all areas are considered in each study. Despite limitations in relation to definition, sample size and standardisation of questionnaire design, a clear description of the international backpacker market in Australia is developed.

Nationality

A constant in all the studies is the dominance of the British and Other European markets (Table 10.2). This may be due in part to Australia's historical ties to Europe, although this is not all that attracts backpackers to Australia. Loker (1993) found that backpackers are motivated to visit Australia for reasons including seeking excitement and adventure and meeting local people and characters. The inconsistency in representation between nationalities could be attributed to each society's tolerance of extended leave (usually required for a visit to Australia) from employment and tertiary education and/or economic conditions (Haigh, 1995). An example of this is Riley's (1988: 319) finding that for Americans 'travel for a

Table 10.2 Major generating regions of backpackers visiting Australia 1989–1999 (% visitors)

Generating region	Pearce 1989	Loker 1991/2	Jarvis 1991/2	Haigh 1992	Buchanan & Rossetto 1995/6	Kininmont 1997	Thoms 1999
United Kingdom	38	37	38	29	20	48	27
Other Europe	28	35	28	36	36	29	33
North America	12	16	14	16	14	12	14
Asia	7	4	2	6	17	4	15
New Zealand	5	3	1	6	6	4	6
Other	0	0	0	7	7	3	5

few months (e.g. a summer in Europe) was viewed as acceptable, but a year or more of travel was likely to be regarded as irresponsible'. Similarly, backpackers may be influenced by the nature and extent of media coverage of tragedies in Australia, such as the Belangalo Backpacker murders in the late 1980s and the fire at a backpacker hostel in Childers, Queensland in 2000. The effects on the backpacker market of recent terrorist activities are not yet known, as government data collected post-1999 have not been released.

Accommodation-based studies tend to report fewer British and more Asian backpackers than those studies based on the social definition of backpacking. It is possible that some British backpackers bypass hostel accommodation and use alternative forms of accommodation such as staying with friends or relatives or camping. The higher proportion of Asian backpackers in Buchanan and Rossetto (1997) and Thoms' (2002) studies could be influenced by international students coming to Australia and staying in backpacker or YHA hostels until they find more appropriate accommodation.

Age

The manner in which data on age were recorded makes it difficult to tabulate. Pearce (1990) found that 84% of backpackers were in the 20–30 year age group. Loker (1993) found 90% of backpackers were less than 30 years of age, while Jarvis (1994) concluded that the average age of backpackers was 24.6 years. Haigh (1995) found 74% of backpackers were 15–29 years, and 14% were 30–39 years. Kininmont (2000) found 89% of backpackers were 18–30 years. Thoms (2002) concluded that the highest

Table 10.3 Gender of backpackers visiting Australia 1989–99 (% visitors)

Gender	Pearce 1989	Loker 1991/2	Jarvis 1991/2	Haigh 1992	Buchanan & Rossetto 1995/6	Kininmont 1997	Thoms 1999
Male	50	51	51	52	61	52	53
Female	49	49	49	48	39	48	47

proportion of backpackers is in the 20–24 year age group (37%) and that most backpackers are under 30 years (71%). Despite these inconsistencies, it is clear that backpackers are relatively young tourists.

Gender

As shown in Table 10.3, there was an even distribution of male and female backpackers. This is not to suggest that backpackers travel as couples. A significant proportion of the backpacker population travel alone – 45% (Pearce, 1990), 51% (Loker, 1993), 38% (Buchanan & Rossetto, 1997), 54% (Kininmont, 2000) and 67% (Thoms, 2002).

Occupation prior to travel

Table 10.4 shows the occupation of backpackers before going to Australia. Although there is general consistency in the findings of each study, there seems to be an increase in the proportion of students who make up the backpacker market. Assuming backpackers from the professional/technical sector have a tertiary education, it is evident that at least half of the backpackers have tertiary qualifications, indicating that they are a well-educated group of travellers.

Length of stay

There is a wide variation in the average period of time backpackers plan to spend in Australia (see Table 10.5), although all studies show back-

Table 10.4 Occupation of backpackers visiting Australia 1989–97 (% visitors)

Occupation	Pearce 1989	Loker 1991/2	Jarvis 1991/2	Haigh 1992	Kininmont 1997
Student	27	27	26	26	36
Professional/ technical	26	26	24	33	29
Clerical/sales	16	21	16	16	17

Table 10.5 Average time backpackers spend in Australia 1989-99 (nights)

	Pearce 1989	*Loker 1991/2*	*Jarvis 1991/2*	*Haigh 1992*	*Buchanan & Rossetto 1995/6*	*Kininmont 1997*	*Thoms 1999*
Travel in Australia	90	156	195	78	83	225	66

packers are long-term travellers, relative to international visitors overall who have an average stay of 23 nights (Bureau of Tourism Research, 2000b). Backpackers spend extended periods of time in Australia but it is often not their sole destination. There are a range of destinations visited by backpackers immediately before and after Australia; although the destinations that attract most backpackers are New Zealand and South East Asia (Buchanan & Rossetto, 1997; Loker, 1993; Kininmont, 2000; Thoms, 2002).

A factor that may have some influence on backpackers' length of stay is the availability of work visas such as the Working Holiday Maker Scheme (WHMS) visa, which allows young people between 18 and 25 years (in 2003, the upper age limit was raised to 30) to work in Australia for one year, though they can work for only three months with each employer (DIMA, 2000). Jarvis (1994) found that 45% of backpackers enter Australia with a WHMS visa, while Loker (1993) found that 49% plan to work or study in Australia, and Kininmont (2000) found that 39% come to Australia for a holiday with casual work. Many of the countries that have reciprocal working rights with Australia have significant numbers of backpackers who come to Australia for a holiday with casual work – United Kingdom 48%, Canada 37%, Ireland 38%, Netherlands 62% and Japan 27%. Of these backpackers, between 90% and 100% are planning to stay in Australia for four or more months (Kininmont, 2000). This suggests that the opportunity to engage in casual work while travelling in Australia increases the time spent in Australia. As noted in the next chapter by Cooper, O'Mahony and Erfurt, it also provides a valuable labour source for many primary producers.

Transport

The main mode of long-distance transport used by backpackers is coach, as shown in Table 10.6. The preference for coach and private vehicle travel may be due to the extensive road network in Australia, in contrast to the limited rail networks. Internal flights are used by approximately half of the backpacker population. This could be attributed to internal flights being included in the price of many international air tickets.

Table 10.6 Transport types used at least once by backpackers in Australia 1991–99 (% visitors)

	Loker 1991/2	Jarvis 1991/2	Haigh 1992	Kininmont 1997	Thoms 1999
Coach	78	80	44	94	43
Air	40	48	21	57	32
Private car	23	31	12	31	19
Shared ride	–	21	–	24	–
Rented car	–	6	5	31	10
Train	9	10	3	37	9
Other	12	–	15	–	–

Note: Percentages do not total to 100 as more than one form of transport could be used during travel in Australia.

Other research in New Zealand shows a similar hierarchy of transport preferences (Newlands, Chapter 13; Vance, Chapter 14 of this volume).

For most types of transport there is consistency in usage across the seven studies. However, inconsistencies are noted with the usage of rented car and train. The variation may be attributed to the wording of the question. Loker (1993: 16) asked 'What mode of transportation (bus, car, etc.) did/will you use to travel between major cities on your route?' Clearly this related to long-distance transport. Although this was also the intention in Kininmont's (2000) study, there it was implied rather than stated. Therefore, backpackers who had visited locations with metropolitan rail services, such as Sydney and Brisbane, may have biased the responses. It is possible that these backpackers may have included 'train' as a major means of transport although they may have used only metropolitan trains and not long-distance rail services. A similar situation may have occurred with rental cars. Responses may have been biased by backpackers who had visited locations such as Hervey Bay, where a popular backpacker activity is to hire a vehicle for use on Fraser Island.

While most of the forms of transport are self-explanatory, 'shared ride' deserves further explanation. Companies such as Travellers Auto Barn in King's Cross in Sydney, sell budget cars complete with a roadworthy certificate, membership to an automobile association and guaranteed title as well as the option of a guaranteed buy back price at the completion of the trip (Travellers Auto Barn, 2000). Backpackers who choose to buy cars can then advertise on hostel noticeboards or Internet bulletin boards for passengers to help share expenses, and backpackers who are looking for a ride to a given destination can advertise using the same medium.

Accommodation

The variation in methods used to collect and analyse data relating to accommodation usage make it impossible to directly compare results, although there are some common trends. All studies show that hostel accommodation (both YHA hostels and backpacker hostels) is the most popular, while staying with friends and relatives and camping should not be overlooked.

Rented houses/units and motels were also nominated by backpackers as accommodation options. While these accommodation types may seem contrary to the budget nature of backpacker travel, backpackers may '... stay in hotels and motels when they first arrive in Australia while they orientate themselves with regard to the availability and position of more traditional backpacker accommodation establishments' (Haigh, 1995: 21). Backpackers who have a WHMS visa may prefer to stay in a rented house/flat rather than in hostel accommodation while working.

Accommodation on farms is used by backpackers taking advantage of such schemes as Willing Workers on Organic Farms (WWOOF). In this instance, travellers are put in contact with farmers looking for people to work in exchange for food and accommodation (WWOOF, 2002). There are also opportunities to stay on host farms, which differ from farms involved in the WWOOF program because they are commercial ventures and guests pay accordingly.

Tours

Contrary to the budget and independent nature of backpacker travel, many backpackers do take tours during their time in Australia. While the types of activities that backpackers engage in is explored in some of the studies, information on the nature of the tours taken by backpackers is limited. Haigh (1995) found that 15% of backpackers take outback safari tours while in Australia. Kininmont (2000) found that at least 41% of backpackers take tours while in Australia, and that at least 20% take more than one tour.

However, tours generally constitute only 1.3% of a backpacker's time in Australia, with the remainder of their time spent travelling independently (Kininmont, 2000). These tours are typically to places (such as national parks) that are difficult to access by public transport, and they are usually only for short periods of time (two to three days). By being selective about the tours they take, backpackers are able to retain their independence and stay within their budget.

Conclusion

Although research on backpackers in Australia was scant prior to the 1990s, industry, government and academic recognition of the backpacker market has led to increased research in the past decade. This research has shown that the backpacker market is a valuable subset of tourists to Australia, and one that should be encouraged. However, efforts to monitor basic socio-demographic and travel characteristics of the backpacker market over time are flawed. While general trends can be identified, small changes in the market (that may be precursors to larger changes) go undetected. For example, Newlands (Chapter 13 of this volume) and Maoz (Chapter 7) suggest that the backpacker market is beginning to attract older backpackers. If this is the case, then there may be changes in the facility preferences shown by backpackers.

Currently the only nationwide longitudinal data collected on the backpacker market is that undertaken by the Australian government via the exit survey of international visitors. While this is commendable and is far more than is being done in many other countries that attract backpackers, the current data collection method is not without its flaws, primarily in relation to the definition of backpacker. Although data collected using the accommodation-based definition do not differ extensively from data collected using the social definition, smaller inconsistencies in the results have been highlighted. The Bureau of Tourism Research is endeavouring to determine the extent of bias resulting from the accommodation-based definition by including a new question in the International Visitor Survey as of 2002 (Thoms, 2002: 12). This question will allow backpackers to be defined on a self-identification basis. The data will then be compared to that collected using the accommodation-based definition of backpackers (Thoms, 2002). Initiatives such as these will allow more effective monitoring of the backpacker market.

Clearly there is much to be learnt about the international backpacker market in Australia, but it is possible to discern that it is currently dominated by backpackers from Europe who are young (18 to 30 years), well-educated, travelling for extended periods of time and making their own travel arrangements for most of their trip. Typically they travel by coach and stay in hostel accommodation, although other forms of transport and accommodation are used. As our knowledge of the backpacker market increases we will be in a better position to develop policies (the beginnings of which are evident in the National Backpacker Tourism Strategy) that will ensure the long-term viability of this potentially lucrative market (Commonwealth Department of Tourism, 1995) .

Chapter 11

Backpackers: Nomads Join the Mainstream? An Analysis of Backpacker Employment on the 'Harvest Trail Circuit' in Australia

MALCOLM COOPER, KIERAN O'MAHONY AND PATRICIA ERFURT

Introduction

This chapter explores the travel patterns and motives of backpackers visiting Australia; concentrating on those who work and those who visit the State of Queensland. The idea of drifters (i.e. backpackers) as 'nomads' (Cohen, 1973) is tested in relation to the actual travel and activity patterns of backpackers visiting Australia in general, and Hervey Bay and Fraser Island in particular. The importance of the flow of backpacker labour to specific areas and types of production in rural areas throughout the country forms a major part of this discussion.

The data on which this discussion is based are derived from a number of sources, including the Tourism Queensland 2001 Market Fact Sheet (International Backpackers Market), the Hervey Bay Tourism and Development Board's Market Research Report for 2001 (HBTDB, 2001), and the Federal Government's Harvest Trails study (DEWSRB, 2000). Both the national and local data show that backpackers are not 'nomads' in the sense of an unstructured travel experience, but are heavily constrained in terms of sites visited and often seek casual employment to pay for these visits. Indeed, the Harvest Trail study was partly conceived and carried out in response to the increasingly obvious disparity between the conventional wisdom relating to backpackers and the reality of regional/rural labour market flows based on backackers receiving payment for their services. This discussion of backpacker behaviour is therefore national in scope, but also concentrates on the local implications in Hervey Bay, Queensland.

Backpackers in Theory and Practice

Backpackers in theory

Cohen's (1972) classic typology of tourists forms the basis for this discussion of backpacker tourism. His construct postulated four tourist types: the organised mass tourist, the individual mass tourist, the explorer, and the nomad (or drifter); with the latter two characterised as non-institutionalised tourists as they were conceptualised as being only loosely attached to the tourist 'establishment' during their travels.

Nomads, a type of tourist that encompassed the archetypal backpacker for early observers of this particular group, were said to be travellers who had no set itinerary and were specialists in discovering and investigating new destinations. Yet until recently this tourism type had rarely been examined in any great depth (Oppermann & Chon, 1997); researchers preferred instead to concentrate on the conventional tourist, while noting that the observed hostility towards and dislike of backpackers (or 'nomads' – Cohen, 1973; 1979; Pearce, 1990; Wood, 1979) made them of little real value as objects of study. In part, this image of backpackers arose through a perception of their low economic value, resulting from their obvious desire to spend as little as possible on accommodation and travel. This notion almost completely missed the fact that backpackers stay longer (in a country, if not in a regional or local destination), and thus can actually spend more in total than other, more fancied tourist groups. In the case of Australia and New Zealand, for example, backpackers spend a significantly greater amount per capita than any other market segment (Kain & King, Chapter 12 of this volume; Oppermann & Chon, 1997).

Research is beginning to show that this expenditure also tends to go to smaller and more local businesses with higher levels of integration into the local economy (Hoivik & Heiberg, 1980; Oppermann & Chon, 1997). This results in less economic leakage and therefore more local economic impact from backpacker visitation than from other forms of tourism. Also, the regional impact of backpackers is much wider because of their more active travel patterns and longer length of stay, which means that peripheral and non-traditional areas also benefit, whereas most expenditure by conventional tourists tends to be made in major gateways and resorts.

In the initial studies of the backpacking phenomenon, backpackers were commonly considered to be pioneers of tourist experiences and/or destinations without much of a structured approach to travel (i.e. 'nomads', Bureau of Tourism Research, 1995; Hoivik & Heiberg, 1980; Smith, 1990). By relating their experiences to others, they set the path for the later arrival of conventional tourism. Backpackers' obvious preferences for low-cost accommodation also meant that a destination could invest in this at much lower cost than hotels and still attract international tourists, in a bottom-up strategy of tourism development (Oppermann & Chon, 1997).

More recently academic and institutional interest in backpacker tourism has markedly increased, particularly as the reality of their economic impact has become more obvious. It has also become increasingly obvious that the original concept of backpackers as 'nomads' needs considerable modification. This chapter is an attempt to reformulate the backpacker concept in relation to the Australian experience in order to take into account the increasing realisation that they are (in many cases) very much not nomadic in the classic sense of being a wanderer. In Australia, the backpacker is a traveller who, while not necessarily conforming to conventional tourism styles, is nevertheless often quite tightly constrained to particular travel routes, types of transport and destinations, for a host of reasons. This chapter also recognises the importance of employment as a major explanatory variable in certain Australian forms of the backpacker phenomenon.

A critique of the drifter concept: Backpacking in practice in Australia

There is increasing evidence that the 'nomad' concept of backpackers is no longer entirely appropriate when applied to the Australian context. Backpackers instead traverse quite specific routes in Australia, constrained by activities and attractions made known to them as 'must see/do' experiences, and by the continent's specific coastal settlement pattern. Even the timing of backpackers' decision to visit a particular attraction or area can be constrained by the practicalities of traversing a route, and taking into account not only attractions to visit, but also employment opportunities and the information gathered from and/or travelling needs of acquaintances and friends along the way. While the individual sense of adventure does of course determine the extent to which something new will be explored, other factors such as employment and 'the beaten track' assume greater importance as predictors of actual behaviour.

Main routes travelled in Australia are concentrated on the east coast (Loker-Murphy, 1996), with some limited forays into the centre and the north/west. Entry points are Sydney, Cairns and to a lesser extent Brisbane. Networks of routes radiate from these centres taking in sun, surf, national parks such as Fraser Island, the Great Barrier Reef, the Red Centre, the Murray River, and a set of subsidiary attractions, bound together by a network of hostels and bus routes. In recent years a layer of work opportunities has been added. Even more recently, these opportunities have been recognised both locally and nationally as a set of specific harvest trails where rural producers rely to a great extent on backpackers and backpacker hostels for their casual labour and, in some cases, for their very existence (DEWSRB, 2000).

For the purposes of this chapter, then, backpacking is probably best understood as a way of combining a holiday and part-time employment in an environment where choice is less constrained than it is for conventional tourism. Nevertheless, backpackers still undertake leisure and recreation in a relatively safe environment and a relaxed, laid back atmosphere away from the cares of the world, just as other tourists do, but with the addition of a significantly longer time factor, some exploration, and a propensity to work. This means that the accepted theoretical construct of backpacker travel behaviour should be modified to incorporate movement along specific routes, not a free-for-all or *smörgåsbord* of choice, and the addition of an increasingly-important employment variable within that movement pattern, in order to take into account the reality of such travel in Australia. The following defining characteristics of backpacking and backpackers in Australia were proposed by the Bureau of Tourism Research (1995) and DEWSRB (2000: 46):

- preference for budget accommodation;
- dominated by international visitors (in 2000 only 17% were Australian);
- predominantly within the 20–35 age group (though older groups also feature);
- flexible itineraries within a set of routes dictated by attractions and activities in vogue at any one time;
- strong interest in adventure and ecotourism activities;
- well educated;
- use train and bus travel more than other forms of travel (internally);
- seek work for some part of their stay.

Some statistics on the Australian backpacker industry

In 1999–2000 backpackers contributed around 9% (404,310) of total international visitors to Australia and accounted for 26.5 million (24%) of total international visitor nights (Tourism Queensland, 2001). International backpackers stayed in Australia for an average duration of 66 nights, and their average expenditure was $A6130 compared with $A4005 for all visitors (Bureau of Tourism Research, 2000a). Of these, 283,900 backpackers (70.2%) came for the main purpose of 'holiday' and stayed for an average duration of 58 nights, and 79% visited New South Wales, 66% visited Queensland and 42% visited Victoria. Queensland attracted 265,746 backpackers and 7.2 million backpacker nights. Transport between sites is mainly by bus (69%); with a smaller percentage hiring a car, using a friend's car, or buying a car (20%), while the rest use a combination of train and air transport (11%).

Within Queensland, Tropical North Queensland attracted the highest percentage of backpackers (71% or 158,718), followed by Brisbane (54% or 143,549), the Whitsunday Islands (43% or 113,048) and Hervey Bay / Maryborough (40% or 107,223). All Queensland regions experienced a growth in backpacker visitors from 1998 to 2000. Of the international backpackers to Queensland in 1999–2000, 74% came to Australia for the main purpose of holidaying, 9% came for the main purpose of visiting friends and relatives, 9% for the main purpose of education, and 3% for the main purpose of employment. Nearly 79% (209,801) were on a first visit to Australia, while 21% (55,945) were on a return visit (Tourism Queensland, 2001). With respect to Hervey Bay, around a million visitors are accommodated each year, of which more than 120,000 were backpackers in 2001.

Backpackers and Employment

Backpackers may in fact be classified as working holidaymakers (WHM) and permitted to supplement their income while they are in Australia, with the restriction that they do not work for more than three months with any one employer. Alternatively, they may be overseas students, who are permitted to work for 20 hours per week (approximately half a normal working week) when their course is in session and full-time during semester breaks (at any one time there are 100,000+ overseas students in Australia,). There are also visitors on a tourist visa who, while not permitted to work, are in fact doing so, which may account for some of the illegal workers mentioned in the Harvest Study Report (DEWSRB, 2000). Some other types of working visa are specific to particular industries, but none of these as yet caters for casual agricultural workers.

Official working holidaymakers are very highly regarded amongst farmers, with most grower organisations regularly lobbying for an increase in this form of visa to alleviate rural labour shortages (DIMA, 1999). The response from various state governments has been to increase the numbers of such visas from 35,000 in 1995, to 78,000 in 2000. However, this is only a fraction of the total number of jobs available (and very much less than total backpacker numbers). Interestingly, hostels also favour WHMs, who tend to be tertiary educated and less likely to cause problems for owners through anti-social behaviour (DEWSRB, 2000).

Harvest Trails

The Australian Job Search website, part of the Australian Federal Government's Job Network system for the unemployed (http://www. jobsearch.gov.au, accessed 23 March, 2002), has on one of its pages a question: *Looking for Seasonal Work?* The site goes on to suggest that there is a way to travel around Australia and also be continuously employed – by following one of the Harvest Trails listed (see Figure 11.1 and Table 11.1). The site gives links to employment providers within the major harvest areas, accommodation along the trails, available transport modes and routes, and links to immigration and other service websites giving authorisation to undertake such work if the traveller is not a resident of Australia.

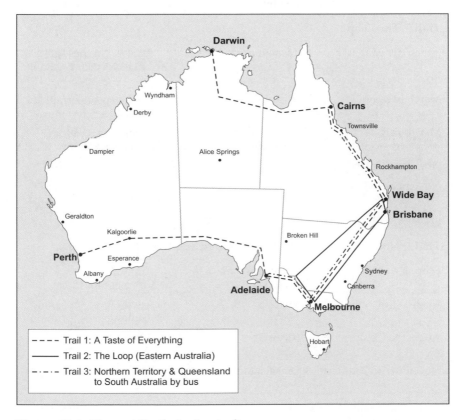

Figure 11.1 Harvest Trails in Australia

Table 11.1 Harvest Trails by area and produce

Time of year	State	Product
Trail 1: A Taste of Everything		
February to April	South Australia Victoria New South Wales	Grapes/citrus Apples Apples/citrus/grapes
April to June	Southern Queensland	Citrus/apples/tomatoes
June to August	Northern Queensland	Vegetables/bananas
September to November	Northern Territory	Mangoes/melons
	Northern Western Australia	Bananas/melons/vegetables
December to January	Southern WA	Vegetables/tomatoes
Trail 2: The Loop		
January to March	Tasmania	Apples/cherries/grapes/strawberries/vegetables
March to May	Victoria	Apples/pears/grapes/vegetables
May to July	South/Central Queensland	Bananas/avocadoes citrus/vegetables
August to October	North Queensland	Bananas/vegetables
November to January	NSW	Blueberries/cherries citrus/cotton
January to March	Back to Tasmania	
Trail 3: Northern Territory & Queensland to South Australia by Bus		
February to March	South Australia Victoria	Apples/pears Citrus/grapes
April to July	Victoria NSW	Apples/pears/pruning Apples/citrus/pruning
August to October	Victoria NSW	Citrus Blueberries
November to February	Queensland	Melons/tomatoes/vegetables

Source: Harvesting Australia: Report of the National Harvest Trail Working Group, Commonwealth of Australia: Canberra. DEWSRB (2000)

This website formalised at a governmental level what had been under discussion for many years: how to assist rural producers to attract sufficient casual labour at harvest time (e.g. Forsyth & Dwyer, 1995; Joint Standing Committee on Migration, 1997). These discussions culminated in the Report of the National Harvest Trail Working Group (DEWSRB, 2000). The terms of reference for that group included establishing harvest trails as a reality, and developing/implementing a strategy for promoting the attractions and benefits of seasonal work both to Australians and to working holidaymakers from other countries.

The study found that both individual farmers and producer organisations greatly favoured the use of backpacker labour, and that this should be encouraged through favourable visa conditions, incentives to develop hostels in strategic locations, and assistance with transport. Even backpackers otherwise drawn to particular areas of Australia for leisure and recreation reasons have rapidly become attracted to the possibility of working, at least when the work is close to their preferred destination.

Two factors were found to be important in the development of de facto harvest trails linked to the movement of backpackers: a growing reluctance on the part of resident Australians (perhaps other than the 17% of all backpackers who are Australian) to undertake seasonal labour in rural areas, and a movement by farmers into servicing growing export markets in fruit and vegetables. Vegetables are especially heavily labour-intensive at harvest time, and farmers require stability in their labour force to be sure of meeting market conditions. Table 11.1 indicates the types of crops by trail and by area.

Backpacker awareness of working opportunities

The Queensland Fruit and Vegetable Growers Association estimated farm losses of $A90 million in 1999 because of the difficulty in finding sufficient casual workers; this represents between 10% and 20% of the gross value of agricultural production in Queensland. For Australia as a whole, between 55,000 and 60,000 full-time equivalent jobs per year are available specifically in harvest areas (DEWRSB, 2000). Depending on turnover and the mobility of harvest labour, the number of workers required to fill these jobs will vary, but will be higher than the full-time job equivalent.

It is not surprising, therefore, that several rural backpacker hostels have emerged in recent years on the Harvest Trails (or at least on the main highways that traverse them). Many of these hostels catering solely for intending harvest workers and have become a major, or in some cases the only, supplier of casual workers to particular growers. Thus, while the harvest trail (and especially its year round aspect) is still not generally well known in Australia, it is well known in backpacker circles. Working holidaymakers and other eligible aliens have thus been identified as an actual source of casual labour, with the Harvest Trails study finding that backpackers with (or without) work permits already form a significant part of the casual workforce, and have done for some time (DEWRSB, 2000).

Frequently, backpacker hostels are requested to supply a specific number of workers, and growers often will employ only workers from a particular hostel. The transport costs of growers are often also reduced by hostels, or the hostels may act as pick up points for buses from local farms. In turn, backpacker magazines focus particularly on information about harvest work and the areas in which it is available. Hostels advertise work in backpacker and tourist magazines, and backpackers also use the Internet – hence the importance of the Australian Job Search website. The downside of this is that a few hostels have been found to take advantage of the lack of local knowledge of the backpackers and other tourists, and to advertise that there is work available before a harvest is ready. This can create a problem for backpackers who are forced by employment pressures to wait locally, incurring debts while waiting for the harvest to start; this also harms the reputation of all backpacker hostels.

Other factors leading to backpacker involvement in Harvest Trails

The generally low incomes to be had in rural areas and the taxation at source may be a disincentive for Australians, but generally not for back-packers as it is supplementary income that they seek. The cost of transport in Australia can also deter residents from travelling to harvest areas, but again this is not so for backpackers, who often enter at the point of harvest (for example in Cairns, Queensland). In addition (and especially when the working period is not scheduled to commence immediately upon entry into the country), backpackers are much more tolerant of long distance travel. This is because their primary reason for coming to Australia is to visit certain attraction/areas and, in terms of distance, these may be located up to half a continent apart.

Uncertainty about getting sufficient work and the cost of accommoda-tion are also known to be barriers to Australians seeking employment in the harvest industry. Again, backpackers do not appear to think these variables are particularly important, given that the work they undertake is generally located somewhere along one of their preferred travel routes, where the hostels they would be using are located anyway. So, since virtually every other aspect of their travel is already determined, there are no further barriers to them taking up casual employment in this way.

For backpackers, there is the added attraction of being able to socialise and have cross-cultural interaction with other workers/travellers (wherever they may be from), as well as the unique opportunity for non-English speaking backpackers to significantly improve their language skills during a given period of work. Increasingly, the 'real' travel experience is when contact is made with locals, partly through integration into local social life (depending on the length of stay) and by meeting other backpackers in a short-term working environment. In other words, venturing off the beaten track is motivated by social experience rather than by the routes travelled or attractions visited outside the conventional tourism itinerary.

Why backpackers are preferred as employees on the Harvest Trails

The Harvest Trail study found that there are distinct preferences for employing overseas backpackers:

> If Australians turn up we tell them we are full. The backpackers from overseas come here to work and they don't cause any trouble ... (manager of a backpacker hostel in Queensland, cited in DEWSRB, 2000: 42)

> Australians are not welcome to the backpacker hostels during harvest season, which runs from September to November. (speaker at a public meeting in Bowen, Queensland in 2000)

> If they are Working Holiday Makers, then a grower is not tempted to use false identities/tax file numbers to secure desperately needed labour. (DEWSRB, 2000: 28–33)

Backpackers generally stay longer and work harder because they are working for a purpose; work is usually recognised as being short term and is not likely to become a lifestyle. Some growers in fact have regulars who return every year, plus a list of locals from which they draw (DEWRSB, 2000). For example, backpacker labour is of considerable importance in Bowen, Queensland, where there are three hostels that specialise in providing labour. Indeed, the Bowen tomato industry would not survive without this labour as between 400 and 500 backpackers are employed in Bowen for this purpose each season.

However, growers also tend to rely on hostels to check visas for work permits. When, as sometimes happens, this is not done, the grower response is to want the Department of Immigration and Multicultural Affairs to 'lighten up' on immigration restrictions, rather than to control the backpackers themselves. In this respect, they are not happy to act as immigration police though they still want the backpacker labour.

Case Study: Backpackers in Hervey Bay and the Wide Bay Region

The phenomenon of backpackers being essential to the harvest industry has also been noted in the Wide Bay region of Queensland (DEWSRB, 2000). This is in spite of the region having a large unemployed population of resident Australians that could easily cope with existing seasonal demands for labour. Therefore, while the popular image of backpackers is that they visit this part of Australia because the Fraser Island UNESCO World Heritage area is immediately accessible from Hervey Bay, the reality is that seasonal employment is also an important secondary motivator for many of them.

Interestingly, the importance of the Fraser Island experience and the importance to the entire nation of backpacker labour on the harvest trails have also come together in the form of a Wide Bay-based organisation that acts as a nationwide clearing house for backpacker labour. VISITOZ (accessed 20 May, 2003) offers those backpackers with a legal right to work, as well as Australians, the opportunity to undertake short-term job placements on outback cattle and sheep stations, on farms and in hospitality establishments. Participants who seek work on cattle, sheep, horse or arable farms are given a short introduction to Australian agricultural techniques, and are then offered a choice of placements to match their interests and skills. All jobs are paid at the union-negotiated rate or better. The choice of available jobs ranges from those suitable for the professional agricultural worker or very experienced horse rider through to those suitable for a motivated person with no previous skills. For the person who wishes to experience life in the outback but not work in agricultural jobs, VISITOZ also offers placements as mother's helps, and also hospitality work in hotels and roadhouses and on host farms. During the ten years that this company has been operating, a network of more than 900 employers has been built up who turn to VISITOZ when they cannot meet their staffing requirements from the local labour market. These employers range from the largest agri-business companies with millions of hectares under crops, to small family farms. Jobs are available throughout the year and in all states except Tasmania.

The importance of backpackers to the Harvest Trails network in the Wide Bay Region is also seen in the local growers' reaction to the problem of intra-regional transport for labour. Lack of public transport forces those backpackers who do wish to work to seek accommodation in centres along the region's main highways where they can be dropped and picked up by long-distance coaches directly. The hostels and/or the growers have then to provide localised transport to regional farms. Where growers are too far away from main transport routes, access to the only certain labour market associated with the Harvest Trail (e.g. backpackers) is problematic. Their ability to find suitable workers is severely compromised and they complain quite strongly, demanding that backpacker hostels be located closer to their operations (DEWSRB, 2000).

Backpackers in Hervey Bay

As a local illustration of the general observations on the actual behaviour of backpackers in Australia, a study of backpackers that formed part of a wider Visitor Profile Survey carried out in 2001–2 by the Hervey Bay Tourism and Development Board was re-examined. This study involved a face-to-face survey of a random sample of visitors staying at motels, caravan parks and backpacker hostel locations in the city of Hervey Bay, Queensland. As Hervey Bay hosts about 120,000 backpackers, a sample of 250 was considered sufficient for reliable results (see Neuman, 1997). At the close of the survey, 235 responses had been obtained, with a ratio of male to female of 57.4% to 42.6% (HBTDB, 2001). Backpackers made up 72.4% of all international visitors, or 129 respondents (Table 11.2), staying in purpose-built hostels, with friends and relations, or in caravan parks.

The main survey compared the 2001 profile of all visitors to the city with those of 2000 and 1999, but concentrated on international visitors. For the first time, supplementary questions on a range of matters were asked of the

Table 11.2 Visitor origin and age

Country or State	Age group (%)					
	< 15	15–29	30–49	50–64	65+	Total
Australia	1.3	27.5	41.3	20.4	5.2	24.1
United Kingdom	–	83.0	3.8	9.4	3.8	11.1
USA/Canada	–	69.2	23.1	7.7	–	8.1
Germany	–	50.0	50.0	–	–	13.4
Other Europe	–	84.1	6.8	6.8	–	45.9
New Zealand	–	100.0	–	–	–	1.7
Japan	–	100.0	–	–	–	1.5
Other	–	81.2	9.1	9.1	–	18.4
Total international visitors		78.2	13.8	6.5	0.4	75.9

Source: Cooper (2001)

respondents identified as backpackers: for example, whether they classified themselves as backpackers or mainstream tourists according to
Pearce's (1990) typology. While such questions were mainly concerned
with determining attitudes to backpackers' use of the Fraser Island
UNESCO World Heritage environment (reported in Cooper, 2001), questions on their length of stay in Australia and their temporary employment
(if any) were also asked. The data gathered on the survey are discussed in
the following section.

Results

More than 78% of international visitors were in the 15–29 age groups,
reflecting the high proportion of backpackers amongst international tourists to Hervey Bay. Most of the remainder were aged between 30 and 49
(Table 11.2). The majority of international tourists surveyed were first-time
visitors while there was a relatively even split between domestic first-time
and repeat visitors.

More than 70% of all visitors had either travelled alone to Hervey Bay, or
were with friends in small groups of two to five people. Groups of more than
five visitors were very rare. Most visitors came for holiday purposes (64%),
with visiting friends and relatives (at 28%), education (6%) and business/
employment travel (6%) making up the remainder. Over 40% of international
visitors came by bus, with 29% in private cars (up from 13% in 2000), 23% by
train, and the remainder (7%) by plane. This is in contrast to the domestic
visitor pattern involving private cars (64%), bus (13%), or train (8%).

The favoured Australian backpacking 'routes' identified by this survey
(Table 11.3) also included Sydney to Cairns plus the 'Red Centre' (Alice
Springs and Uluru/Ayers Rock) and the East and West coasts (essentially
incorporating the city of Perth in the East Coast route). All backpackers had
visited Sydney, Melbourne, Brisbane, and Cairns, but not just as entry
points into the country. These centres also provide many of the attractions,
alternative life styles, and working opportunities to be found in Australia,
outside of the harvest trails.

Backpacker respondents were asked to state the places they had visited,
or intended to visit, in order of visiting during their present visit to
Australia. The majority (82.9%: Cooper, 2001) had visited Hervey Bay in
order to experience Fraser Island as part of a planned route covering the
East Coast of Australia incorporating Sydney, Byron Bay, Fraser Island, the
Whitsunday Islands and Cairns. Some 7% cited friends and family as
reasons for visiting, and the remainder stated that they were looking for
work. Hervey Bay thus forms an essential waypoint on the East Coast of

Table 11.3   Travel routes of backpackers

	Percentage of respondents
Planned route:	
Melbourne to Sydney to Cairns (the extended East Coast route)	46.3
Sydney to Cairns plus the Centre (East Coast plus)	19.5
East and West C:oasts combined	17.1
No particular route	17.1
Places visited:	
Capital Cities (Sydney, Melbourne, Brisbane)	100.0
Hervey Bay/Fraser Island	100.0
Byron Bay (NSW)	36.6
Noosa (Sunshine Coast, Queensland)	7.3
Whitsundays (Queensland)	34.1
Uluru(Ayers Rock)/Alice Springs (Northern Territory)	14.6
Great Barrier Reef (Queensland)	2.4
Why chosen?	
Must see	21.9
Word of mouth recommendation	19.4
Limited time	17.1
Lonely Planet Guide recommendation	9.7
Diving	9.7
Coastal location	9.7
Ease of access by plane	4.8
Wherever I could get work	2.4
No answer	5.3

Source: Cooper (2001)

Australia 'circuit' (see Table 11.3), above all other reasons for visiting. Nevertheless, 12% of backpackers had worked in the Wide Bay Region, most notably in the harvesting areas of the region (Childers–Bundaberg), before visiting Hervey Bay (Table 11.4).

Table 11.3 also provides evidence of why these routes are chosen. It is noticeable that working does not appear to be an imperative of choice compared with the sightseeing icons of Australia such as the capital cities, Fraser Island, the Whitsunday Islands and Alice Springs/Uluru (Ayers Rock), or in relation to the limited time available for travel. The attractions listed come into the 'must see' category, reinforced by word of mouth and the travel guides, and work is for supplementing the income required to undertake such trips. Nevertheless, backpackers arguably do work during their travels. Table 11.4 shows that around 42% of the sample had worked, 53% of those in agriculture. A further 24% had worked in the hospitality industry (in Hervey Bay a number of these jobs are in the backpacker hostels themselves), or in occupations such as retail, legal offices and transport.

Most backpackers find jobs in New South Wales or Queensland, with Sydney and Brisbane featuring strongly, but with a significant proportion gaining employment on the harvest trails listed in Table 11.1 and depicted in Figure 11.1. Table 11.4 also shows that the most common time span for this work is between one and six months; this is significant, since the median length of stay in Australia of backpackers is around five months (Kain & King, Chapter 12). This implies that working takes up a considerable proportion of backpackers' time in the country, contrary to the impression that working is not of particular importance to them.

Conclusions

This chapter has shown that any attempt to understand the phenomenon of backpacking in Australia has to at least acknowledge that they are independent travellers who are often quite tightly bound for a host of reasons to particular travel routes, types of transport and to particular sets of destinations. It has also demonstrated that employment is a major explanatory variable that should be included in the Australian form of the backpacker phenomenon. Even the timing of a backpacker's decision to visit a particular site can be constrained by the practicalities of meeting harvest deadlines while traversing a particular route during their stay in Australia. Main backpacker routes in Australia are concentrated on the East Coast, with some limited forays into the centre and the North or West. Entry points are Sydney, Cairns, and to a lesser extent Brisbane, but all coincide with or incorporate at least one harvest trail. Indeed, the emergence of the Harvest Trails has (to a considerable extent) been based on the routes travelled by backpackers. At the very least, the existence of a potential labour force in backpackers was recognised very early in the development of the trails.

In recent years agricultural work opportunities have been recognised

Table 11.4 Working patterns

Working patterns	Percentage of respondents
Work in Australia?	
Yes	41.7
No	58.3
In what industry?	
Agriculture	52.9
Hospitality	23.5
Retail	11.8
Other	11.8
How long?	
less than 1 month	29.4
1– 6 months	64.7
7–12 months	5.9
Where?	
Sydney/NSW	35.3
Melbourne/Victoria	5.9
Brisbane	23.5
Wide Bay	11.8
Other Queensland	11.8
Other	11.7

Source: Cooper (2001)

both locally and nationally as a set of Harvest Trails has emerged, relying to an important extent on backpacker hostels for their casual labour and, in some cases, for their very existence. Indeed, the Harvest Trail study was partly conceived and carried out in response to the increasingly obvious disparity between the 'conventional' wisdom relating to backpackers and the reality of regional/rural labour market flows based on payment for backpackers' services (DEWSRB, 2000). In other words, backpackers are very definitely *on the beaten track* with respect to employment opportunities in rural areas of Australia and arguably are not – in any real sense of the word – nomads.

Chapter 12

Destination-Based Product Selections by International Backpackers in Australia

DENISE KAIN AND BRIAN KING

Introduction

Within the backpacking phenomenon there has been an increasing blurring of the distinction between free independent traveller (FIT) backpackers and youth travellers undertaking extended tours offered by commercial operators. This has had consequences for the suppliers of tour and related products that are likely to appeal to backpackers. At the same time, there has been a proliferation of commercial backpacker hostels and destination-based tour products targeted specifically at backpackers' needs. This chapter investigates the provision of tours (both day and extended) targeted at backpackers, how backpackers source information about such products, the extent to which they engage in advanced product booking and purchases, and the various segments that exist within the backpacker market. The research was conducted exclusively in Australia but doubtless has broader applicability since its focus is on international backpackers.

Backpacking in Australia is a significant and growing phenomenon. International backpackers contribute more than $A1.5 billion each year to the Australian economy, and backpackers in Australia spend around $A6130 per head compared with an average spend of $A4005 for all visitors (Bureau of Tourism Research, 2002). In 1996, the average length of stay for backpackers was 83 nights compared with 23 nights for all other visitors (Buchanan & Rossetto, 1997). As was shown by Pearce (1990), most backpackers adopt an informal approach to itinerary planning, and the economic benefits of backpacking appear to be retained to a substantial degree within local communities. If backpackers are receptive to alternative products, then this retention could be enhanced.

A key aspect of backpacking is the effect of clustering in particular areas, and Australia follows this pattern. It is important to understand this clustering if we are to gain a proper insight into the relationship between back-packers and the products that are targeted at them. A limited number of routes have gained popularity with backpackers such as the East Coast route between Sydney, Brisbane and Cairns – sometimes including Melbourne (Loker-Murphy, 1996). Each stopover has developed its own enclave characterised by a backpacker 'culture' with accommodation facili-ties and other businesses that target backpackers forming clusters that in turn attract more backpackers to the area. City gateways act as the major points of entry and exit into Australia, but backpackers visit a range of other cities and towns. It has been noted that many backpackers follow the mainstream backpacker guidebooks (Wheeler, 1999) and indeed, it has been accepted for many years that the popularity and use of such books has led to the creation of well-established backpacker routes and clusters (Hampton, 1998; Pearce, 1990). A major focus of the present study is the pattern of backpacking in Australia, including the information that back-packers gather about products after their arrival at their destination.

Literature Review

As has been discussed in previous chapters, the Australian Government has produced a backpacking strategy, thereby giving a level of official recognition to the phenomenon (Commonwealth Department of Tourism, 1995; Hampton, 1998; Tourism Victoria, 1995; Woodrow, 1994), although the backpacker market is often perceived as less lucrative than other tourism segments (Loker-Murphy, 1996; Loker-Murphy & Pearce, 1995). Backpackers arguably contribute significantly to businesses and to host economies in diverse locations (Carr, 1998; Jarvis, 1994; Loker-Murphy & Pearce, 1995). In venturing far afield from major gateways and destina-tions, backpackers can spread the benefits into host communities that are less exposed to conventional tourism. Backpackers' spending also covers a range of smaller locally-owned businesses as opposed to multinationals such as international hotel chains and duty free stores (Hampton, 1998). Carr observes that younger tourists make greater use of the type of facilities (aside from accommodation) used by the local population, thus lessening the need for infrastructural investment (1998). Indeed, according to Pearce (1990), backpackers prefer budget accommodation and favour encoun-tering like-minded travellers. They pursue extended independ-ently-organised and flexible travel schedules, and express a preference for informal and participatory holiday activities. For the purpose of the present chapter, these characteristics may impact on backpacker informa-tion-gathering about available products, as well as on purchase patterns.

The term 'backpacker' is used in the present study, though many international studies prefer the term 'youth market' or 'young independent travellers'. Of the authors who have examined youth travellers, Desforges (1998) is one of the few who has referred specifically to backpackers. Desforge's study affirmed that young independent travellers attach importance to authenticity as an integral component of the destination experience. Pearce's (1990) definition applies no age-based criterion and many of his subjects would be excluded from studies focusing on 'young' tourists. He views the backpacker market as heterogeneous and complex. Authors who have relied on the definitions in official statistics struggle to make meaningful international comparisons owing to a lack of standardisation. This heterogeneity may influence product selection where the product has been developed specifically for consumption by young travellers, rather than for FITs generally.

Australia's Bureau of Tourism Research (BTR) defines a backpacker as aged fifteen years or over and spending at least one night at a backpacker or youth hostel (Commonwealth Department of Tourism, 1995). No distinction is drawn between short- and long-term visitors, or between those on work/tourist visas and those purchasing a fully-inclusive tour utilising backpacker or youth hostel accommodation. Despite their disparate behavioural characteristics, these inclusive travellers are grouped together with FITs. It is risky to ignore such characteristics, since they may determine the economic contribution and the effectiveness of particular marketing activities. Products targeted specifically at FIT backpackers may be offered as an option within tours by commercial operators such as Contiki, thereby creating an overlap between target groups as well as a blurring of distinctions.

In less-developed countries, backpackers may avoid many types of service provider by, for example, walking rather than taking taxis or local transport and by guiding themselves rather than making use of local tour guides. By contrast, backpackers in Australia appear to make greater use of backpacker organisations and touring companies owned by local operators, thereby keeping their spending within the local economy. It is this characteristic of backpackers in Australia that adds potency to the current investigation. Consistent with Pearce's (1990) contention, backpackers spend more on activities and experiences than on accommodation. Budget accommodation within backpacker cluster areas can provide a meeting place for like-minded people, who enhance the travel experience by providing advice and stories on current and planned destinations.

An interesting issue influencing backpacker product choices is the incidence of advance purchase. Jarvis notes the increasing share of tourists arriving in Australia who have pre-purchased a plane ticket. This practice increased from 52% of travellers in 1988 to 60% in 1990 (Jarvis, 1994). Loker-Murphy and Pearce (1995), however, noted that backpackers were more likely not to have made prepaid bookings for any part of their trip, particularly accommodation (98% compared with 78%) and tours (97% compared with 87%).

The backpacker decision-making model proposed by Jarvis is shown in Figure 12.1. This model is similar to many other consumer choice models as cited in Kucukkurt (1981). The 'object' of backpacking is often to signify the completion of either work or study. This activates need recognition or an 'attitude' that in turn alters the current status. The information search involves both internal and external sources, and destination choice is the culmination of a combination of the drive and expectancy factors. A job that may have generated the funds to facilitate travel and the completion of work

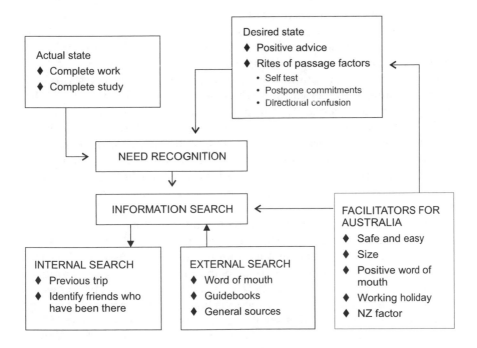

Figure 12.1 Backpacker decision-making model
Source: Jarvis (1994)

and/or study are described as the 'actual state'. For youth travellers (most backpackers fall into this category), eliminating the 'burdens' of work and study by travelling may postpone further commitment. This is described by Cohen as the assumption of 'adult, middle class responsibility' (Jarvis, 1994) and by Graburn (1983) as a *rite de passage*.

Loker-Murphy (1996) characterises backpackers as motivated by excitement and adventure, as well as by the opportunity to meet local people. The status of travel is viewed as less important than the opportunity for personal growth and development. Following Bourdieu, Desforges (1998) characterises backpacker travel as a form of cultural capital that depends on a shared interest between the backpacker and his/her audience. If a backpacker's family, friends and associates are not interested in hearing about the travel experience, then the value is diminished. Backpackers may undermine the perceived value of the experiences of fellow backpackers if they characterise them as less *'authentic'* than their own (Desforges, 1998: 182–3). Cohen (1972, cited in Gnoth 1997: 284) explains that, in terms of destination and experience, travellers may be positioned on a continuum between authenticity and artificiality. Different backpackers may view the cultural capital or authenticity associated with a given situation very differently. This provides a framework for the importance (or otherwise) of product purchases made prior to arrival.

Length of stay and nationality are also likely to influence product purchase patterns. American students who travel for a couple of months between semesters constitute an important segment. Typically, they stay in Australia for shorter periods than their British counterparts, who have generally arrived on working holiday visas. Whilst many tourism products may be more suited to shorter-term visitors, this market has been given only scant mention in the literature. Short-term backpackers may also have a higher daily spend on internal travel and touring costs, since they have less time to experience Australia.

There is, however, substantial research on consumer impressions of destinations and products, albeit with little emphasis on the purchase of locally-based services. For example, Hampton (1998) discusses backpacker purchases of locally-made goods; a better understanding of products targeted at backpackers would help to identify any mismatch between supply and demand. Carr (1998) suggests that products targeted at young travellers may help to define what it means to be a young tourist. If, for example, a tour operator focusing on the youth market sets age limits, then these limits form the parameters for what comes to be known as a 'young tourist'. Similarly, if backpacker lodges exclude couples or families, then backpackers are increasingly viewed as being synonymous with single travellers.

Is an organised 'backpacker' tour then a contradiction in terms? Or is the notion of backpacker travel simply evolving? Independent travellers may participate in inclusive packages comprising accommodation, transport, meals and sightseeing with commentary, and many day tours are available at backpacker lodges and youth hostels in Australia. Whilst many incorporate destinations and experiences not offered by mainstream tour operators, some tours are scarcely distinguishable from conventional itineraries. In such cases, their appeal depends on distribution through the hostel network and the deliberate targeting of like-minded travellers. Small operators may benefit from low overheads, and thus be able to offer competitive prices.

According to Gnoth (1997), consumers base their decisions about destinations on the attributes, facilities and experiences that they anticipate. Selby and Morgan (1996) and Murphy (1999) have examined the process of choosing between competing destinations. Um and Crompton (1992) view the key motives for travel as 'travelability,' need satisfaction and social acceptance. Kucukkurt (1981) emphasises practical concerns such as increased media exposure and safer, speedier and more comfortable travel as factors influencing the appeal of destinations. He notes that visitors may tolerate negative destination features if doing so allows them to access the 'positives' (c.f. dissonance theory). Lower standards of accommodation may be tolerated in settings that offer the prospect of experiencing a different culture. A backpacker may choose to sleep on an airport bench rather than purchase accommodation, if recounting the experience to fellow travellers also brings additional kudos.

Jarvis (1994) examined backpacking as a *rite de passage*, as proposed by Graburn (1983) for tourists more generally. However, backpacker participation in more 'mainstream' products such as backpacker tours has not been considered to date. Such products may appeal because they help overcome time constraints, or facilitate independent travel within an expansive and varied terrain such as Australia. Despite the negative association of organised tours for many backpackers, specially-targeted activities and transport have proved popular. New Zealand, for example, has developed a network of transport options and activities (particularly adventure-based activities) that are priced and packaged to appeal to the budget-conscious traveller (Muir, 1994; Vance, Chapter 14 of this volume). Consistent with Graburn's (1983) theory on challenges and personal growth, Australia may also be categorised as an appealing and even 'exotic' destination for international travellers.

Fodness and Murray (1997) have suggested that search behaviour may form the basis of market segmentation, but that many tourism operators overlook the motivating factors that lead to travel decisions and consumption behaviour. In attempting to target potential backpackers, Internet sites and coverage in backpacker-oriented guidebooks may be more effective than advertising in a mainstream print medium (such as a metropolitan daily newspaper), or participating in a brochure distributed through conventional travel agency channels. In seeking a social experience with like-minded travellers, backpackers may be willing to substitute quadruple -share for triple-share accommodation. However, participation in a more 'mainstream' touring package may diminish the desired experience.

Jarvis (1994) and Perdue and Botkin (1988) have argued that international travel is a 'big ticket item', involving a risk in terms of time and expense. According to Buchanan and Rossetto (1997), long-haul backpackers to Australia plan for more than six months, whereas the planning undertaken by shorter-haul visitors from Japan and other Asian countries averages only three months. Though somewhat at odds with the attitude of 'I will work it out when I get there', travellers who spend time gathering information about Australia can make financial savings, thereby enhancing their peer group status, consistent with Desforge's (1998) notion of backpacking as the accumulation of 'cultural capital'. Backpackers may gather general background information in preference to pre-organising specific activities.

The preliminary information search may vary between backpackers, particularly on the basis of their underlying motives (Fodness & Murray, 1997). The inexperienced may feel a greater need for information about pre-arranged components. Kucukkurt (1981) has applied the concept of mass and transformation points to the travel decision making process. Mass refers to the intensity of attitude and transformation refers to the point at which consistent behaviour occurs in a given situation. A backpacker may, for example, receive (and follow) advice from fellow travellers regarding facilities or attractions en route. Providing that the ensuing experience is positive, the transformation point may be lowered where the traveller defaults to such word of mouth information, rather than relying on guidebooks. The incidence of guidebook use may increase amongst those with previous experience who require less intensity. An understanding of how the travel product decision-making process differs during the various stages of the trip may be useful for product providers.

Guidebooks also seem to be an influential factor, although Hampton (1998) has observed that outdated guidebooks may give the wrong impression of prevailing prices within the destination. The rapid obsolescence of information printed in guidebooks is sometimes used as an argument for

Internet-based solutions. The use of the Internet is increasing amongst travellers including backpackers (Schonland & Williams, 1997), and the current study examines its role in the purchase decision.

Backpacker Information Use and Decision Making

Research questions and conceptual framework

A conceptual framework (Figure 12.2) highlights the key characteristics of international backpackers to Australia and the interface between operators (information providers) and information users in the context of the decision-making process. The four key research questions were:

(1) What is the profile of international backpackers to Australia?
(2) How do backpackers gather information about the destination following their arrival in Australia?
(3) What factors influence their decision making?
(4) What general products and services and what specific organised tours appeal to backpackers and what marketing techniques are most effective?

Following discussions with backpacker operators and tourism authorities about key issues facing them, four propositions were drawn up:

(1) that information search would vary on the basis of gender, age, country of residence, party size and travel experience to Australia and elsewhere;
(2) that product selection would vary by party size and travel experience;
(3) that the time and effort involved in the information search would vary according to the product costs, with more time invested for 'big ticket' items; and
(4) that planning and/or purchase lead-time would vary with the degree of travel experience.

The discussions with backpacker operators provided guidance in designing questionnaires that reflected a number of current industry concerns. The data were analysed using simple cross tabulations to identify patterns on the basis of gender, age and country of origin. ANOVA and chi-squared tests were applied to test for significance. Two limitations of the study are acknowledged: (1) the data were collected during a particular period and may not take full account of any seasonal differences and (2) a disproportionate share of the sample is made up of native English speakers.

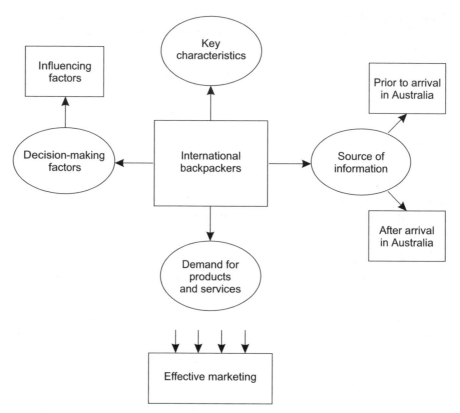

Figure 12.2 Conceptual framework

Methods

Previous Australian research on backpacker decision making has generally focused on the choice of Australia as a destination (Jarvis, 1994; Loker-Murphy & Pearce, 1995; Ross, 1993), rather than the purchase of travel-related products such as accommodation, transport, food, tours and attractions. In the present study, the research methods chosen focused on information gathering and decision making after arrival. The study used a combination of qualitative and quantitative methods including a survey-based consumer questionnaire and an examination of the marketing activities of tourism operators. The latter was included with a view to understanding whether current marketing activities are consistent with traveller decision making.

To supplement the consumer-based survey, the researchers approached operators participating in a consumer show, the Melbourne Backpacker Expo. A pilot of the consumer questionnaire was administered to both day- and extended-tour operators and to the operators of backpacker properties, which led to the inclusion of questions about visa status and traveller expectations about value for money. This piloting helped to improve the survey instrument.

During a series of semi-structured interviews, operators were asked about their marketing research activity, including any tracking that they undertook. They subsequently distributed the self-completion questionnaires to their customers. The questionnaire aimed to identify how purchase decisions are made for particular tourist services such as accommodation and touring. It also requested demographic and profile information, and investigated the factors that influence decisions including party size, the extent of planning undertaken prior to travel, and the extent of advance purchase.

During late 1999 and early 2000, 400 questionnaires were distributed to backpackers through the participating operators. Of the 151 questionnaires that were completed and returned, 139 were deemed to be usable – a response rate of about 35%. The tour operator response rate (42%) was superior to the response rate for accommodation operators (18%). In the present study the operators were largely Melbourne-based, so most respondents are likely to be backpackers who have included Melbourne in their itinerary.

In drawing up the key decision-making influences, the researchers drew upon the work of Snepenger *et al.* (cited in Fodness & Murray, 1997) who note four determinants influencing the tourism information search process: travelling party composition, the presence of friends or relatives at the destination, past experience, and the degree of novelty associated with the destination. Reinforcing the importance of the 'friends and relatives' factor, one tour operator noted that older local residents often come into the office requesting touring information on behalf of the visiting backpackers they are hosting.

Consistent with the findings of Fodness and Murray (1997), the study acknowledged the practice of using multiple information sources during the decision-making process. Another area of examination was the 'New Zealand factor' – the inclusion of New Zealand within the respondents' travel itineraries. Visits to other countries were also considered, particularly as there is a potential for product development that combines different countries in the form of air or accommodation passes.

It was anticipated that there would be obvious differences between experienced backpackers and first-time backpackers in terms of information sources and the extent of planning, and also that the former would pre-book fewer components prior to their arrival in Australia. It was also predicted that experienced backpackers would rely on recommendations by other backpackers and by local friends or relatives, rather than on guide-books or product brochures. Also those travellers who had visited Australia before were expected to take less time planning their trip prior to their arrival than did those who had not previously visited Australia.

Analysis and Discussion

To increase validity and replicability, the profile of the sample group must approximate to the known profile of the population. Murphy (1999) notes that the inbound backpacker was most likely to originate from the UK/Ireland, Germany or North America, to stay approximately 25 weeks, to be female rather than male, and to be on average 26 years old.

As indicated in Table 12.1, the current study approximates the profile of previous studies to a considerable degree (see Slaughter in Chapter 10), although respondents from UK/Ireland are over-represented (44.1%) and respondents from Germany were under-represented (4.3%). Classifying travellers from the UK/Ireland, United States, Canada and New Zealand as being from English-speaking backgrounds (ESB), and respondents from other countries as Non English-speaking backgrounds (NESB), 77 of the 139 respondents (55%) are native English speakers (43% in the case of the 1999 Murphy study). In view of the dominance of UK and Ireland

Table 12.1 Profile of respondents

	Present study	*Murphy study*
Origin		
UK/Ireland	44.0%	28.0%
North America	9.0%	15.0%
Germany	4.3%	15.0%
Netherlands	5.8%	
Japan	6.5%	
Gender		
Male	41.7%	47.4%
Female	58.3%	52.6%

respondents, it was not practical to make a meaningful analysis by individual country.

The gender balance was fairly consistent both with the Australian BTR statistics and with Murphy's (1999) study. A chi-squared goodness of fit test to the level of 95% confidence supported the fit of the data from the current study with the known gender profile of the population based on Murphy's study. Of the total respondents, 48% ($n = 67$) were in the 20–24 years age group, almost double the number in the second most frequent age bracket of 25–29 years (25%; $n = 35$), and 11.5% ($n = 16$) aged 30–34 years. The sample is broadly representative of the known profile of inbound backpackers in terms of age and gender. Since the present study was focused on Melbourne, the respondents' country of residence is not necessarily representative of those who visit Australia.

Information search

The questionnaire investigated the influence of information sources on the decision to purchase accommodation, day tours, air, coach and rail passes (i.e. multiple sectors), activities, and overnight or extended tours. Using a scale of 1 to 5 (where 1 is 'not influential' and 5 is 'very influential'), respondents were asked to assess information sources used to purchase various tourism products. Recommendation by other backpackers emerged as the most influential source of information, even in the case of air passes, where it may have been expected that guidebooks, hostel/travel agents and discount card programmes would play a significant role. In practice it is often cheaper for inbound visitors to purchase the domestic flight sectors as an adjunct to their international ticket prior to their arrival in Australia. These fares are usually obtainable only through travel agents.

Backpackers tend to rely on guidebooks to provide information about accommodation, while friends and relatives were noted as key influences in the actual choice of accommodation (47%), as well as day tours (40%) and activities (36%). In the case of day tours, such recommendations were (perhaps surprisingly) more influential than guidebooks (36%). Whether a traveller books a mainstream tour or a tour specifically tailored to backpackers depends considerably on whether the relevant information is made available to local friends and relatives. Local friends and relatives may be more familiar with booking mainstream brands. Also, some mainstream tours may be inconsistent with backpacker travel objectives, such as socialising with like-minded travellers, and such purchases could lead to consumer dissatisfaction.

The strong social, cultural and familial ties with Australia amongst UK and Irish backpackers may account for the strong influence of local friends and relatives on the purchase decision for activities (3.79 on a scale of 1 to 5 compared with NESB of 3.3). UK and Irish respondents also attach greater importance to recommendations by other backpackers (3.93) than travellers from non-English speaking countries (3.44). The latter may prefer to receive information in their native language.

Fellow travellers undoubtedly influence purchase decisions. It is noteworthy that 56% ($n = 78$) of respondents cited recommendations by other backpackers as being influential or very influential in their decision to purchase activity-based products such as adventure-based, nature-based, cultural, or other destination-based activities. The influence of other backpackers is consistent with Pearce's (1990) profile, which highlighted the role of informal itinerary planning and a desire to socialise with like-minded travellers. Guidebooks were cited as an influence by 42% of the respondents ($n = 59$). The importance of fellow backpackers in the decision-making process is a reminder of the importance of customer satisfaction and the associated positive word of mouth recommendations.

In the case of extended tours (those including at least one night's accommodation) backpacker recommendation was the major influence (42%: n =59), followed by product brochures (37%: $n = 51$). This suggests that backpackers undertake little preliminary research and that research proposition (3) was not confirmed. The type of information found in brochures and flyers typically includes itinerary, inclusions, cost and sometimes pictorial representation. Backpackers tend to seek value for money (see Pearce, 1990) and are diligent in comparing inclusions such as meals and accommodation. Product comparisons may be difficult since the entrance fees that are included in the overall price vary considerably between tours and companies.

Perhaps surprisingly, the influence of product-specific websites appears to be minimal, particularly amongst female respondents. Websites were the least influential source of information for all product types except for accommodation, where backpacker magazine advertisements rated even lower. Although online information is generally more up-to-date than guidebook-based information, the ease of consulting books appears to make them popular compared with paying for access time in an Internet café. However, given the rapid evolution of the latter method of distribution, it would be useful to conduct further research on emerging online products targeted at backpackers.

The method of information search was also examined on the basis of country of residence. Respondents from the UK and Ireland were more likely to use travel agents and hostel centres than others, who were more likely to be influenced by product brochures. Whether this can be related back to English language proficiency is another potential area for further investigation. NESB backpackers may be either more reliant on photographic depictions of the product, or may prefer to read the brochure at their leisure to establish if it suits their requirements, in preference to a discussion with an English speaker. The average number of information sources used by respondents ranged from 1 (in the case of rail passes) to 3 (accommodation), with a mean of 2.18 sources. More detailed information might assist operators in the allocation of their marketing and advertising budgets.

Travel experience

A positive relationship was predicted between first-time backpackers / first-time visitors to Australia and advanced purchase: research proposition (4). Consistent with Jarvis (1994) who noted that 60% of all arrivals into Australia make no prior land arrangements, the present study concluded that of the 46% of respondents who identified themselves as both first-time visitors to Australia and first-time backpackers, only half had pre-booked any components of their trip. As indicated in Table 12.2, half of the experienced backpackers had pre-booked a component of their trip despite an expectation that they would be confident enough to make all their arrangements when they arrived. An alternative explanation is that the more experienced travellers have learnt from previous experiences and are aware of alternative ways of travelling, such as pre-purchasing cheaper flight or rail passes overseas prior to their arrival in Australia. As expected, a substantial proportion of those with previous backpacking experience did not pre-book any components prior to their arrival into Australia. Surprisingly, about half of the first-time backpackers arrived in Australia without any pre-booking whatsoever.

Table 12.2 Pre-booked components by travel experience (number)

Travel Experience	*Components booked prior arrival into Australia*	*Have not pre-booked components prior arrival into Australia*
First-time visitor to Australia / first-time backpacker	29	30
First-time visitor to Australia / previous backpacking experience	16	28
Previously visited Australia / first-time backpacker	3	3

Do backpackers feel more comfortable travelling in Australia than other destinations, and does this vary according to travel experience or proficiency in the language of the host country? First-time backpackers booked more coach and rail passes and extended tours in advance than experienced backpackers did. These three product types were commonly booked at least seven days prior to their use, in some cases before the traveller departed from his or her country of origin. About a third of those purchasing air passes were experienced backpackers. It was expected that travellers who had previously backpacked would pre-purchase fewer components of their trip. This assumes that backpackers wish to behave as 'intrepid' travellers, and that it is only lack of confidence and experience that gets in the way. However it is possible that those experienced backpackers who did pre-purchase an air pass did so for the more prosaic reason of cost-minimisation rather than in the interest of pre-planning their itinerary. Almost half of air pass purchasers (11 out of 26) were planning to stay in Australia for three months or less. It is also possible that prior experience had made them aware of the difficulty of travelling around a country as large as Australia within such a limited time frame.

It was also anticipated that experienced backpackers would have a shorter lead-time than first-timers in planning their trip prior to their arrival in Australia. Whilst the differences were not significant (owing to the small sample size), Table 12.3 shows that experienced backpackers generally booked less than three months before departure, whereas first-timers booked between three and twelve months ahead. There are distinct differences between respondents from ESB and those from NESB. The chi-squared test indicated a strong relationship with first-time travellers (both native English speakers and those from NESBs) who had previously backpacked. This was indicated with a significant difference at

Table 12.3 Trip planning lead-time related to backpacking experience ($n = 125$)

Lead-time	*First timers* (*n = 64*)	*Experienced backpackers* (*n = 61*)
<1 month	13%	23%
1–3 months	19%	30%
3–6 months	27%	21%
6–12 months	25%	21%
1–2 years	11%	5%
2+ years	6%	0%

the 0.05 level ($X = 5.253$, df = 1, $p < 0.022$) though this may have been attributable to the small sample. A majority of ESB respondents were first-time backpackers, and a majority of NESB respondents were more experienced (i.e. repeat visitor) backpackers. Collectively, respondents were divided roughly equally between the experienced and the inexperienced. To determine the resources worth devoting to promotional material targeted at NESBs, further research is required relating to the specific sources of information that influence the decision making of speakers of different languages.

Age

As indicated in Table 12.4, younger visitors (defined as younger than 25) were more commonly first-time backpackers, whilst older visitors (30 years plus) had often visited Australia previously and this was confirmed using the chi-squared test. Whilst there are many first-time travellers to Australia, many end up having diverse travel experiences.

Table 12.4 Age by travel experience

Age group	First-time backpacker (number)		Total
	Yes	No	
Under 25	42	27	69
25–29	17	16	33
30 plus	6	20	26
Total	65	63	128

$X = 10.801$, df = 2, $p < 0.005$

Party size

The study aimed to investigate whether travel companions influence decisions about length of stay in Australia, and purchase patterns: research proposition (2). 'Travel companions' prompted 19% of the respondents to stay in Australia longer, although it is unclear who or what influenced their original decision to stay in Australia for a particular period. Two possible explanations are that their current companions did not wish to stay longer (or were not able to do so), or conversely, that the traveller would remain longer if they had a travel companion.

Almost two thirds (65%: $n = 91$) of respondents left their point of origin accompanied by at least one other person. The average travel party size increased from approximately 2.3 to 2.6 people after arrival in Australia. Respondents appear to have travelled with new companions over short periods within Australia, indicative of a changing party composition. Given the extended average length of stay for backpackers, the capacity to vary party size provides flexibility. Overall, solo travel was most common, followed by travel with one other person. The high incidence of two people travelling together could provide an opportunity for operators to provide 'two for one' offers during off-peak periods. Some significant differences were evident across the groups based upon party size from point of origin.

Gender

Gender had little influence on decision making. Female respondents were somewhat more influenced by 'organic' images (Gunn, 1988) derived from non-commercial sources than male travellers who place more reliance on information contained in guidebooks (which may be regarded as 'induced' since they are intended to 'attract' tourists). There was some evidence that male travellers were more likely to consult a website for information than females were. It remains to be determined whether travellers of either gender, with or without previous backpacking experience would be more reliant upon organic rather than induced (Gunn, 1988) sources of information.

Length of stay

Most respondents would prefer to travel within Australia for considerably longer than their current trip. An extended stay of six or more months (approximately 180 days) in Australia was favoured by 40% of respondents ($n = 55$). Of these respondents, 35 intended to stay for one year. This exceeds the average actual backpacker stay noted by the Bureau of Tourism Research (2000a) of 24.7 weeks (175 days). On average, respondents to that survey expressed a preference to travel around Australia for a period of 284 days, 63% more than the typical amount of time that they currently spend. This suggests that removal of travel impediments could increase backpacker expenditure and associated economic impact. However, as noted by the Joint Standing Committee on Migration (1997), the implications of amending the conditions attached to the Working Holidaymakers Programme extend beyond tourism into the immigration portfolio. The reasons for backpackers not staying longer in Australia are specified in Table 12.5 on the basis of country of origin.

The average stay of respondents from the UK/Ireland was 200 days, whilst the average stay of the other respondents was 128 days. Whilst financial constraints were cited as the key reason by both groups for not

Table 12.5 Barriers to an extended trip duration

Barrier	UK/Ireland	Other
Financial constraints	43	34
Work restrictions	20	21
Study restrictions	3	15
Work visa restrictions	30	17
Study visa restrictions	2	6
Travel companions	8	18
Total	61	78

extending their stay in Australia, some other major differences were evident. UK/Ireland respondents were less likely than others to cite study commitments. Like Australian backpackers, travellers from the UK and Ireland may be more likely than those from other countries to defer their study for a year in order to travel, and therefore may not need to cut short their ideal travel time.

Of the 61 respondents originating from the UK and Ireland, 30 were travelling on a working holiday (WHMS) visa, whilst only 11 of the other 78 respondents from other countries were doing so. The close ties between Australia and UK/Ireland, and the high level of awareness of the working holidaymaker visa programme within the two source countries may explain this difference. It may also explain the discrepancy between UK/Ireland residents and others wishing to extend their length of stay. The working holidaymaker visa programme currently allows visa holders to work for the same employer for up to 3 months within a maximum total length of stay in Australia of 12 months (Joint Standing Committee on Migration, 1997). The substantial number of UK/Ireland respondents citing work visa restrictions as preventing them from staying longer in Australia is notable.

The 'New Zealand factor'

Of all respondents, 54% ($n = 74$) were including New Zealand on their trip. Just over 35% of all respondents – or 68% of respondents visiting another country other than New Zealand during their current trip ($n = 48$) – had included Fiji and/or Thailand on their trip. This may provide an opportunity to develop further destination product combinations. The 'New Zealand factor' may develop into the 'South Pacific' or 'South East Asian' factors of the future. Given Australia's relative isolation from its regional neighbours (relative to the proximity of countries in Europe, for example), it may be difficult to be definitive about practical country pairings. There may however be potential for further multinational product development to incorporate Northern Australian cities such as Darwin and Cairns.

Visa category

As a result of the operator interest expressed, a question was included about visa category. Over half of the respondents (56%, $n = 78$) were travelling on a holiday visa, and 10% were on student visas. Unfortunately, the small number of respondents travelling on student visas did not allow for any meaningful analysis of purchase patterns. It is clear, however, that this segment constitutes a pool of potential travellers within Australia, particularly in view of the growth of overseas student numbers attending Australian tertiary institutions. This issue could form the basis of a study in its own right.

Of all respondents, 30% ($n = 41$) were on working holiday maker (WHMS) visas. According to the Joint Standing Committee on Migration (1997) backpackers constituted a significant number of the 40,000 WHMS visa holders who visited Australia in 1995/96. The committee also noted that 200,000 backpackers were reported as having visited Australia during the same period. In view of their visa status, many of the respondents to the present study are allowed to work during their visit. As discussed above, conditions of the WHMS visa may inhibit backpackers from extending their stay in Australia.

Given the continuing reliance on word of mouth recommendation, businesses focusing on the backpacker sector may need to attend to issues of product quality in their marketing. If backpackers have negative experiences, a high level of product awareness will not necessarily result in a high level of patronage, since dissatisfied customers tend to relate their experiences more widely than satisfied customers do. Personal recommendation by other backpackers and family or friends may be classed as 'organic' whereas other forms are 'induced' (Gunn, 1988). Backpackers may solicit travel agent and hostel recommendations, believing them to be organic. In reality, these recommendations may be prompted by potential commission earned through the sale of preferred products in a commercially-negotiated relationship, rather than by the interests of the traveller. Within the current study, travel agent / hostel recommendations influenced about one third of purchases of day tours and of extended tours. The findings indicate that the most influential sources of information are the traditional forms of promotion, such as brochures and guidebooks, as well as word of mouth recommendations by backpackers and local friends and relatives.

Conclusions and Recommendations for Further Research

This chapter has profiled inbound backpackers to Australia, how they gather information and what factors influence their decision making. Most backpackers seem to undertake their own research on Australian-based products and services prior to leaving their country of origin. Backpackers are price-conscious, but relative to recommendations by guidebooks or other backpackers, they attach little importance to discount programs during the decision-making process. Discounting may be a useful mechanism for stimulating demand during off-peak periods, but many backpackers appear to be looking for higher-quality experiences and may be willing to pay for them. Online information currently appears to be less influential than product brochures. This finding challenges the expectation that the Internet will rapidly replace the established distribution channels and is surprising in view of the prominence of backpacker and Internet cafés in backpacker precincts.

A number of opportunities for further research are evident. Future studies could be conducted during both the peak and off-peak periods with a view to investigating the extent to which the influence of word of mouth recommendations increases when there is a higher concentration of fellow travellers to provide advice. A better understanding of seasonality would also assist operators to target their promotional activities more effectively, while cross-cultural comparisons between ESB and NESB backpackers could be extended in future studies. The present chapter has also identified contrasts between the backpacking behaviour of UK/Irish travellers (with their more extended stays) and US backpackers (with their shorter-duration trips). Further research on backpacker travel by visa type (i.e. those on working holidays, or students) may also provide insights into travel patterns and into the decision-making processes of different traveller segments. Perhaps those who arrive on working visas create a different dynamic in backpacker clusters because of their longer average length of stay.

Looking at the research propositions at the beginning of the chapter, the research has shown that information search behaviour is influenced by age, but not necessarily by gender or by country of residence. The second proposition concerning information search on the basis of size of travel party and travel experience was not supported. Differences were evident between ESB and NESB respondents, while lead-times and types of information used differ across product categories. The high reliance placed on word of mouth recommendations, both by other backpackers and by local friends and relatives, is consistent with Pearce's earlier (1990) findings. As such, the desire to mix with like-minded travellers and the importance attached to flexibility of planning increases the reliance on such information sources. The wide range of businesses targeting backpackers would benefit from a more open dialogue with their customers with a view to understanding their needs and behaviours and ensuring that their products remain competitive, relevant and accessible.

Finally, a number of supply issues are worthy of further consideration. What is the scale and value of backpacker activity on mainstream tourist products and on backpacker-dedicated products? How is the backpacker 'sector' of the travel industry performing and developing, and which types of marketing activity have been most successful? Understanding some of these issues will help to provide insights into backpacking as a free independent activity and the extent to which it has an active involvement with the mainstream travel sector.

Chapter 13

Setting Out on the Road Less Travelled: A Study of Backpacker Travel in New Zealand

KEN NEWLANDS

Introduction

The 'backpacker' market segment is firmly established as a significant element of the international visitor market mix for New Zealand, nonetheless, a comprehensive review of the composition and behaviour of the backpacker market segment is somewhat overdue. In response to the consequent gap in the literature, this chapter examines the backpacker market from a New Zealand perspective.

The chapter takes a systemic approach to the study of backpacking as a social phenomenon, touching on different aspects of the tourism industry in New Zealand, but with a particular focus on the demographics and travel motivation of the backpacking visitor. Much of the chapter content is derived from the findings of a survey of visitors staying in backpacker establishments, which sought to address the underlying question, 'who are the backpackers and why do they backpack'?

The chapter opens with a background to the New Zealand tourism scene, and the role of backpacker travel in the development of tourism, before reviewing the relevant literature, with an emphasis on New Zealand-specific research. The objectives of the current project are identified, the methods used are described, and findings are reported against each of six original research objectives. The chapter closes with an analysis of the results obtained, and a series of recommendations for potentially useful future work.

Background

Prior to 1990, there were several reviews of what was until then known as 'youth tourism' (e.g. Adler, 1985; Cohen, 1982; Vogt, 1976), but these tended to focus on the seventeenth-century 'Grand Tours' and their counterpoint – the religious and labour-related travel of the lower classes. The first recorded academic use of the term 'backpacker' appears to have been in 1990 (Pearce, 1990) and, for reasons of clarity, this chapter adopts the five defining characteristics of backpacker travel suggested by Pearce, and later supported by others including Ryan and Mohsin (2001) and Slaughter (2001):

(1) preference for budget style accommodation;
(2) rejection of a rigid travel timetable, in favour of an independently organised and flexible itinerary;
(3) predominance of long vacations over short breaks;
(4) emphasis on the social aspect of travelling, i.e. developing an understanding of other cultures through the process of meeting people (both locals and fellow travellers);
(5) emphasis on informality and a desire for adventurous participation in a range of activities.

In Australia, a considerable amount of research has been carried out in relation to backpacker motivations and behaviours (e.g. Australian Tourist Commission, 1995; Buchanan & Rosetto, 1997; Commonwealth Department of Tourism, 1995; 1996; Haigh, 1995; Hancock, 1998; Hillman, 1999; Loker, 1993; Murphy, 1999; Pearce, 1990; Ross, 1992; 1993), perhaps because, as Slaughter (2001) suggests, the Australian Government has a tradition of active support for such research. However, this chapter's specific focus on backpacking in New Zealand means that the research must be set within the context of previous research on New Zealand. In this respect, there have been ten investigations over the past decade that are particularly worthy of acknowledgement.

One of the earliest studies, by Parr (1989), used an extensive 107-item questionnaire to examine the activities of 1565 travellers into Auckland and Christchurch airports, and found five distinct lifestyle segments based on demographic and holiday characteristics. Although some of Parr's questions are now included in New Zealand's International Visitor Survey, the project is otherwise ripe for replication 15 years on.

Ware (1992) undertook a study of 190 winter backpackers at 17 separate Youth Hostels Association (YHA) hostels and backpacker lodges throughout New Zealand. The survey approach was supplemented with interviews and focus groups of industry practitioners, including Department of Conservation staff, hostel managers and University staff. Ware's work complements Parr's summer research, by discovering the activities and accommodation preferred by winter backpackers, and brings an international (British) perspective to bear on situations faced by New Zealand.

Garnham's (1993) work addressed the distribution of backpacker establishments in relation to the (jump-on, jump-off) Kiwi Experience bus routes of the time. In a similar approach to that of the current research, Garnham presents the backpacking sector within a systemic model of tourism, and takes a political-economy perspective to explain the developing relationship between tourism operators, all of whom wish to maximise the yield from each backpacker in New Zealand.

The concept of backpacker impact on host communities has been an important one for New Zealand. First, Doorne (1994) studied the relationship of backpackers to two local communities, and argues that the process of integration of a developing tourism industry will influence industry–community relationships to the extent that the status and role of the host community in the development process will ultimately be diminished. Second, working within the prime tourism destination of Rotorua, Ateljevic and Doorne (2000) identified four broad areas for further discussion, including the link between entrepreneurship and the backpacker industry, and the need for further research into community attitudes.

From a demand perspective, Farrell (1999) examined the motivations of 60 international backpackers, administering a 29-item instrument to guests at five separate backpacker hostels. She concluded that the key motivators of backpackers significantly influence pre-travel decisions such as destination choice. Similarly, Toxward (1999) investigated backpacker expectations of (and satisfaction with) three areas within the service sector (accommodation, transport and tourism activities) in the Northland region. She found that service quality expectations were most often met and frequently exceeded, and that backpacker travellers were predominantly young, well-educated, and often travelling for an extended period of time.

From an industry perspective, Tourism New Zealand (1999) commissioned a qualitative study for the Backpacker Tourism Network based on in-depth interviews with 24 backpackers. This report recognised that backpackers are overwhelmingly positive about their time in New Zealand, and that their decision making is influenced by images of New Zealand, word of mouth recommendations, and by feedback from other travellers. Three barriers to travel to New Zealand were identified as cost, isolation and a lack of awareness. The study categorises backpackers into two demographic segments: young first-timers, away on a study break between secondary and tertiary study; and older backpackers (aged 25–35), usually single and tertiary-educated, with no dependants. The latter have often worked for a few years and have chosen a backpacking holiday as an extended break before settling down. They chose New Zealand because they perceived it as a relatively safe location, exotic, but with no requirement to cope with extreme cultural differences. New Zealand provides an opportunity to attain a sense of freedom and independence, have an inexpensive but adventurous time, meet new people, and experience the outdoors.

In support of the type of study discussed above, Moran (1999, 2000) successfully combined quantitative and qualitative social research methods such as questionnaires on coaches, participant observation, semi-structured interviews, analysis of passengers' photographs and post-tour questionnaires, to indicate patterns in backpacker profiles and tour preferences.

More recently, Ateljevic and Doorne (2001) have argued that backpackers do not constitute a simple and homogeneous market. In a study conducted over a two-year period, 106 in-depth interviews were conducted with visitors who were free independent travellers (FIT), alongside a series of backpacker focus groups and a participant observation programme. These methods allowed the authors to conclude that the backpacker market is significantly segmented, 'particularly with respect to consumer behaviour and the underlying cultural values which guide that behaviour' (Ateljevic & Doorne, 2001: 185).

There are also a number of other studies focusing on more specific issues such as service quality (e.g. Logan, 2000); these are often produced by students as outputs of research projects.

The contemporary backpacker market segment in New Zealand is substantial, generating an estimated 11% of all guest (bed) nights (Tourism New Zealand, 2000). In the year to August 2002, the country welcomed approximately 210,000 international backpacker visitors (Tourism New Zealand, 2002), and both the Commercial Accommodation Monitor (Statistics New Zealand, 2002) and the Tourism Leading Indicators Monitor (Tourism Research Council for New Zealand, 2002) continue to report a steady increase in backpacker accommodation guest nights. For example, accommodation guest nights increased 9.7% for the year ending August 2001 and a further 11.9% for the year ending August 2002 to reach 3,261,877 backpacker guest nights (Tourism Research Council, 2002). Backpackers also stay in a range of other types of accommodation, so their value to the New Zealand economy is often underestimated.

Backpackers tend to stay for long periods, and their total spend has been estimated at up to $NZ3533 per person (Tourism New Zealand, 2000). More recent figures are a little more conservative at $NZ3331, but even this is 8% more than the average international tourist (Tourism New Zealand, 2002). Based on these 2002 figures, the international backpacker market is worth $NZ701 million annually, clearly an important component of New Zealand's tourism earnings.

The 2002 summer season was an excellent one for the backpacker industry, extending well into April, and this has encouraged two of the larger operators in Auckland to plan significant expansions. Auckland Central Backpackers opened a 500-bed hostel in Queen Street (in the heart of Auckland's Central Business District); while the Youth Hostel Association plans to expand one of their city hostels by up to 400 extra beds (Gibson, 2001). In addition, the French multinational hotel chain Accor announced plans for a global backpacker brand 'Rocca', initially with three New Zealand hostels (Dominey, 2002). Accor subsequently changed the brand name to 'Base' and delayed opening in the main cities until 2003, but in the interim they took over an existing backpacker hostel in Rotorua (see also Richards and Wilson, Chapter 15). This picture presents a vision of an exciting and innovative industry sector in which to conduct research.

Objectives and Methodology

Six initial objectives were defined for the study:

(1) to analyse the profile of New Zealand's backpacker market;
(2) to establish the main motivations for backpacker travel;
(3) to examine the primary sources of information used whilst travelling;
(4) to establish the main motivations for specific destination choice;
(5) to identify the main destinations visited by backpacker travellers;
(6) to identify the main forms of transport and accommodation used.

Data were collected through administration of a self-completion survey, with questions adapted from the international ATLAS Backpacker Research Group questionnaire. In order to pre-test the instrument for use with respondents who were in mid-journey, a pilot survey was conducted in December 2001 with 13 volunteers staying at Auckland's major YHA hostel and at Auckland Central Backpackers, the city's largest backpacker establishment. Respondents made a number of useful suggestions, and some minor adjustments were made prior to field implementation.

For the present New Zealand study, a number of additional questions were included, as suggested by the local industry's Backpacker Marketing Group (BMG) and by academic colleagues. Inclusion of these local-market questions was instrumental in obtaining researcher access to BMG member establishments, and provided an important database of information specifically related to the New Zealand backpacker industry. Preliminary results of this 'domestic' section have been reported separately (Newlands, 2002).

The revised survey instrument was completed by a sample of guests staying at, or visiting, a wide cross-section of 18 large and small backpacker establishments in both Auckland and Christchurch – interviewing in two cities was considered to be particularly important, as not all backpackers visit every region (or even visit both of the two main islands) of New Zealand. The selection of establishments was stratified to mirror the composition of the four major marketing networks existing at the time: the non-profit and worldwide Youth Hostel Association (YHA), and three private sector networks – Budget Backpacker Hostels New Zealand (BBH), VIP Backpacker Resorts New Zealand (VIP), and Nomad.

Respondents were asked to complete the survey while the researcher was on the premises, but were also given the option of taking it away for completion and returning it to the hostel office at their leisure, or returning it by mail directly to the researcher. Of these two extra options, the former method proved to be most successful in terms of response rate, but the latter suited those who were about to leave. A total of 480 questionnaires were distributed, and 381 returned. After five incomplete questionnaires had been discarded, a total of 376 (a response rate of 78.3%) were analysed using SPSS statistical software.

The Research Findings

Backpacker demographics

Of the 376 respondents, 39% were male and 61% female. This is a surprising result, as previous backpacker research tends to indicate a more even gender balance (see Slaughter, Chapter 10). In fact, Garnham (1993) comments that the backpacker of the early 1990s was typically male.

However, this predominance of female respondents matches the findings of the global nomad survey already reported in Chapter 2. A director of the BBH network (M. Dumble, personal communication, May, 2002) also reported that a sample of 4344 travellers who completed a voluntary survey in February 2002 was split 53:47 in favour of women; while the Youth Hostel Association (G. Burrow, personal communication, May 2002) suggests that a 60/40 female dominance would be expected because 'females tend more to YHA because of security'. In the current research, the researcher consciously attempted to alternate requests between males and females, but it appears that more females chose to accept the invitation to complete the survey.

Over three quarters of the respondents ($n = 212$) were single. However, this finding should not necessarily be taken as a justification for the creation of more single dormitories, as many hostellers travel in small groups and prefer to share accommodation.

Table 13.1 shows that 91% of backpackers surveyed were aged under 35 years, a result that indicates a slight increase in older backpackers compared to the 99% under 35 reported by Doorne (1994). Although Doorne's sample size was small, there is some suggestion that an older generation of backpackers is becoming more common.

Though more than 100 individual occupations were recorded (including a number who were 'between jobs' or had 'no occupation at present'), a clustering into general categories revealed a substantial proportion of students, service sector employees and professional people. These clusters of employment categories may help to explain the two noticeable peaks in

Table 13.1 New Zealand backpacker survey basic demographic data

	Count	%	Age group	Count	%
Male	146	38.8	Up to 19	35	9.3
Female	230	61.2	20–24	155	41.2
			25–29	99	26.3
Single	212	77.1	30–34	53	14.1
Married	63	22.9	35–39	12	3.2
			40 and over	22	5.9
Occupation (n = 376)	*Count*	*%*	*Nationality (n = 376)*	*Count*	*%*
Student	106	28.2	UK Ireland	181	48.0
Service sector	93	24.7	Other Europe	92	24.5
Professional	93	24.7	North America	29	7.5
Manufacturing/production	29	7.7	Asia	29	7.5
None	39	10.4	Africa /Middle East	29	7.5
Other	16	4.3	South America	10	2.5
			Other	6	2.0
Education (n = 365)	*Count*	*%*	*Annual income ($US) (n = 253)*	*Count*	*%*
Primary/secondary	83	22.7	0–10,000	95	37.5
Tertiary cert, diploma	84	23.0	10–20,000	41	16.2
Undergraduate degree	144	39.5	20–30,000	27	10.7
Postgraduate degree	54	14.8	40–50,000	18	7.1
			50,001 +	72	28.5

income distribution, the first at $US30–40,000, and the second at $US50,000 or more.

Respondent nationalities were widely spread over more than 40 countries, although the majority of visitors were of European origin – in particular, the United Kingdom and Ireland provided nearly half of all respondents. Although the UK has always constituted a strong element in the backpacker market in New Zealand, the Tourism Research Council (2002) also reported a significant increase in UK visitors to New Zealand, although this might have been related to the concurrent tour of New Zealand by the English cricket team.

Other countries providing a significant number of arrivals were Israel (6.4%), Germany (5.9%), Canada (4.8%), Sweden (4.8%), and Japan (4.5%). Australia and the United States each recorded just 2.4% of respondents, which is significantly lower than expected – Australia, the United States, and Germany are historically important sources of backpacker visitors (Tourism New Zealand, 2002). One possible reason for the relative absence of Australians may be that they are more likely to have friends or relatives to stay with, or that they are repeat visitors who simply choose to bypass the gateway cities.

The respondents were exceptionally well qualified, with 54% of respondents holding at least a university degree and a further 23% with a tertiary-level qualification. This result mirrors earlier findings that back-packers are generally well educated (Toxward, 1999). There were also a number of students holidaying in New Zealand whilst studying in Australia. This finding indicates the existence of a potentially valuable market segment, as long as international student numbers continue to increase in Australia.

Travel motivations

Respondents were asked to respond to 18 possible motivations for their destination choice. Basic descriptive statistics for these questions are shown in Table 13.2.

A Kaiser-Meyer-Olkin test for data suitability was performed, the 0.803 result obtained suggested that the data were suitable for factor analysis, and a Principal Component Analysis was carried out using the conventional Varimax rotation. Instructed to retain any factor with an eigenvalue greater than 1.0, the process revealed a four-factor solution that explained 54.778% of total variation. Some 15 of the 18 criteria clearly loaded on to one of the four factors, whilst two criteria displayed ambiguous loading – criterion 13 ('explore other cultures') loaded 0.557 on factor 1 and 0.516 on factor 3, while criterion 15 ('to interact with local people') loaded 0.524 on

Table 13.2 Destination choice motivators: Basic descriptive statistics

Criterion	Mean score (1 = very important, 5 = of no importance)	Standard deviation
Explore other cultures	2.23	1.67
Interact with local people	2.61	1.51
Increase my knowledge	2.68	1.65
Relax mentally	2.83	1.78
Challenge my abilities	2.87	1.78
Have a good time with friends	2.89	1.89
Associate with other travellers	3.18	1.69
Build friendships with others	3.19	1.68
Avoid the hustle and bustle of daily life	3.34	1.93
Use my imagination	3.37	1.80
Find myself	3.60	2.21
Relax physically	3.62	1.95
Be in a calm atmosphere	3.63	1.83
Use my physical abilities/skills	3.70	1.78
Develop close friendships	3.71	1.79
Contribute something to the places I visit	4.21	1.85
Gain a feeling of belonging	4.39	2.01
Visit friends and relations	4.71	2.35

factor 3 and 0.506 on factor 1. Criterion 18 ('to find myself') did not significantly associate with any of the four factors, and has been discarded.

Analysis and interpretation of the four factors suggested that respondent motivations were not homogeneous, but could be categorised under four headings:

(1) physical–mental challenge;
(2) responsible sociability;
(3) fun times with friends;
(4) relaxation and reflection.

The items in the second column of Table 13.3 help to explain the attitudes that underlie each factor. For example, the items in factor 2 were 'gain a feeling of belonging', 'contribute something to the places I visit', 'visit friends and relations' and 'develop close friendships'; they all suggest a feeling of some sense of responsibility to the community, family, and old friends, allied to a parallel need to belong, to build friendships and to socialise. These attitudes are indicative of responsibility and sociability and thus the label 'responsible sociability' was given to this factor.

Table 13.3 Principal component analysis (PCA) for motivation to choose destination

Factor	Item	Factor loading
(1) **Physical-mental challenge**	Challenge my abilities	0.724
Eigenvalue 2.632 4.624% of variance	Use my imagination	0.719
	Increase my knowledge	0.688
	Use my physical abilities/skills	0.564
	Explore other cultures	0.557
(2) **Responsible sociability**	Gain a feeling of belonging	0.707
Eigenvalue 2.512 13.955% of variance	Contribute something to the places I visit	0.682
	Visit friends & relations	0.654
	Develop close friendships	0.605
(3) **Fun times with friends**	Associate with other travelers	0.722
Eigenvalue 2.363 13.130% of variance	Have a good time with friends	0.709
	Build friendships with others	0.642
	Interact with local people	0.524
(4) **Relaxation** and reflection	Relax mentally	0.803
Eigenvalue 2.352 13.069% of variance	Relax physically	0.709
	Be in a calm atmosphere	0.665
	Avoid the hustle and bustle of daily life	0.619
Summarised data	*Alpha coefficient (factors)*	*Alpha coefficient (total scale)*
Cumulative Eigenvalues	Factor (1) 0.700	
9.859	Factor (2) 0.669	0.821
Total Explained Variance	Factor (3) 0.711	
54.778%	Factor (4) 0.704	

Travel booking and information sources

Nearly 90% of respondents had pre-booked some aspect of their journey; 43% had booked transport only, and a further 7% booked both accommodation and transport, through a travel agent. Around 30% had used, or also used, a specialist travel agency, but only 13% had used the Internet for bookings. Around one third of respondents made their own travel arrangements directly with accommodation or transport suppliers.

Bookings for travel were made, on average, two months in advance ($n = 322$), although 10% booked more than five months ahead. However, for accommodation, a smaller number of respondents reported that they had booked ahead ($n = 105$) and, of these, 43% booked in the week prior to arrival. Only 10% booked their accommodation well ahead of time.

Perhaps of more interest to the travel industry is the range of sources the backpacker community uses to obtain information before departure. A wide variety of sources of information was used, including brochures, newspapers and magazines; but the principal source for nearly 75% of respondents was a guidebook – *Lonely Planet* was the most extensively cited. A cross-tabulation of the three most popular sources of information against self- description, age groupings, and gender reveals that before departure, females (80%) are more likely than males (67%) to use guide-books, and younger respondents under the age of 24 are more likely (65%) than older respondents (48%) to rely on family and friends for information. More than half the respondents turned to family and friends or to the Internet for information, and nearly a third obtained their information from travel agencies or experienced travellers. Information Centres (12.3%), staff at backpacker hostels (11.5%), and local people (10.7%) were used less often. A few backpackers were inspired by the *Discovery* TV channel, and other intrepid explorers just looked at the globe and 'went for it'. As one respondent wrote 'I hardly planned ... the nature of trip was that I never knew what was happening at all'.

Once the journey had started, the primary source of information was again guidebooks, which were used by 85% of respondents. *Lonely Planet* (60.6%) was the most frequently used publication, well ahead of *Moon Handbooks* and more than 20 other guidebooks (Table 13.4). Members of staff at backpacker lodges and hostels, visitor information centres, and experienced travellers were more important sources of information once respondents are on the road, and the Internet decreases in importance as an information source. This may be because of the lack of Internet facilities within accommodation establishments, or simply because the other sources are easier and cheaper to access.

Closer inspection of the data highlighted three significant differences in sources of information:

(1)   males (39%) were slightly more likely to use family and friends as a source of information than females (30%);
(2)   females (64%) were more likely to use the staff at backpacker accommodation and information centres than males (55%) as a source of information;
(3)   information centres were most commonly used by respondents aged 25–34 (67%) and less well patronised by younger and older age groups (55%).

When asked about their communications while travelling, respondents indicated that they regularly communicated with family (84%) and friends (80%), but only occasionally with the tourism industry (8%). Contact was also made with financial institutions and the employment sector. Younger respondents under 24 (88%) and female respondents in general (88%), were slightly more likely to communicate with family members than older respondents (77%) and male respondents in general (77%). Reported communications outcomes included 'peace of mind' contacts (52%),

Table 13.4   Sources of information used during the journey (n = 376, multiple response possible)

Sources of information used during the journey	Frequency	Percentage
Guide books*	318	84.6
Staff at backpackers / hostels	227	60.4
Information Centres	226	60.1
Experienced travellers	187	49.7
Local people	158	42.0
Family and friends	127	33.8
Internet	108	28.7
Tour operators brochure	86	22.9
Newspapers, magazines	72	19.1
Tourist board	71	18.9
Travel agency	55	14.6
Others	78	20.8
*of which *Lonely Planet* guidebook	228	60.6

seeking news of others (49%), and taking an opportunity to share experiences (17%). Travel industry-specific communications were less frequent, with respondents arranging bookings for future travel (13%) or accommodation (6%). Selected quotes on respondent's motivations for communicating include:

'Let them know that I am safe and enjoying my time.'

'Kept my business going by email and phone en route.'

'Get updates from home; tell people what I'd done on travels.'

'Give them some idea of my experiences, remind them I exist.'

'Job and flat search.'

At another level, some respondent comments were quite illuminating in terms of evaluating their own backpacking experience:

'Contact with home, conversations with people I really know (not just "how long are you in New Zealand" and "where are you from" ... it gets boring!)'

'Learn culture, got to know new friends.'

'Nearly all people I got to know a little bit better.'

E-mail was used by nearly all respondents, and rated as their most important means of communication.

Travel route selection

In an effort to determine what motivated backpackers to visit specific New Zealand destinations, the research sought to discover which of 15 separate activities had been experienced by respondents during their trip (Table 13.5).

The most highly-rated activities were those that involved natural attractions such as the beach or the bush. There was little recorded difference in response by gender, age and self-descriptions, though 'hanging out at the beach' was much more popular with respondents under 35. Similarly, cultural events and sporting or adrenaline-producing activities were less likely to be undertaken by those over 35, and night clubs were far more frequently patronised by the under 19s (89%) than the over 35s (35%). Males (79%) were more frequent nightclub patrons than females (67%), and were also more likely to attend sporting events (53% to 41%).

Approximately one third of all respondents claimed to have earned money while in New Zealand, although the over 35's were only half as

Table 13.5 Activities undertaken during the journey (*n* = 376, multiple responses possible)

Activity	Frequency	Percentage
Walking/hiking/trekking	354	94
Observing wildlife/nature	339	90
Hanging out on the beach	338	90
Sitting in cafes/restaurants	332	88
Visiting historical sites/monuments	321	85
Shopping	307	82
Visiting museums	304	81
Cultural events/performances	282	75
Nightclubs	270	72
Sporting activities/adrenaline activities	268	71
Attending sporting events	171	45
Earning money	128	34
Working as a volunteer	46	12
Participating in an academic study programme	28	7
Others	32	8

likely as their younger counterparts to have taken paid employment. This may reflect either the age restrictions that apply to New Zealand's working holiday visa regulations or the lesser need of older backpackers to work during their journey.

Previous backpacker travel experience

Somewhat surprisingly, respondents did not appear to be particularly experienced travellers. When presented with a list of destination regions across the world, and asked to indicate whether that region had been visited independently (as opposed to being an organised tour passenger), only Australasia/Pacific and, to a much lesser extent, Southern Europe were familiar destinations. The relative lack of travel experience shown in Table 13.6 suggests that Australasia may well enjoy a frequent 'first choice' status amongst long-haul backpacker destinations. The high score for Australasia may also reflect a practice of visiting Australia before arrival in New Zealand, a pattern that is already well established amongst more conventional market segments.

Table 13.6 Respondents' prior travel experience to regions of the world (number of respondents, n = 376)

Destination	1 visit	2–3 visits	3+ visits	Never visited	Never visited (%)
Australasia/Pacific	242	70	20	44	11.7
Southern Europe	63	42	94	177	47.1
Northern Europe	66	29	76	205	54.5
North America	82	44	30	220	58.5
South East Asia	105	28	14	229	60.9
Eastern Europe	47	33	17	279	74.2
Central America/Caribbean	41	12	4	319	84.8
Central/Southern Africa	40	8	6	322	85.6
China/Japan	36	8	5	327	87.0
North Africa	29	12	5	30	87.8
Middle East	22	9	10	335	89.1
Indian sub-continent	35	2	4	335	89.1
Central Asia	27	11	2	336	89.4
South America	27	8	4	337	89.6

For many respondents, length-of-stay statistics suggest that their trip to the region was intended to be a major, once-in a-lifetime experience – 95% of respondents had never been to either Australia or New Zealand before. Respondents reported a mean number of 2.44 trips in the last year. For 32% of respondents the 'main' trip (usually the one that encompassed New Zealand) occupied less than 90 days, for another 30% it occupied 91–180 days, while 33% stayed away all year and 5% travelled for longer than a year.

Although analysis of respondents' travel itineraries is not yet complete, there are some early signs that many backpackers will circumnavigate the world. Around 15% of respondents had visited one of the Pacific Islands (e.g. Fiji or the Cook Islands) on their outbound journey, and most of these visitors planned to continue on a round-the-world itinerary rather than to return home the way they came. However, many respondents admitted that their forward plans were a little fluid after their time in New Zealand.

Transport and accommodation

New Zealand is an island nation, and virtually all respondents travelled to and from the country by air, using the international airports of Auckland or Christchurch. Only one respondent planned to leave the country as crew on a yacht.

All of the respondents had used an aircraft at some stage of their journey; Qantas was the preferred carrier for approximately half of all respondents, Air New Zealand the choice of 28%, with less use of British Airways, Singapore Airlines, Thai International Airlines and Air Pacific. Coach or long-distance buses were used by 35% of respondents, water transport (ferries, boats or yachts) by 22%, and trains by 19%. Tram/metro/local bus, rental cars, walking, hitchhiking, overland truck, bicycles and campervans were used by fewer respondents, and a scattering of backpackers had used taxis, shared cars and ridden horses (or even camels) on their journey to their destination.

A wide variety of transport modes was used within New Zealand (Table 13.7). Coaches, and long-distance buses, were the most frequently used mode of transport (65%), which may be a reflection of the array of public transport and backpacker networks available in New Zealand. The high incidence of ferry use (48%) is explained by the need to travel across water between the two main islands.

Respondents used a variety of modes of accommodation, with back-packer lodges and independent hostels the most frequently cited, and the well-established Youth Hostel Association (YHA) attracting 38% of all survey respondents (Table 13.8). The next two most frequently used forms of accommodation were 'with family and friends, or 'tent/caravan' at a little under 20% each.

Table 13.7 Modes of transport used within New Zealand ($n = 376$, multiple responses possible)

Transport modes	Percentage
Coach, long distance bus	65.2
Ferry, boat, yacht	48.4
Tram, Metro, local bus	46.0
Walking	45.2
Train	40.2
Domestic air	39.9
Rental car	36.7
Own car, motorcycle, van, joined others in car	32.2
Hitch hiking	16.5
Bicycle	13.3
Campervan, motorhome, overland truck	13.3

Table 13.8 Predominant use of accommodation by gender, age and self-description

Accommodation mode	Total sample %		Total count	% of respondents using accommodation
	Male 38.8	Female 61.2		
Backpacker/independent	40.1	59.9	314	83.5
Youth Hostel Association (YHA)	35.2	64.8	142	37.8
Family and friends	38.7	61.3	75	19.9
Tent and caravan	43.7	56.3	71	18.9

Other forms of accommodation, reported by fewer than 10% of the respondents, were independent hotels, self-catering accommodation, guesthouses, campervans/motor homes and 'bed and breakfast' style private houses. The survey uncovered a few plucky individuals who sleep in their own vehicles or in huts, and some longer-term backpackers who used rental accommodation.

A cross-tabulation of the four principal accommodation types was undertaken against gender, age groupings and self-description, revealing a slight tendency for females to prefer YHA hostels, and males to use camping grounds and caravans. In terms of age, YHA has a slight over-representation of both younger and older hostellers, and tent users are over-represented in the 20–24 years age group (Table 13.9). Family and friends do not appear to be quite so attractive a proposition for the 25–29 years age group.

Table 13.9 Predominant use of accommodation by age ($n = 376$, multiple responses possible)

	Percentage usage by age category				
Age category	0–19	20–24	25–29	30–34	35+
Total sample	9.3	41.2	26.3	14.1	9.0
Accommodation mode					
Backpacker	10.2	40.4	27.1	14.3	8.0
YHA	13.4	33.8	23.9	17.65	11.3
Family and friends	12.0	42.7	14.7	14.7	11.3
Tent	8.5	46.5	26.8	7.0	8.0

Table 13.10 Predominant use of accommodation by age (*n* =376, multiple responses possible)

	Percentage accommodation use by self description			
Self description	*Backpacker*	*Traveller*	*Tourist*	*Other*
Total sample	53.1	41.6	4.0	1.3
Accommodation mode				
Backpacker	57.2	37.9	3.2	1.6
YHA	59.6	37.6	2.8	
Family and friends	47.9	47.9	4.1	
Tent	55.1	42.0		2.9

Backpacker establishments and YHAs both attract more 'backpackers', while family and friends attract more self-proclaimed 'travellers' than their sample size might suggest (Table 13.10).

Conclusions and recommendations

This chapter has produced a snapshot of backpacker tourism in two major New Zealand gateway cities, and the research has been contextualised with reference to earlier studies and recent secondary data.

The surveys confirmed the importance of the United Kingdom as a major backpacker market for New Zealand, and this is clearly related to the close cultural ties between the two countries. However, this may change as increasing numbers of international visitors are expected from Asia and particularly from China. One indication that the industry is already responding to new markets is to be found on the Auckland Central Backpackers website, which has links to Asian language translation sites. Future research could target a larger sample of these 'new Asian backpackers' to determine if their needs are being met. Such research should include the international students studying in Australia who were identified in this research.

The principle motivations for visiting New Zealand identified in this study included exploring other cultures and interacting with local people. This suggests that New Zealand should continue to develop and promote opportunities for travellers to meet 'real' New Zealanders and experience Maori culture. Backpacker establishments may find it advantageous to employ people from a cross section of New Zealand society to ensure that backpackers have every opportunity to mix with genuine New Zealanders. These members of staff need to be well trained in customer service, selling and destination knowledge to ensure enhanced interactions with back-packers. They need to have knowledge of the principal activities under-taken by backpackers, which this study highlighted – such as walking, hiking, trekking, and opportunities to observe wildlife or nature as well as simply hanging out on a beach. It appears that many activities are fairly unique (bungee jumping, caving, rafting), or are cheaper in New Zealand (scuba diving, sky diving).

The industry would be well advised to continue to develop innovative products to meet the needs of the increasingly diverse backpacker market because the market is not homogeneous. The identification of four backpacker segments in the survey provides opportunities for the develop-ment of niche products. For example, the YHA in New Zealand are recognising that among their 68 locations they need to provide a mix of city hostels but also provide for a niche market that seeks seclusion, peace, quiet and privacy with easy access to the bush and natural wonders. YHA report dramatic increases in September 2002 occupancy for locations meeting this market need (Coventry, 2002).

While guidebooks are frequently used for information (both prior to and during the journey) staff at backpackers' hostels and information centres and other people were all more frequently used on the journey than the Internet. This may explain the complaints received about insufficient Internet facilities at backpacker accommodation (Newlands, 2002). More importantly it shows the importance of personal contact with people as a source of information and guidance, which underlines the need to train the front line staff who deal with backpackers.

The trip to New Zealand appears to be 'a trip of a lifetime' and is typi-cally part of a trip of six months in duration, taking in an average of 3.65 countries including Australia – 5% of respondents had already been away for more than one year. Two issues arise from these findings. First in marketing terms, the positioning of New Zealand as the 'trip of a lifetime' poses a challenge to ensuring that backpackers do make return journeys to New Zealand. Second, although general biosecurity risks (e.g. transmis-sion of plant diseases) seem low in view of the low number of destinations visited by most backpackers prior to visiting New Zealand, some entrants, such as backpackers who have worked on farms in Australia (see Cooper, O'Mahony and Erfurt, Chapter 11) may be a particularly high-risk group.

In terms of transport choice, most backpackers use public transport, underlining the growth of backpacker transport networks described by Vance in the next chapter. Although there has been little change in the use of private vehicles or hitchhiking in 2002 compared with 1989, this may change in future if the current proposal to introduce taxes on consumption of fossil fuels in order to reduce green house gases is implemented. The relatively flexible travel itineraries of backpackers are highlighted by the short lead-time for accommodation booking. Only one third of respondents booked their accommodation ahead of time and, of these, 43% booked their accommodation less than one week ahead. This provides an opportunity for last-minute marketing at departure points or on transport links such as airport buses.

In overall conclusion then, the research presented here generally supports the backpacker definition proposed by Pearce (1990). Backpackers in New Zealand generally make extensive use of budget accommodation, are visiting the country for a long period of time, and have flexible travel itineraries. However, it is clear that the New Zealand backpacker market is not homogeneous, as respondents vary considerably in terms of their motivations, activities and travelstyles. These variations present opportunities for the suppliers of backpacker services to develop targeted niche products in future.

Acknowledgements

I have learnt a great deal personally through working with the ATLAS BRG. I would also like to acknowledge the support of colleagues including Ken Simpson, Charles Johnston, Peter Wiltshier, Peter Carswell, Greg Richards and Julie Wilson, the 18 backpacker establishments and their 376 guests. My thanks to Marie Stuart, Julie Puia and Cathy Mahoney for data entry assistance (and especially to Cathy for understanding, 'I'll just be a few more hours').

Chapter 14

Backpacker Transport Choice: A Conceptual Framework Applied to New Zealand

PAUL VANCE

Introduction

In spite of the growing interest in backpacking or independent travel as an academic research area, backpackers' choice of transport modes has scarcely been considered in the literature. This chapter goes some way to addressing this gap by constructing a conceptual framework for analysing transport choice and applying this framework in New Zealand. This is a complex issue, because as Dellaert et al., (1998) point out, the selection of travel methods does not involve simple, independent choices. Rather, many transport decisions interrelate with the use of other tourism services, such as accommodation and activities. Indeed, the complexity of transport choice might help to explain the dearth of research on this particular issue in backpacker travel.

The chapter begins with a review of relevant literature and then presents a conceptual framework of backpacker transport choice derived from previous research findings. It concludes with the preliminary findings of a study that applies the conceptual framework to backpackers in New Zealand.

Research Aim and Rationale

This chapter focuses on the first stages of a wider piece of research, the aim of which is to 'develop a comprehensive understanding of the factors that influence backpacker transport choice'. The first step in the research was to perform a literature review.

The transport choices of independent travellers are a significant issue in the tourism market as a whole. For example, Mintel (2000) estimated that independent travel as a whole in the UK market alone was worth £8.3 billion. Backpackers seem to be a growing segment of this overall market, and very few tourism sectors hold such promise of economic development (see Hampton, 1998; Schevyens, 2002) or the opportunity for developing small, more sustainable business networks. In spite of this apparent potential, however, academic research on backpacker transport networks has been scarce, and little attention has been paid to backpacker-style transport operators and transport method choices. Specifically, little consideration appears to have been given to the decision-making process and underlying causal factors.

There is a clear need for research that examines the issue of transport method choice, particularly in those markets that are serviced by a range of operators offering a range of products and services. This is underlined by commentary from Ryan and Mohsin (2001: 89) who suggest that: 'future research on backpackers may need to consider more carefully the nature of the location and the nature of the backpacker networks it is sustaining'. Such research would allow more effective marketing of products and services and it could inform the development of new, targeted transport services.

Literature Review

This section considers a number of key areas within the literature. Among these are various considerations of what constitutes a backpacker, and literature concerning backpacker transport operators.

As previous chapters in the current volume have indicated, exactly who or what constitutes a backpacker is open to much debate, and the relationship between the terms 'backpacker', 'independent traveller' or 'fully independent traveller' may be just as complex. For example, Pearce (1990) considers backpackers to be predominantly young travellers on an extended holiday. They are said to have a preference for budget accommodation, with a flexible and informal travel itinerary and place an emphasis on meeting people and participating in a range of activities. On the other hand, Sorenson (1999) utilises a more general definition: 'they are self-organised, multiple destination pleasure tourists who ascribe much importance to the spatial and organisational matters of their mode of tourism'.

Alternatively, there is a motivation-based focus to the backpacker definitions proposed by many authors. One of the most extensive and all-inclusive is the seven categories model identified by Loker-Murphy and Pearce (1995). Others, such as those discussed by Ateljevic and Doorne (2000) consider the travellers' need for new and unexplored areas, or the need to play with identity. Elsrud (2001) continues this thread, with discussion of a need for risk-taking (real or perceived) during long-term travel. More specifically, Sorenson (1999) considers that the key parameter for defining who or what a backpacker is should be the backpacker's own perception of his or her travelling and tourism activities.

Adopting a definition of backpackers for the current study was therefore problematic. The definition proposed by Pearce (1990) is probably the most useful, in that it captures elements of the accommodation, travel and informal nature of backpacking. Also, the issues of risk-taking and self-perception are crucial to this study, as these arguably influence the choice of transport method. The Pearce definition is therefore utilised within the conceptual framework developed in this chapter.

Whilst there is a great deal of literature on transport in tourism and specifically on transport method choice, particularly with regard to urban transport (see Bradley, 1988; Fowkes & Wardman, 1988), the field of backpacker transport has been neglected. Significantly, little consideration is given to the question of *why* backpackers choose the method or methods of transport they use and the importance of each. Consideration of transport use also features sparsely within the literature on backpackers or independent travel. Whilst this is hardly surprising, given that backpacker-orientated transport operators are relative newcomers to the market, the absence of discussion of the *general* transport use by backpackers is remarkable. Hampton (1998) notes that the transport needs of backpackers are often considered minimalist – but transport operators have recognised backpackers as a valuable revenue source, and are beginning to operate in many backpacker 'destinations'.

One of the few studies that specifically considers backpacker transport operators is that of Ateljevic and Doorne (2000), who discuss the growth of transport operators in New Zealand. Ateljevic and Doorne focus on some of the development drivers of backpacker transport operators – such as the demand for flexibility and independence in travel, with a degree of organisation. Subsequent developments such as flexible ticketing are also highlighted. They note that the transport networks play a role in developing the tourism sector, but that the reverse relationship could also be possible. Much of their commentary on the situation in New Zealand is equally valid for other emerging backpacker tourism destinations. For example, Ireland, Scotland and South Africa have a number of backpacker-oriented transport operators offering jump-on, jump-off services with operating characteristics similar to those in New Zealand and Australia (see Speed and Harrison in Chapter 9).

Moran (1999) examines the experiences of travellers on structured backpacker tours in New Zealand. The material is wide ranging, but lacks depth of analysis, examining a narrow range of tours with a limited survey sample and adopting a loose definition of a 'backpacker tour'. It focuses largely on the environment and how this impacts on the tourist experience, and does not directly examine why people have chosen a particular tour.

In his commentary on backpacker tourism in South-East Asia, Hampton (1998) considers (albeit briefly) backpacker-oriented transport operators. Whilst none of these services presently displays a level of development seen in other destinations, they appear to offer services targeted towards the backpacker market. Tourism New Zealand (2000) has also considered backpacker transport operators, discussing the range of options available for organised backpacker travel in New Zealand, but significantly also highlighting the high proportion of travellers who use other methods such as domestic buses and hitchhiking.

A range of other literature also informs the conceptual framework illustrated in Figure 14.1, including the work by Moran (2000) on structured

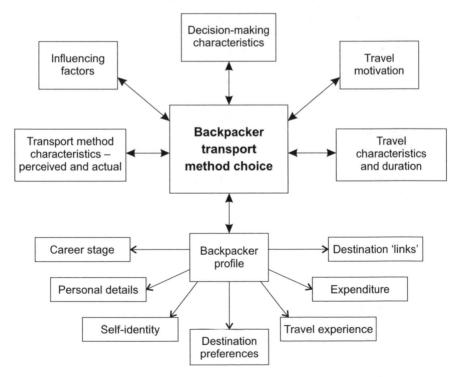

Figure 14.1 Conceptual framework of backpacker transport choice

backpacker tours in New Zealand, Tickell (2001) on traveller identity, and Uriely *et al.* (2002) on backpacking experiences. The following section describes the different elements used to construct the conceptual framework.

Conceptual Framework

The conceptual framework (Figure 14.1) derived from the literature encompasses two basic sets of factors that can influence transport choice. The framework links the characteristics of the individual backpacker (such as travel experience, demographic background and preferences) to factors likely to influence or limit the choice of specific transport modes (such as the characteristics of the backpackers' journey and their destination).

Backpacker profile

Integral to the understanding of backpacker transport choices is an understanding of the travellers themselves. In keeping with the primarily qualitative nature of the study, the aim of building a profile of respondents was to develop a brief 'pen-picture' to aid understanding of individual transport choice. Data were collected in a number of areas:

Career stage

Traditionally, backpacker travel has been an experience that people engage in before starting a career. Anecdotal evidence from the fieldwork suggests that this is changing, with a growing number of people taking a career break or leaving jobs to travel. The career stage of the traveller (and of course related to this, their age and life experience) is likely to impact upon travel methods utilised.

Self-identity

The issue of identity has been discussed by a number of authors in the current volume, although few links have been made to its impact on transport choice. Desforges (2000) considers that the initial decision to travel can result from a questioning and exploration of self-identity. Related to this, Sirgy and Su (2000) consider that the match between destination image and the traveller's self concept and social image is what influences destination choice. Evidence from dialogue with backpackers in 'popular' destinations suggests that this is particularly the case with backpacking experiences. Murphy (2001)'s work on the social interaction of backpackers states that meeting people is second only to economic imperatives in transport method choice. All of these highlight the fact that self-identity and the social aspects of backpacking are important to the transport method choice.

Destination links

Anecdotal evidence from conversations with backpackers suggests that if they have family connections within a destination, these can influence the choice of transport method. Relatives may provide information or lend means of transport.

Expenditure

Murphy (2001) highlighted the role of economic factors in transport choice, suggesting that the level of expenditure on travel plays a primary role in guiding purchase decisions for travel products and/or services.

Prior travel experience

Previous studies suggest that travel experience, both within the destination and in other destinations, influences the choice of transport method and the decision-making process – particularly the role and level of planning undertaken. For example, McCabe (2000) suggests that the decision process is a result of previous experiences, and this idea is supported by Elsrud (2001), who suggests that using a pre-booked ticket in a destination is a sign of inexperience.

Destination preferences

Destination image plays a role in this area. Other factors, such as the activities available in the destination, the possibility of meeting local people or, conversely, of avoiding other travellers, have also been high-lighted as key motivators in destination and transport method choice.

Socio-demographic profile

Data concerning the nationality, citizenship and life experience of the independent traveller (i.e. factors that impact upon the choice of transport mode) are considered an important area. Schevyens (2002) argues that the demographic profile of backpackers is changing (for example, the rising numbers of career-break travellers affects the average age of backpackers worldwide), while Newlands (in Chapter 13 of this volume) also suggests that backpackers visiting New Zealand are increasingly older.

Although the characteristics of the individual backpacker may influence his or her choice of transport method, that choice is in turn determined or limited by a range of factors related to the destination and the choice process itself.

Market and destination characteristics

The characteristics of the destination and the independent travel market within that destination play a role in determining transport method choice. Characteristics of the destination include the ease of access to transport services, the cost of those services and the array of transport services available. The geography of the destination, the distribution of population and business activities and the services offered to independent travellers, will also vary widely. For example, Shipway (2000) reports that international backpackers visiting Britain criticised its fragmented transport system, which is largely the legacy of the privatisation of rail and bus services.

The nature and context of the independent travel market within the destination also plays an important role in determining transport choice. Anecdotal evidence (such as the popularity of those destinations with a more developed infrastructure) suggests that, the more developed the independent travel market is, the more travellers it attracts, often through perceptions of 'ease of travel' that then create a demand for more transport services. It can be observed that this ultimately leads towards a conventional tourism orientation, which may subsequently be rejected by travellers oriented towards a more independent travelstyle (see Atlejevic & Doorne, 2000).

Particularly for first-time visitors to a destination and for the 'less-experienced' traveller, the marketing and image of the destination in the tourism-generating countries may influence transport choices. The tourism literature suggests that the image of the destination is all-important in destination choice. Using New Zealand as an example, Tourism New Zealand (1999) considers that the decision to travel to that destination is influenced by images of the country, word of mouth and feedback. So the conceptual framework includes the images of the destination prior to travel, as well as the information sources used by backpackers.

Transport method characteristics

The independent traveller has many options for travel in some of the popular international destinations. In destinations such as Victoria, Australia, these include domestic networks, specialist backpacker transport networks, and a variety of tours. These transport methods vary in terms of facilities on board, the frequency of 'stops', on-journey activities and the profile of fellow travellers.

Perhaps more important than some of the physical or service characteristics is the traveller's own perception of the transport method and operator. Anecdotal evidence gained from dialogue with backpackers in destinations such as Australia and New Zealand suggests that some operators have reputations as 'party buses', whilst others are considered as 'boring' (and so attract different types of customers). This is important in the context of this study for, as Murphy (2001) notes, social interaction is an integral part of backpacking.

It is important to note that each travel experience may be different (even if the service, vehicle and driver are the same), as the group dynamics in the individual situation can impact upon the experience. Whilst it is recognised that this is an important part of this section of the conceptual framework and of the study as a whole, assessing or quantifying the impact of this is very problematic. Certain 'clues' to the differing group dynamics can be drawn out during the data analysis – but even these are open to interpretation. This remains an unresolved issue in the study.

Travel motivation

There is a large body of research on travel motivations in general, but motivations for independent travel are less well known. Several themes emerge from the literature on motivation. First of these is the 'need to escape', either from a career job or from mundane, everyday life experiences. The second of the themes is the requirement by travellers to gain life experience or to have new and novel experiences. The last major theme is the desire to visit and to see new destinations, led partly by the experience hunger described by Richards and Wilson in Chapter 1.

The motivation for travel obviously impacts on the length of the trip, which in turn influences the transport choice made – be it the 'party' oriented transport, domestic transport networks, or vehicle hire or purchase. Similarly, motivation to travel appears to be closely linked with other aspects of the conceptual framework, such as expenditure, age, career stage of the traveller and particularly the destination chosen.

Travel characteristics and duration

Backpacker studies have observed many variations in travel mode, ranging from structured backpacker tours to fully independent travel that attracts a range of customer profiles. There is little conformity to a specific model of a backpacker transport product, although there are many common characteristics.

The duration of the trip (both in total and within New Zealand) is important within the context of this study. In a destination such as New Zealand with multiple transport operators and multiple transport options, the time available both for travel and for spending within the country visited influences the transport method chosen. With the option of visiting many attractions during travel, more time can be spent reaching a destination – although this depends on the travel product being considered.

Decision-making characteristics

Decision making is a complex area, and so the conceptual framework examines only those particular aspects that are considered central to this study. Particularly important is the location of the decision making – whether the traveller decides on the method of transport in his or her home country, or on arrival in the destination. Linked to this is the influence on transport choice of promotions, special offers or discounts. Decision making may also be influenced by previous travel and there are links between the transport methods used in previous trips and the method(s) used on the current trip.

In summary, the range of factors that potentially exert an influence on transport choice illustrates the complexity of the processes at work. It is not possible to validate such a complex conceptual framework with a single empirical study, as this would require a series of observations across different traveller types and destinations. The following application of the conceptual framework is therefore an initial attempt to examine some of the elements of the framework in one specific destination.

Empirical Research

This section of the chapter explores the empirical application of the conceptual framework to the backpacker transport market segment in New Zealand.

The fieldwork was carried out in New Zealand for a number of reasons. The backpacker or independent travel market within New Zealand arguably makes it one of the most developed backpacker destinations. Whilst New Zealand is not one of the original independent travel destinations, the market displays a level of maturity. This is particularly evident when the transport networks used by and available to backpackers are examined. Indeed Kiwi Experience (one of New Zealand's backpacker operators) appears to be one of the first jump-on, jump-off backpacker transport operators.

New Zealand is also a relatively small country, but it has a wide variety of attractions and activities that support the backpacker market and transport networks. This simplifies the process of transport choice to a certain extent, allowing observations to be made of the relationships between different variables in the framework.

The respondents

The sampling method chosen was quota sampling, based on the nationality of the interviewee. Such a sample is simple to implement, as data on international arrivals to New Zealand are readily available.[1] More specifically, anecdotal evidence gained in many 'backpacking' visits to destinations suggests that different nationalities have different expected 'norms' of travel behaviour (see Cohen, Chapter 3; Maoz, Chapter 7).

Table 14.1 Proposed sampling frame for interviews

Origin country/region	No. of interviews
United Kingdom	21
Japan	16
European	12
China, Hong Kong and Taiwan	11
Total	60

The proposed sampling frame (Table 14.1) was developed using visitor origin statistics gained from Tourism New Zealand (1999; 2000) for the twelve months prior to September 2001.[2] In some cases a pragmatic approach was used in consolidating the originating countries to enable the sampling frame to be implemented. The consolidation process also excluded from the sample frame those with American and Canadian nationality, as experience suggests that this market segment in backpacking is very small and may be have been over-represented in the sample of backpackers. For example Newlands (Chapter 13) recorded only 7.5% of his respondents from North America.

During the fieldwork, language difficulties made it difficult to get visitors from Japan, China, Hong Kong and Taiwan to agree to be interviewed, and the actual distribution of nationalities subsequently differed from that intended (see Table 14.2). There is a dominance of United

Table 14.2 Actual sample of interviewees

Nationality	Count	%
United Kingdom	28	45.2
Canada	5	8.1
Holland	4	6.5
Japan	2	3.2
Germany	5	8.1
Israel	3	4.8
United States	4	6.5
Ireland	3	4.8
Switzerland	2	3.2
Other nationality	6	9.7
Total	62	100.0

Kingdom nationals, although the actual number interviewed is not far out of line with the anticipated sample. The distribution also matches the profile of respondents for the much larger survey conducted by Newlands in New Zealand (see Chapter 13). A further restriction placed on the sample was that, in order to gain a broader cross section within the sample, when a couple (or group of friends) were travelling together, only one member of the group was interviewed.

The interviews took place in eight backpacker hostels, located both in the North and South Islands of New Zealand. The hostels had a range of affiliations – with some being members of the Budget Backpacker Hostel (BBH) organisation, some being Youth Hostel Association (YHA) hostels or YHA associate members, and one hostel being affiliated to both.

Research Findings

Travel behaviour

Multiple travel methods

The research revealed that many respondents used a number of transport methods for travelling in New Zealand. Out of 62 respondents, 9 stated that they used two methods equally for travelling within the country. A significant number of respondents also stated that they had used a bus, train or some other mode of transport occasionally,[3] but when questioned did not classify this as a 'primary' mode of transport. It appears that the decision to use a second mode of transport is a matter of circumstance. When questioned about other issues that affect the method of transport chosen, a small number of respondents highlighted cost. This emerged as a secondary or underlying factor in the decision-making process – but not a significant issue. This may be due to the comparatively low cost of transport within New Zealand.

Low levels of exposure to marketing material

Even though Tourism New Zealand recognises the importance of the backpacker market to the tourism industry, there appears to be little marketing activity directed towards this segment. Of the 62 respondents questioned, 25 could not identify any marketing material seen or used before they came to New Zealand. It was also interesting to note that only one respondent could recall exposure to specific transport-related marketing material, in this case a Kiwi Experience brochure distributed at the time of buying an air ticket. The influence of direct marketing from the tourism industry therefore seems to be small. In contrast, television, travel documentaries and films[4] appear to play a large part in marketing New

Zealand as a destination for backpackers, with 16 out of 62 respondents identifying these items as 'marketing material' they had seen. The impact of this material on the unconscious decision-making process remains to be explored. It is also interesting to note that Moran (1999) confirms this impact of film and the media on the choice of a travel destination. Contrary to findings by Tourism New Zealand (2000), word of mouth did not play a significant part in marketing New Zealand to the respondents.

Low levels of pre-arrival purchasing

In view of the lack of marketing impact, it was perhaps not surprising that the research found little evidence of the purchase of travel tickets prior to arrival in New Zealand. Only four respondents stated they had purchased a non-air travel ticket prior to arrival in New Zealand. Of these, only one had actually purchased a backpacker-operator transport pass for New Zealand prior to arrival (a Kiwi Experience ticket). There also seems to be little evidence that the purchase of tickets is influenced by specific offers or discounts.

Factors affecting transport choice

Previous travel experience

Previous travel experience was loosely defined as a trip in excess of three weeks out of the home country and not taken as part of a 'package' tour product.[5] The respondents had a significant amount of previous travel experience, with 41 of the 62 respondents stating that they had travelled before. This contrasts strongly with the perception of New Zealand as 'an easy place to travel' and one that is particularly attractive to first-time travellers.

There was a relationship between previous travel experience and the method of transport chosen for the visit to New Zealand (see Table 14.3). Of the 23 primarily using national domestic bus networks, 17 had travelled

Table 14.3 Transport use and travel experience (number of respondents)

| | *Have you been travelling before?* | | |
Transport method used	*Yes*	*No*	*Total*
Jump-on, jump-off backpacker transport services	8	6	14
Domestic buses or coaches	17	6	23
Hire cars	4	3	7
Car that you purchased	9	5	14
Hitchhiking	3	1	4
Total	41	21	62

previously, whilst only 8 of the 14 using backpacker-type transport services had travelled before. Of the 4 hitchhikers, 3 had travelled previously. The use of domestic transport networks is more prevalent among those who have travelled before.

Travel characteristics and duration

The data collected indicate a number of trends in transport usage. The first concerns the use of domestic transport services, with 30% of those using domestic transport services staying in New Zealand for just one month, and 48% staying for longer than three months. Purchasing a vehicle proved to be most popular with those visiting in excess of four months, whilst hiring a car proved to be popular with those visiting New Zealand for two months. Organised backpacker transport services tended to be most popular with those visiting New Zealand for less than two months (43% of those using backpacker type services).

As a result of the relatively short stay for those utilising domestic transport services, their total expenditure was relatively low: 77% of respondents spent 1000–2000 euros in New Zealand). Those spending in excess of 3000 euros were most likely to buy or hire a car in New Zealand (66% of respondents). Hitchhikers also appeared to be in the high spending category – although this may be due to extended stays. It appears that the length of stay of the respondent has a major impact on choice of transport method.

Travel motivation

Most common among the stated reasons for travel were the desires to 'meet new people', to 'try something different' and to 'travel first and see what I want to do'. The feelings of 'I don't know what I want to be in life' also featured in six cases and the desire to 'put off a job' featured strongly in six others. Numerous other reasons were also cited, including a desire to 'see the world', to 'experience other cultures' and 'always wanting to travel'. However, there was no direct relationship between the motivation for travel and the transport method used.

Destination links

The impact on transport use of family links to the destination is complex. Many of the respondents professed to have family or close friends who are resident in New Zealand. However, it was interesting to note that many of the respondents had not made contact with their relatives or, if they had made contact, could not identify any impact of the family on their transport choice. Only in one case had the relatives assisted in travel arrangements – in this case, the purchase of a vehicle.

Conclusions

The application of the conceptual framework to backpackers in New Zealand indicates that the complexity of transport choice processes suggested in the conceptual framework is reflected even in a relatively small destination with a well-developed backpacker transport network.

Some of the relationships proposed in the conceptual framework could be examined through the fieldwork. One indication is that experienced travellers are less likely to make use of tailor-made backpacker transport services. This could be a problem for suppliers of such services in future if the supply of first-time visitors begins to decline. There may be a need to develop more flexible transport options in order to meet the needs of more demanding repeat visitors. On the other hand, there was little indication that travel motivation affected transport choice. The duration of the trip seemed much more influential, as those staying longer tended to use private vehicles and did not make use of either specific backpacker transport or public transport options. In addition, the research indicated that marketing activity by transport providers had little impact outside the destination itself, which indicates a problem for suppliers in communicating with backpackers before they arrive in New Zealand. On the other hand, the use of multiple transport methods by respondents in this study also indicates a great deal of potential for collaborative arrangements between transport providers.

This chapter has made a contribution to understanding the influences on transport choice in backpacking – an area that has been the focus of little attention to date. Although this work is at an early stage, the application of the framework to the New Zealand market (albeit with a fairly modest sample) has provided a basis for future development and empirical application of the conceptual framework.

Notes

1. The data available are not sub-classified for backpackers or independent travellers.
2. The fieldwork was carried out in March/April 2002, so year end September 2001 were the latest data available for use at the time.
3. Two examples of this were where respondents used a public bus to depart from the backpacker transport network routing and where they had hitchhiked when short of money.
4. This was particularly evident with the release of the first *Lord of the Rings* film, stated by some respondents as a major influence. Travel documentary programmes such as the Discovery Channel/ National Geographic also play a large part in marketing New Zealand as a destination.
5. The definition of a 'package tour' used when questioning respondents was deliberately flexible.

Part 4

Conclusions

Chapter 15

Widening Perspectives in Backpacker Research

GREG RICHARDS AND JULIE WILSON

The study of backpacking is becoming increasingly important because of the symbolic role that the backpacker has assumed in more general debates about tourism and youth culture. In *The Tourist*, MacCannell (1976) argued that the tourist had become a symbol of modernity. By worshipping the differentiations of modernity through visiting tourist attractions, the tourist re-affirms the structures of modern society. If the tourist is (or was) the model for modern social life, the backpacker now seems to have become the model for the tourist. The contributors to this volume show the extent to which meaning is created through discourse between the back-packer, the traveller and the tourist. Backpackers in particular become the major affirmation of the modernity of tourism, not only through their attempts to escape the modernisation of backpacker consumption, but also through their failure to do so. These failed escape attempts underline the gap between the ideology and practice of backpacking, identified by Erik Cohen in Chapter 3. This gap is also reproduced in the structure of this volume and the composition of the ATLAS Backpacker Research Group. If academics have been relatively slow to catch up with the growth of the backpacker phenomenon, however, it is clear that the backpacking 'scene' or market has attracted a lot of attention from tourism destinations and individual entrepreneurs. The backpacker 'industry' is particularly inter-ested in finding out more about the motivations and behaviour of young travellers, and policy makers seem most concerned with the economic contribution that backpacking can make to destinations. Most of the issues presented in this volume can therefore be viewed from many different perspectives. Is backpacking an important ideology of a travel subculture, or is it an expanding market niche to be tapped by tourist destinations? Or as Cohen asks in Chapter 3, are backpackers the vanguard of post-tourism, or the rearguard of modern tourism?

This concluding chapter considers these and other important questions arising from our attempts to review the field of backpacker research. It discusses a number of dimensions that feature in the contributions to this volume, the debates within the ATLAS Backpacker Research Group and previous studies of backpacking and independent travel. As the chapters in this volume have underlined the role of the backpacker as a collector of experiences, the nature of the backpacker experience is the first topic of discussion. Subsequent sections deal with specific aspects of the back-packing experience. Given the role of backpackers as 'time rich' travellers, the temporal dimension of backpacking is considered, including issues of identity. The spatial framing of experience in the creation of specific backpacker spaces or 'enclaves' is the subject of the next section. The final area of discussion considers the question of the impact of backpacking, not only in terms of the impact that backpackers have on the areas they visit, but also the impact of travel on the backpackers themselves. The chapter concludes with a review of potential areas for future research.

The Experience of Backpacking

One of the important areas of discussion in terms of the driving forces behind the rise of backpacking revolves around the issue of the social–psychological function that it fulfils. The development of conventional tourism has often been traced to the onset of modernity and increasing alienation from the material values of Western society. Because the original drifter was conceived of as a lone outsider (Cohen, 1973), alienation was also often assumed to be a major driving force for backpacking. People travelled to seek out experiences and values that they felt to be missing in their own (modern) society. This idea links with Turner's (1973) idea of a *rite de passage*, as Cohen discusses in Chapter 3. Just as Turner sees the *rite de passage* as involving a reversal of the everyday, many commentators hold that tourists essentially seek out difference or even a different reality through travel (e.g. Lengkeek, 1996; Urry, 1990). In practice, however, many tourism experiences tend to be extensions of what people do in their everyday lives (e.g. Richards, 2001; Thrane, 2000). The ideology of consuming difference has to be maintained in order to justify travel, but the practice of travel is often a 'home plus' experience.

As the number of backpackers has increased and the range of facilities available in backpacker enclaves has grown, it has been increasingly diffi-cult to assert that backpacking is driven by alienation, and that backpacker travel necessarily involves reversal. One might argue that for many modern backpackers the experience has become more akin to an extension of their everyday lives. As we have seen in this volume, the backpacker 'scene' is increasingly characterised by the extension of customised services, familiar comforts and contact with home. Travelling to 'find oneself' did not feature strongly as a motivation for travel among those backpackers we surveyed (see Chapter 2). As Cohen notes in Chapter 3, neither alienation nor *rite de passage* can offer completely satisfactory models of the backpacking experience.

Modern backpacking therefore seems to involve elements of both extension and reversal. Extension is provided by contacts with Western culture and facilities during travel, particularly through a high level of contact with fellow travellers. Reversal is provided for many not so much by deep cultural experiences, ritualistic behaviour and culture shock but by a physical shift in location and a distancing from restrictions encountered at home. The ability to take on new identities is a good example of this (see Ateljevic and Doorne, Chapter 4). The identities that travellers assume are not usually identities drawn from the cultures they visit, but are more likely to be derived from the global backpacker culture or from their home culture. In this sense, there is no reversal of identity, rather a hybridisation of identities that combine elements of different cultures at will.

Backpacking as suspension

Perhaps many modern backpackers are not so much engaged in either reversal or a strict extension of everyday life, but rather in a suspension of it. This suspension can be both temporal and spatial. The norms and values of the home region are temporarily suspended during the trip. However, at any time the backpacker can opt in again, simply by reaching for an American Express card (see Binder, Chapter 6). The trip may therefore involve multiple periods of suspension, as periods of roughing it are interspersed with periods of hotel beds, air conditioning and other 'home comforts'. In spatial terms the Western backpacker may be suspended between two cultures in a backpacker enclave that combines elements of the 'West' and the 'Other' in digestible doses and is, as Noy (forthcoming) suggests, neither 'here' nor 'there'. Backpackers cannot be 'here' because the 'real' experience is outside the enclave, but they are also not 'there', because they are surrounded by the familiarity of the enclave.

Just as particles may be suspended in a solution, backpackers are effectively floating in an environment in which identities, relationships and communities are more fluid. During a prolonged stay in a backpacker enclave or traveller centre, different strata of travellers may settle out of solution and become more clearly visible. The hardened travellers don native garb and ditch their watches to distinguish themselves from the red-faced new arrivals. These distinctions are not formed by adopting elements of a totally alien culture, but rather through adopting hybrid cultural codes, such as wearing Thai language Coca Cola T-shirts, donning the backpacker 'hippy uniform' or eating banana pancakes (see Binder, Chapter 6; Welk, Chapter 5).

Of course, at any time the state of suspension may be ended, as the traveller gets fed up of a diet of banana pancakes and videos. There may be a desire for change, for new experiences, but does this always lead to a *rite de passage*, as suggested by Turner (1987)? Perhaps for some groups the journey as an initiation into the world is still important. For example, Bell (2002) argues that for young people in New Zealand the overseas experience (or big 'OE') is still a vital part of the maturation process. The relative isolation of New Zealand does make it more likely that such trips will still be viewed as a 'once in a lifetime experience'. Similarly Maoz (Chapter 7) shows that many Israelis become independent of the army and their families through their travel, but such *rites de passage* are unlikely to be experienced by all backpackers. The respondents to the global nomad survey generally have a high level of travel experience, and seem to view long-distance travel as a relatively normal part of everyday life. As Newlands shows in Chapter 13, many backpackers keep up regular email contact with home, and even carry on business activities and hunt for jobs and flats via the Internet.

The ideas of reversal and the *rite de passage* suppose a profound change in state for the traveller. As Cohen points out in Chapter 3, most backpackers do not undergo the kind of 'communitas' suggested by Turner, nor are they really separated from home as much as they used to be. The reversal is therefore not complete, but seems to represent an extension of youth culture in the home society. The evidence gained from the global nomad research also suggests that a more subtle shift occurs for most people. Backpackers may engage in behaviour that challenges the norms of their home environment (such as taking drugs or hanging around 'doing nothing'), but at the same time they conform not so much to the norms of the host culture they are visiting, but to those of the backpacker subculture in which they are suspended.

The concept of suspension therefore poses a dialectic relationship between extension and reversal. Backpackers may seek a reversal of the norms and values of the home environment, but they are prevented from fully entering into the host culture by the confines of the 'Lonely Planet Bubble' (Giesbers, 2002). Most backpackers express a desire for reversal, as 'exploring other cultures' is their main motivation for travel, but the practice of backpacking is bound largely by the cultural norms of life at home. The gap between the ideology and the practice of backpacking noted by several authors in this volume may help to explain one of the apparent contradictions in theoretical studies of tourist behaviour and motivation. As Cohen suggests in Chapter 3, while individual backpackers want to 'do their own thing', they all end up doing much the same, because what they actually seem to want is 'hedonistic enjoyment, experimentation and self-fulfilment under relatively simple (and affordable) circumstances'. The other reality is desired, and even sought, but the traveller remains firmly suspended between desire and fulfilment. As Speed and Harrison indicate in Chapter 9, the expressed desire of backpackers to meet local people is not fulfilled (even in the absence of a significant language barrier, as in the case of most visitors to Scotland), but the desired encounters with locals are replaced by contacts with other travellers. Even though back-packers may be meeting people from their own home culture, the need for difference is satisfied by the 'neither here nor there' suspension of the enclave or life on the backpacker trail.

Time

Time spent on the road may well be one of the most important defining characteristics of backpacking. As one respondent remarked in the Khao San Road in Bangkok, 'I do not consider myself to be a backpacker because I am on the road for only short lengths of time'.

Almost all definitions of backpacking concentrate on the fact that back-packers are money-poor, budget travellers. The global nomad survey and various chapters in Part 3 of this volume indicate that the daily budget of most backpackers is relatively low. However, relatively little attention has been paid to the logical corollary of this – a low daily expenditure also enables them to be relatively 'time-rich' travellers (Richards, 1999). Various chapters in the current volume indicate some of the consequences of this. For example, in Chapter 5 Welk shows how travelling as long as possible is one of the defining elements of backpacking. Travelling for a long time allows more experiences to be crammed in to the trip, and more material to be gathered for good travel stories. Travel journalist Mary Fitzgerald (2000) argues that bona fide travellers don't believe in time, and feign to have forgotten when they started travelling, even when the reality is rather different:

> ... Disdain is reserved for those who don't know any better and tell everyone that they are 'on holiday' for two weeks or admit that they have to leave to go back to university. To be accepted as a 'real' traveller, you must lug your rucksack around for at least three months; anything less and you're just a tourist. (Fitzgerald, 2000: online source)

Time is important in backpacking, not just in terms of quantity, but also quality. The attraction of many travel destinations is that they have a different sense of time from the home culture of the tourists. As J.B. Priestley once remarked, 'a good holiday is one spent among people whose notions of time are vaguer than yours' (Anon., 1994: 90). 'Conventional' tourists have little chance to enjoy this source of difference, caught as they are in the iron cage of the holiday schedule. Backpackers, on the other hand, can attempt to integrate themselves into a different time culture. Catching the local bus, spending time bargaining for the cheapest room, or hanging around Bangkok waiting for a visa can all be experienced as a new perspective on time.

Because backpackers are time-rich individuals, they can also engage in time-intensive activities that they may not be able to indulge in at home – such as 'doing nothing'. The time-richness of the destination allows them to adjust their expectations to suit the time culture they are in. It is no problem to the backpacker to arrive a day late, particularly if this generates a usable story of travel hardship, but for the package tourist this is a disaster and grounds for compensation. For the tourist, delay is a loss of experience; for the backpacker, it is an integral part of the experience.

The time-richness of backpacking can easily be observed in backpacker enclaves. In the Khao San Road, much of the day appears to be spent hanging around in the cafés; reading, writing journals, watching pirate Western DVD movies in the bars. Killing time may become a necessary investment in extending the trip and gaining another backpacker 'badge of honour' (Welk, Chapter 5). The shift to another time culture may also be a way of establishing your identity as a seasoned traveller. Discarding one's watch seems to be a statement of discarding the Western values that attach so strongly to a linear sense of time. It is a statement of wealth – being in possession of so much time that individual seconds, minutes, hours or even days are no longer of any consequence. For some travellers there may even be a reaction against the experience-seeking behaviour that characterises most backpackers. 'Doing nothing' becomes a statement of freedom from the necessity of experience (been there, seen that, done it), but it may also be a means of extending the trip experientially: 'The more your days resemble each other, the less you notice time's passage' (Marlowe, 1999: 229).

Risk

One of the things that may mark out backpacking as a different time is the degree of risk experienced or perceived. Goffman (1971) argues that risk and adventure are no longer a part of everyday life, so risk increasingly has to be sought in travel. As one backpacker service provider in Sydney remarked: 'I feel backpackers are doing the things they want to do. Their adventures and experiences make them who they are; often for the better where there is a risk involved'. Thrill-seeking and risk taking indeed seem to have become an integral part of backpacking (Cater, 2002; Cloke & Perkins, 1998, 2002; Elsrud, 2001), as growing numbers of backpackers head for less developed destinations or take up more dangerous activities in established destinations. This presents the suppliers of backpacker products with the problem of organising risk, or 'safe danger' (Graeme Warring, 2002, personal communication). This is what Cohen refers to in Chapter 3 as part of the 'staged authenticity' of backpacking. Real danger of course has to be avoided, as the death of a backpacker will tend to dissuade others, but unless there is a perception of risk, the experience will not be interesting enough. The explosion of risky activities has, however, created its own problems for backpacker businesses. The biggest problem is dealing with compensation claims from injured clients or on behalf of dead ones. In North America the development of adventure sports has been curtailed by the high propensity for legal action in the case of accidents. In New Zealand this is less of a concern for the operators, because individuals cannot sue for any injuries. Instead, residents and visitors are covered by the Accident Compensation Corporation, which takes care of medical costs and loss of earnings resulting from tourism-related and other accidents. Indirect government support, which is not specifically aimed at tourism, has therefore helped to underwrite the development of the backpacker industry in New Zealand.

But not only is the backpacker industry engaged in manufacturing risk; the backpackers themselves work at building elements of risk into their travel. In Chapter 6, Binder shows how backpackers will save money on accommodation in order to go diving. The dive itself becomes an unforgettable experience to be recounted later, while the cheap cock-roach-infested hostel room may itself generate risks that can be recycled into stories. This idea links closely with Cederholm's (1999) qualitative study of Swedish backpackers, which revealed that 'planned unexpected-ness' was an important aspect of their experience. Essentially, backpackers may try to 'have their cake and eat it – the back of beyond with frequent connecting flights – and finding themselves disappointed when this proves difficult' (Wilderness.com, 2003).

A perception of increased risk or the availability of 'thrills' can also influence destination choice. In the global nomad survey, for example, backpackers visiting New Zealand agreed more strongly than other travellers that they were motivated by a search for excitement. Some backpackers also see destinations that can be perceived of as more dangerous as being more attractive for 'hardcore' backpackers (Graeme Warring, 2002, personal communication). However, danger is perhaps more attractive if it is perceived rather than actual. Warring argues that experiences in Australia do not have to be that far off the beaten track to be successful. The Australian backpacker industry uses the trappings of adventure and 'hardcore' travel (such as four-wheel drive vehicles) to suggest danger or difficulty even when in fact little exists. The development of 'safe danger' and 'planned unexpectedness' may also have influenced the travel careers of backpackers, as noted by Richards and Wilson in Chapter 2. Australia and New Zealand may be visited early on in a backpacker career as a rehearsal for more adventurous destinations, such as Latin America, where the danger is perceived to be more 'real' or 'hardcore'.

Space

Covering as much space as possible seems to be an aim of many backpackers, but backpacking also has important spatial consequences in the destinations visited. The number of backpacker enclaves is growing, and the range of specific backpacker services provided is expanding rapidly, as Vance illustrates in Chapter 14.

The existence of a relaxed, tolerant and socially permissive atmosphere is a sought-after touristic commodity among backpackers worldwide (Westerhausen & MacBeth, 2003). This is arguably one of the major reasons for the development of backpacker 'enclaves' in different parts of the world. The concentration of backpacker-related services and the congregation of predominantly young people with time on their hands looking for fun give these places an atmosphere of their own. Because the enclaves tend to become areas in which traveller norms become mixed with the values of the host culture, these enclaves are demarcated not just spatially but also socially and psychologically.

Different types of enclaves have developed, depending largely on their surroundings. As Erik Cohen shows in Chapter 3, urban enclaves such as the Khao San Road in Bangkok or King's Cross in Sydney differ widely from their rural counterparts such as Ubud in Bali or Koh Phangan in Thailand. There is evidence that rural enclaves may be sought out as being more 'authentic', whereas urban enclaves are more likely to be service centres or transit points. Timmermans (2002), for example, found that backpackers view Ubud as an unspoilt, authentic enclave, whereas in reality it has long been part of the mainstream Balinese tourist industry.

The demarcation of enclaves may serve to turn such areas into contested spaces. For example in urban areas, local residents often complain about the disorder and disruption caused by partying youth. To others, however, this may in itself be attractive. The Khao San Road, for example, has increasingly seen local Thai young people beginning to occupy the leisure spaces previously inhabited only by Western tourists. Newspaper reports (Rojanaphruk, 2001: 4A) indicate that some backpackers are even moving out of Khao San, at least partly because 'they don't like people looking at them'; on the other hand, young locals assert, 'it's our right to be here. We're Thais' .

Others argue that the impact of backpacker tourism is much greater in idyllic rural enclaves:

> While cities such as Bangkok and Kathmandu can absorb these ghettos, smaller places can have their characters irreversibly changed by pandering to travellers' demands for Western food, bars, and other home comforts. The *Lonely Planet* guidebook series helps promote, however unwittingly, this rash of traveller-oriented centres. (Fitzgerald, 2000: online source)

The indications are that the backpacker experience in such enclaves is increasingly similar to that of the 'tourist bubble' (Judd, 1999) in that very few travellers encounter local people in non-commercial settings (Fitzgerald, 2000). The very process of differentiation may itself become a repellent for some travellers. The development of well-established enclaves has followed a pattern of increasing sophistication of backpacker services. One can compare the modern backpacker enclave to the 'homogenous spaces' of tourist performance identified by Edensor (2001). As the range and quality of services has grown, so the 'hard line' backpackers have also sought to avoid the 'touristification' of the enclaves, and have gone to find new destinations elsewhere. This in turn leads to the development of new enclaves as their fellow travellers attempt to imitate the escape act performed by their role models.

The enclaves created by backpackers take on a central function in the maintenance of backpacker (sub)culture. The enclave is the quintessential 'refuelling station' where road-weary travellers can take a hot shower, buy an imported beer, use the Internet and watch the latest movies. Most importantly, however, they are also places to meet fellow travellers. These encounters have become crucial to the maintenance of the (sub)culture, because as the global nomad surveys show, the most important source of information 'on the road' is fellow backpackers. This information is not just factual – the stories and urban myths of the backpacker subculture are reproduced and exchanged in the enclave. From the point of view of the individual backpacker, the enclave is also the place where status can be established through storytelling. It is no good telling stories about out-of-the-way-places to those encountered in peripheral locations – they share the same experience. You really need to return to the enclave (i.e. the core) to find those who can relate to your tales and will be impressed by them – those who have not yet ventured to the edge themselves. In Chapter 6 Binder emphasises not only the need to return to the enclave to be able to communicate your stories to other backpackers but also the need to return home to make them sound more impressive and exotic to those who haven't had similar travelling experiences.

Backpackers not only colonise enclaves, they also carve out their own routes and produce their own events. There are well-established back-packer trails that follow the availability of work (Cooper *et al.*, Chapter 11) or the staging of major events, such as the Oktoberfest, Glastonbury Festival and the running of the bulls in Pamplona (Andy Lyon, 2002, personal communication; Welk, Chapter 5). Specific events, such as the Full Moon parties in Thailand, are also created by the very presence of back-packers.

These observations indicate that most backpackers behave very differently today from the 'drifters' described by Cohen (1973) as alienated individuals travelling to remote areas alone. In Chapter 3, Cohen suggests referring to such travellers as the 'original drifters', to distinguish them from modern backpackers, who may pursue the ideology of drifting but end up following the crowd. In Chapter 11, Cooper, Erfurt and O'Mahony also raise the question whether backpackers can really be considered 'nomads', given the extent to which the backpacker trail has now become a 'circuit'. But in fact, one could argue that this is precisely why the backpacker is a model for the global nomad. Classic nomadic travel is cyclical, following well-trodden routes in search of fresh pastures. The backpacker, as a modern global nomad, follows the enclave circuit in search of fresh experi-ences. Another link between traditional and global nomads lies in their development of a verbal culture. Stories become for the backpacker not only a source of identity, but also their 'map of the desert'.

Identity

One of the classic notions about backpacking is that people travel 'to find themselves'. Although the respondents to the global nomad survey did not identify very strongly with this sentiment, the question of identity is a recurring theme in backpacker research and in many of the chapters in the current volume. The social construction of backpacking study (Chapter 2) illustrates that the identity of the backpacker or traveller or tourist is far from simple. Some people identify very strongly with the backpacker label, while others may recognise themselves as 'backpackers' but still not be totally happy with their membership of the 'culture'.

Studies of backpacking have often used the subculture metaphor: defining the group as individuals who reject the 'mainstream'. Welk argues in Chapter 5 that the rejection of the label 'tourist' in particular is what seems to unite many backpackers. They are clear on the object of their disdain (tourists travel in groups, tourists stay in hotels, etc.) even though they are less clear about what a 'backpacker' is. However, the social construction research presented in Chapter Two suggests an even more complex relationship between backpackers, travellers and tourists, where not only do individuals adopt multiple identities (backpacker, traveller *and* tourist, for example) but can also reject members of their own group. For example, one 'backpacker' in Sydney said, 'I hate backpackers who trash places and don't respect the local culture. We should always respect our hosts and the environment'.

Whatever the basis on which backpackers define themselves as a group, it is clear that the rituals and symbols associated with backpacker culture are becoming more complex as the culture of 'scene' develops (Wilson & Richards, Chapter 8). Ateljevic and Doorne have argued in Chapter 4 that the backpacker community is characterised by the emergence of hybrid identities, with the freedom offered by backpacker travel being used as a means of assuming new identities or playing with existing ones. In Chapter 6, Binder also underlines the fact that through backpacking, you can 'become a different person'. Part of the process of becoming different is the adoption of various elements of the material culture of backpacking, such as the backpack itself, 'hippy' clothes or destination markers that show where you have been travelling.

> As in any other tribe, there is a subtle hierarchy, born of fierce snobbery headed by those who believe themselves to be hardcore 'real' travellers and filtering down to the 'cut-them-and-they-bleed-tourist-blood' minions. (Fitzgerald, 2000)

Fitzgerald argues that, although the differences between backpackers and travellers are often difficult to ascertain, there are some definite demarcation points. These include appearance, choice of luggage (including reading matter), concepts of money, and ways of spending time. For example, a large backpack offers people the opportunity of showing their strength by carrying bigger packs than their companions (although this can also be construed as a sign of inexperience and lack of skill, i.e. the inability to travel light). The widespread practice of displaying symbols of nationality on the backpack can also be a source of shifting identity. It is sometimes practical to adopt a new national symbol when travelling through areas hostile to your home country. Some Americans take on a more neutral Canadian flag of convenience, to 'separate the "genuine" travellers from the pretenders', which is one of the most popular conversation/bragging topics'. Interestingly, however, the backpack itself is hardly ever considered as a defining characteristic of backpackers in the tourism literature (Timmermans, 2002), as was noted in Chapter 2.

Gender issues

The chapters in the present volume indicate that women are becoming an increasingly important part of the backpacker community, and may well constitute the majority in some areas. This highlights even more strongly the relative lack of consideration for gender issues in backpacking research.

The social construction study (Chapter 2) shows that women's experiences of backpacking are clearly different. One female respondent commented: 'being female and travelling makes it difficult to be as much of the community in some countries as there are countries where women are portrayed and treated as animals'. Perhaps because of the additional restrictions often placed on their movement and behaviour, women see backpacking differently. Compared with their male counterparts, females consider backpacking to be less sexy, less thrilling, less drug-related and less of a lonely pursuit than their male counterparts do. The global nomad surveys show that women are significantly more likely than men to be travelling in order to develop friendships with others and to end up developing close friendships. These views are in stark contrast to the macho image of backpacking as a cheap, rough, individualistic and potentially dangerous form of travel. Perhaps the reality is that most of the people writing about backpacking (particularly in novels) tend to be men. It will be interesting to see how perceptions change as more women start analysing the backpacking scene (e.g. Cederholm, 1999; Elsrud, 2001).

Unfortunately, recent events show that backpacking is not always a 'safe' form of danger, particularly for women. In April 2002, for example, *The Guardian* newspaper in the UK featured articles (Thompson, 2002; Zinn & Hall, 2002) on two female backpackers who had been murdered, one on the rural fruit picking route in Australia described by Cooper, O'Mahony and Erfurt in Chapter 11, and the other in a backpacker hostel in the Khao San Road in Bangkok. The parents of the second victim were reported as saying, 'she was very eager to go travelling and didn't think twice about going alone'. But reports of these and other deaths of female tourists (inevitably referred to as 'backpackers' in the media) may well limit the number of females willing to travel alone. The supposed freedom of backpacker travel is probably more curtailed for women by the need to preserve personal safety. The global nomad survey indicates that women are significantly less likely than men to have visited South America, which is regarded by many as more 'hardcore' backpacking territory because of the perceived dangers and hardships of travelling there, as well as the increased language barriers.

The need for personal safety may also cause women to travel in groups more frequently than men do. These data were not gathered in the global nomad survey, but a series of observations in Bangkok indicated that that men were more likely to be travelling alone than women.

Impacts

The growth of backpacking has undoubtedly had an impact, not just on the places that backpackers visit, but also on the nature of backpacking itself. The backpacker literature is sprinkled with nostalgia for the decline of 'real' backpacking. There is often a feeling that backpacker travel is 'not what it used to be' or has been spoilt by the onslaught of conventional tourism. For example, Westerhausen (2002) argues that travellers today are forced to abandon many backpacker paradises in order to keep one step ahead of the onslaught of 'conventional mass tourism'. For him, former backpacker preserves such as Koh Samui have now become lost paradises for the backpacker community.

For other commentators this lament rings a bit hollow:

> Today's travellers are the love children of bored boho eighteenth-century aristos such as Byron, Shelley *et al.*, who slummed around on their Grand Tour of Europe, and the tie-dyed hippies of the twentieth century who did the overland Morocco-to-India odyssey in search of the finest stimulants and their own personal guru. Their offsprings' experience differs in that it often appears that it was so much better 10, 20, 30 years ago when there were parts of the world relatively untouched by the greedy hand of tourism, whereas now it seems, despite the travelers' protests otherwise, there is little difference between their experience and that of the Fodor's-toting, air-con-insisting, luxury-coach-traveling 'tourists' whom they despise. (Fitzgerald, 2000)

The idea that backpacking is now little different from conventional tourism (at least in practice) has many echoes in the current volume. In fact, one could argue that some backpackers, far from fleeing the onslaught of conventional tourism are actively helping to reproduce it. Ateljevic and Doorne (2000) illustrate how former backpackers in New Zealand have become lifestyle entrepreneurs in adventure tourism or backpacking, enabling them to extend the travelling lifestyle even when they have stopped travelling.

The backpacker 'industry' now exists as an organised phenomenon in a number of countries. As suppliers of travel, accommodation and activities begin to work together to provide a comprehensive service, backpacking may also become more packaged than the package tour. In countries such as Australia and New Zealand the backpacker travel industry is becoming a force to be reckoned with. For example Backpackers World has a number of branches in Sydney, Melbourne and other Australian cities offering a one-stop shop for all backpacker needs: an employment agency, a travel agency, an accommodation-finding service, boards with job adverts, vehicles for sale, expatriate food items, a lecture room for briefings, employment orientation schemes, and assistance with visas and work permits. Staff will collect backpackers from the airport, give them an orientation briefing, provide details of the job they have arranged for them, and drop them at their accommodation.

As well as providing more packaged services, the backpacker industry exhibits an increasing clustering of backpacker businesses in many enclaves. The availability of a wide range of individual suppliers in close proximity probably appeals more to some backpackers than integrated businesses do, since it allows them to assemble their own package of travel services. There is also a tendency for new clusters to form in the wake of successful individual enterprises. In the Khao San Road area of Bangkok, for example, there was only one Internet café in late 1997, but this had grown to 16 outlets by April 1998 and had reached 100 by August 1999 (Jaturapattarakij, 1999). The King's Cross area in Sydney had only three backpacker hostels in 1987, and now there are dozens. The Coogee and Glebe backpacker areas of the city also began with single hostels and grew rapidly. This seems to fit well with a pattern of some backpackers deliberately seeking out new areas away from existing enclaves, until they are joined by fellow backpackers, when the process begins again.

The success of backpacker businesses has not gone unnoticed by major conglomerates either. Accor hotels, for example, are developing the 'first globally branded backpacker network', starting with the Base Backpackers brand of hostels in Australia and New Zealand (Travel Scene International, 2003, online source). The brand is being led by Graeme Warring, who has 15 years' experience in building other backpacker 'brands', including Backpackers World, Backpacker Headquarters network, VIP Backpacker Resorts International, Oz Experience and Kiwi Experience. Warring said:

The launch of Base will completely transform the face of backpacking by offering, for the first time, a reliable international name on the scene that guarantees a consistent standard of accommodation. We are not going to change the 'face' of backpacking, but the new breed of backpackers expect better standards behind the scenes and a greater range of services from a hostel, so Accor is using its enormous experience in hospitality to create a new way of backpacking. (Travel Scene International, 2003, online source)

The backpacker industry doesn't just follow market trends, but has also played a direct role in the creation of backpacker markets.

A specific example of industry-led backpacker tourism development was to be found in Australia in the late 1990s. A postcard campaign was issued with student travel magazines and also marketed via Australian universities through first year student induction packs (Graeme Warring, 2002, personal communication). On offer were bus trips to Australian locations (including Byron Bay and Cairns – popular destinations for foreign backpackers) aimed at young Australians, emphasising the benefit of meeting lots of foreign backpackers, whose addresses would ensure free accommodation on a subsequent European trip. The slogan for the campaign also offered further 'benefits' along the lines of ' ... why bother with Bruce from Byron Bay when you could be copping off with Sven from Sweden?' In this respect, not only is it possible to treat backpacking as a rehearsal for later life, but also to undertake a 'rehearsal' for overseas backpacking in the home country prior to departure.

As the backpacker travel industry expands, so do the media and communications associated with it. This is most noticeable in the growth of *Lonely Planet* as the 'backpackers' bible', but there is a growing range of other information sources for, by and about backpackers. In Australia, British backpackers started a magazine in 1988: *For Backpackers by Backpackers* that became *TNT*. Later, *British Balls* set up in competition with *TNT* using the slogan 'For Backpackers by Backpackers' to underline the fact that this was a 'real' backpacker publication.

Backpacking also increasingly provides material for television. One of the hostels on the veritable 'hostel alley' in King's Cross, Sydney – Victoria Street – was the setting for a reasonably gritty soap opera called *Crash Palace* which featured international backpackers in King's Cross. The international cast included backpackers of varying ages (for example, a woman travelling with her 15-year-old daughter, singles, couples, long- and short-term travellers, surfers, those in temporary employment and a 'patriarch' figure as the hostel owner). The storylines emphasise the fleeting relationships between the constantly changing clientele. The fact that the soap is filmed there is advertised on a board outside the hostel: 'As Featured in *Crash Palace*'. At the time of writing there are also at least two substantial documentaries in preparation on the subject of backpacking. One is an MTV programme on the experience of American backpackers in Europe (a sure sign that the 'backpacker' label is beginning to make its way across the Atlantic), and the other is a UK Channel Four documentary about travellers who never return.

The growth of the backpacker industry is one sign that backpacker travel is now beginning to have a significant economic impact on the destinations they visit. A number of recent studies have pointed to the economic benefits that can be derived from backpacking tourism (Hampton, 1998; Scheyvens, 2002). This point is underlined by the empirical research presented in Chapter 2 and some of the other contributions to this volume (Kain and King, Chapter 12; Slaughter, Chapter 10). The impact of backpacking has been a relatively under-researched area in the past. This is beginning to change as official approaches to backpacking move from 'demarketing' to encouragement (Ateljevic & Doorne, Chapter 4).

The repositioning of backpacking as a 'good' form of tourism has not been without criticism, however. As Cooper, Erfurt and O'Mahony show in Chapter 11, backpackers can have a considerable impact on the natural environment. It seems that many are determined to seek out 'unique' or 'thrilling' experiences, even if these come at the cost of the environment, as the thrill element for some outweighs the social and environmental responsibility, a notion supported by the global nomad survey. As a New Zealand Maori working in Sydney (and a respondent in the global nomad survey described in Chapter 2) commented: 'Not all backpackers care about the environment, especially if it's not there [*sic*] own country (disposing of rubbish, destruction of vegetation, etc.)'. These problems are likely to increase as backpacking reaches more marginal and environmentally-fragile environments.

Considering all the contributions to the current volume and the broad survey of other sources they contain, it is clear that the conceptual model of backpacking initially developed by the ATLAS Backpacker Research Group is in need of revision. In contrast to the simple combination of 'push factors' and 'pull factors' that were seen to generate backpacker tourism in the original model, one might argue for a more central role for 'experience' in the revised model. The desire for experiences not only stimulates backpacker travel, but also determines to a large extent the form and content of the journey. Because the actual experiences gathered during travel often do not meet the original expectations of the backpacker, there is

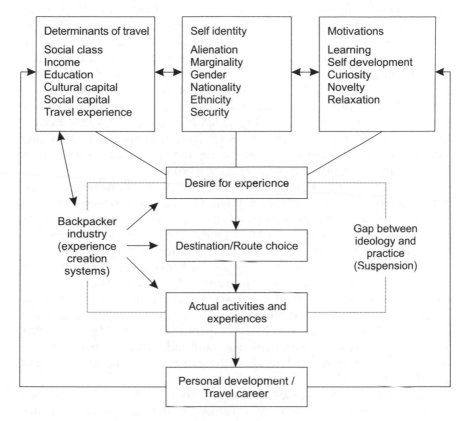

Figure 15.1 Revised conceptual model of backpacker travel

a gap between the ideology and practice of backpacking. This gap is increased by the experience production system of the backpacker industry, which caters to the contradictions inherent in the backpacker experience, including a desire for safe danger, distant intimacy and planned unexpectedness (Cederholm, 1999). A revised model of backpacker travel is therefore presented in Figure 15.1. We hope that this model will be further altered and refined in future, as more research becomes available on the nature and experience of backpacking.

Conclusions

The contributions to this volume have not just increased our knowledge of the backpacking phenomenon, they have also raised a wide range of new questions for the future. One of the key areas of debate among the various contributions is the role of backpacking. Is backpacking a travelstyle or an ideology? Is it an imagined community or a (sub)culture? Is it a social phenomenon or a market niche? Are backpackers a mirror for society, for modern tourism or simply for themselves? The answers to these questions depend on your disciplinary perspective or involvement with back-packing. What is reasonably clear, however, is that backpacking is a highly dynamic field of contested meanings, identities, travelstyles and product development. This dynamism, whether driven by alienation or a longing for experience, is increasingly attracting the attention of academics, industry suppliers, policy makers and the media.

The global nomads appear to have come full circle, journeying from the margins of society to the centre of conventional tourism and then seeking to distance themselves again as freer, more creative tourists. In this process, the position of the backpacker in the wider social field has also changed. In the past the 'tourist' was seen as a metaphor for modern life (Urry, 1990) or the social world (Dann, 2002), but now it is the backpacker who has become a metaphor for modern tourism or even modern youth. Backpacking is tourism caught between modern idealism and postmodern playfulness, suspended between the homogenous spaces of the backpacker tourism industry and the heterogeneity of the authentic world outside the enclave. The backpacker is suspended between desire and fulfilment, driven by the need to experience in order to close the gap between the ideology and practice of backpacking.

Perhaps this apparent 'false consciousness' of the backpacker will become ever harder to sustain in future, as the backpacker industry expands and major corporations move into the market. Moves to 'officially recognise' or 'formalise' backpacking on the part of policy makers may well sharpen the contradiction. Is it not paradoxical to formalise an informal activity such as backpacking? Or does this simply underline the fact that backpacking has long since become part of the 'formal' tourism system? The growing importance of backpacking in many destinations, particularly in Asia and Australasia already suggests that backpacking has achieved sufficient critical mass to be considered a 'conventional' form of tourism. As some of the contributions to this volume have suggested, the realisation of this fact is likely to drive the 'real' backpackers further afield – and further away from our current concepts of 'backpacking'. Perhaps another homology between the traditional and global nomads is that, just like their older counterparts, the global nomads are disappearing just at the point of their discovery by (post)modern society.

Future Research Directions

Given the lack of previous research on backpacking and the relatively limited coverage of the current volume, it is clear that many gaps remain to be filled in the developing picture of the (post)modern backpacker. In Chapter 3 Cohen suggests that more attention should be paid to the dynamism and diversity of backpacking, the gap between the ideology and practice of backpackers, and the historical and social context that motivates and influences their behaviour. In Chapter 4, Ateljevic and Doorne identify additional research 'gaps' in terms of hybrid identities, gender and the relationship between work and leisure. Binder in Chapter 6 argues that more attention should be paid to the backpacker community and to the transnational mechanisms of distinction that it creates. As well as these gaps in backpacker theory, there are also large areas of backpacker practice that remain relatively unexplored. The contributions from Australia and New Zealand in the current volume provide a relatively clear picture of the backpacker, but much work remains in other world regions and in other backpacking contexts. Elements of backpacking behaviour such as social interaction, communications, the recording of experiences and different travelstyles also require much more attention. The contribution of Speed and Harrison (Chapter 9) also underlines the need to investigate the policy context of backpacking and the potential to use backpacking as a 'good' form of tourism in tourism marketing and development. Finally, one area of the original global nomad research to which very little attention has been paid is the changes in backpacking over the course of the traveller's life, and the influence of early backpacking experiences on future travel choices. Within this wide range of future research possibilities, we have chosen to discuss a few areas in more detail. As in the ATLAS BRG research programme, these themes are organised in the form of a backpacker 'route', from preparation, through travel to return.

The ritual of preparation

The real or perceived risks involved in backpacking also place a great emphasis on the time invested in preparation. Particularly as backpacker travel becomes more global, the business of obtaining visas, saving for the trip, getting immunised against tropical diseases, and gathering information about strange cultures and new experience opportunities becomes all the more important.

The departure for a major 'trip' and the process of return have not been studied in any detail in this volume or in other backpacker literature. But, given the tendency for many theoretical perspectives on backpacker travel to be based on the concept of liminality, it would seem a logical step to pay more attention to the preparation for travel and the re-integration of returning travellers. In principle, the development of the Internet and the growth of the backpacker industry should reduce the need for preparation and the reverse culture shock of return. But is this true? Is it more 'hardcore' not to book in advance? Do more experienced backpackers avoid the popular backpacker enclaves altogether?

Many chapters in the current volume have looked at the issue of backpacker destination choice, but there still remains much work to be done in this area. In particular, the decision-making process could be examined for backpackers from different origin countries. Do people originating from different cultural contexts or social backgrounds have the same image or expectations of the places they travel to? Maoz (Chapter 7) indicates that there are significant differences even for backpackers coming from the same origin country, but how far is this true for other backpacker groups?

The mainstreaming of backpacker travel means that increasing numbers of backpackers are using the services of the backpacker industry to save time during their trip. Booking a package from one of the major bus companies in Australia and New Zealand saves a lot of time in terms of searching travel timetables, booking tickets and looking for hotels. This may well also take away one of the important aspects of the backpacker (sub)culture, which is the search for information and 'insider tips' prior to travel (Welk, Chapter 5).

The context from which backpacker travel derives is also ripe for more research. In contrast to the idea of the 'original drifter' (Cohen, Chapter 3) many current studies of backpacking present a picture of relatively privileged individuals moving from the 'centre' of their own society to the margins of others. Perhaps those on the margin of their own society are not just limited by a lack of cash, but might also feel they don't need to be marginalised elsewhere? Is backpacker travel the preserve of those with a solid 'centre' who can afford the physical and psychological risks of travel to the margin?

On the road: Forming communities

Once the journey begins, many questions arise about how backpackers adjust to life on the road. Most backpacker research concentrates on people who have been travelling for a while or have even finished their journeys, and the research therefore misses much of the dynamism of the process of 'becoming' a backpacker. We might ask, what is the role of stories in creating backpacker expectations and backpacker communities and in forming individual identities? Is backpacking a good way to make friends, or are loners drawn to backpacking?

How do backpackers actually experience life on the road? Even those who don't find paid employment during the trip may experience back-packing as a form of 'work'. The labour required to gather information, to find accommodation and obtain visas or simply to carry the backpack may be experienced as arduous. Although many backpackers may view travel as a state of 'being' rather than of 'doing', much of the actual travel experience revolves around 'doing'. Perhaps only those who remain in one place for a long time actually find time to 'be'. Could it be – paradoxically – that tourists (reviled by backpackers for their 'easy' forms of travel and sedentary forms of consumption) can actually spend more time 'being' because they spend a lot less time 'doing'?

How do backpackers actually spend their time? Do they spend most of their time with other backpackers, and avoid the other tourists in the desti-nations they visit? Are women more sociable and more willing to forge friendships with their fellow travellers? Is the expressed desire of back-packers to interact with local people actually fulfilled in practice? Do people tend to mix with backpackers from their own origin country or culture rather than experiencing difference through contact with a wide range of other backpackers?

Adaptive behaviour while travelling

As Cohen notes in Chapter 3, backpackers are distinguished more through their behaviour or conduct rather than a particular style of travel. Presumably, therefore, 'new' backpackers have to be initiated into the behavioural codes appropriate to each backpacker (sub)culture, taking on the guise of a 'backpacker' rather than a 'traveller' or a 'taxi backpacker' rather than a 'hippy'. The process by which people adapt to the backpacker (sub)culture may therefore be interesting to investigate. Arriving in Thai-land, paying 10 baht for a bowl of rice may seem ridiculously cheap for a Westerner but, after the money has been stretched in order to prolong the stay as much as possible, rice that costs any more may subsequently be seen as a rip-off. How far does bargaining become an important element of the backpacker culture? Is such bargaining perfectly acceptable 'on the road', but perhaps a source of embarrassment on return to the relative luxury of 'home'?

In terms of the material culture, looking at the change in appearance of backpackers may also be revealing. The gradual (or sometimes very sudden) replacement of Western clothes with more ethnic garb may indicate a desire not to be identified as a 'tourist' (see Welk, Chapter 5). On the other hand, the new clothes might cause the backpacker to be identified as a 'hippy'. The diversity of those identified as backpackers has been strongly underlined in the current volume. There is much work to be done on the emerging groups within the backpacker (sub)culture or 'scene', for example on the way in which music or drugs mark out different groups as well as providing an important source of backpacker activity.

One important issue identified in most chapters in the current volume is the apparent gap between the ideology of backpacking as an expression of freedom and consumption of difference and the practice of most back-packers, who seem to be more and more like the conventional tourists they try and escape. How and when do such gaps emerge? Are the gaps the same for most backpackers? Cohen (Chapter 3) suggests that backpackers must develop coping mechanisms to close the gap between ideology and practice – but what are these and how are they developed?

The backpacker enclave

The formation of backpacker communities takes place to a large extent in backpacker enclaves. The development and function of enclaves has been discussed in this volume, but our picture of the structure, development and dynamics of enclaves is still poor.

For example, what are the differences between rural and urban enclaves? Do rural enclaves function as places to 'chill out', with urban enclaves being seen more as essential stopovers? How do backpackers use different spaces within enclaves? How are such spaces engaged with physically and emotionally? How do backpackers behave within enclaves? Is their conduct different while suspended in the enclave than while in direct contact with the host community? How are the enclaves viewed by hosts and travellers? How much time do backpackers actually spend in enclaves as opposed to being 'on the road'? Time and space-time diaries of backpackers' use of time while 'on the road' and 'off the beaten track' could give an insight into this.

The development of enclaves as contested spaces could also be a fruitful avenue for research. The development of enclaves such as the Khao San Road in Bangkok indicates that tensions between locals and backpackers may occur even in relatively well-established urban enclaves. There are also tensions between different types of travellers and between the suppliers fighting for a share of an increasingly competitive market. How does the local culture adapt to the enclave (for example, learning different languages, adopting banana pancakes as a 'local' dish)?

Maintaining backpacker communities

The concept of a backpacker community has been approached from different angles in this volume. Welk (Chapter 5) and Binder (Chapter 6) both argue for the existence of a backpacker community, although they acknowledge that this is perhaps more an 'imagined community' (Anderson, 1991) formed through shared ideology(ies) than a 'real' community. There is still much research to be done on the basis of this community, its shared beliefs, ideas and practices.

Another important issue concerns the way in which this imagined community might be sustained. A nation as an imagined community has a number of clearly structured means of maintaining itself, but the backpacker community is far more diffuse and diverse. The way in which information is circulated through the community and reproduced should therefore be an interesting research avenue of research. For example, word of mouth is a fundamental conduit for information exchange, but we still know relatively little about the form and content of the 'insider tips' being passed from one traveller to another (Welk, Chapter 5). To what extent are modern means of communication such as mobile phones, text messages (SMS), email and chat rooms forming global bonds between backpackers and home or between backpackers in different parts of the world? Are written letters and postcards still important, or are these being replaced by electronic media?

The way in which backpackers record their experiences is also of potential interest. Some authors have argued that backpackers avoid 'traditional' tourist recording devices, such as photographs (Uriely *et al.*, 2002; Welk, Chapter 5), whereas others argue that photos are an integral part of the backpacker experience. For example, Cederholm (1999) analysed the collector mentality of traveller (i.e. backpacker) photography as well as the role of photography in allowing travellers to frame the 'extraordinary sphere'. Cederholm concluded that such 'framing' takes place both in the situation where the traveller takes the photograph and also when showing the photos back home after the trip.

What is the relationship between backpacking and youth culture in general? For example, how does the trance music scene in Goa impact on the listening habits of young people at home? To what extent does the proliferation of music encourage people to travel to new destinations?

To what extent are postmodern playfulness and hedonism replacing the search for authenticity as cultural symbols of backpacking? Perhaps many backpackers are managing to combine both in their search for experience. Perhaps the long duration of backpacking trips means that 'fun' can still be experienced as a compensation for the 'hard work' of the backpacker trail? Does the 'fun' of Goa have to be compensated for by 'serious' trekking in the Himalayas?

Backpacking as an alternative reality

Perhaps the role of the backpacker as a rebel or a role model for alternative ways of living has diminished over the years. But there is still some evidence that backpackers experience backpacking as different from the everyday reality they have left behind. The difference between everyday life and the existence of the backpacker could fruitfully be analysed in a number of ways.

For example, the use of time while backpacking seems to be different from everyday life at home, everyday life in the destination (backpackers don't have to work, while their hosts do) and the time use of other tourists (who are forced to live a more hurried existence on holiday). Do backpackers consciously avoid wearing a watch in some destinations? Wearing a watch represents normal life, punctuality, 'structure' and 'conformity'. Perhaps 'forgetting' to wear a watch when 'on the road' is a sign of distinction, a badge of honour for those who have transcended time? One of the interesting potential areas for research is the extent to which individual experiences begin to act as time markers in the absence of a linear time pattern. In particular, do 'bad' experiences become significant markers of backpacker maturation, supplying more material for the relating of stories?

The backpacker experience is also a contradictory package, involving as it does safe danger, exotic home comforts, searching for the unexpected on the beaten track, Internet intimacy, packaged spontaneity, and other apparent tensions. Does this create a 'new reality' for backpackers, willing as they often are to sacrifice personal comfort for the ultimate experience?

Impact

The growing perception that backpacking is 'good' tourism is based on the fact that backpackers tend to spend more in total than conventional tourists do, and also buy more services from local people, increasing the impact of their purchases on the local economy. The social construction research and the global nomad survey both show that backpackers themselves feel that they have more contact with locals than other tourists do. There is, however, a lack of empirical research on the actual spending of backpackers in local communities or on the impact of that expenditure compared with that of other visitors. Do backpackers give more back to the communities they visit than other tourists do? Are they more motivated to help local people? It may be that the growth of the backpacker industry and its penetration by larger suppliers (such as the Accor Base Backpackers brand) is beginning to siphon off some of the economic benefits that originally went directly to the local community.

We also know very little about the social, cultural and environmental impacts of backpackers. To what extent does the presence of backpackers cause irritation and/or resentment among local people? Does the backpackers' search for experience lead them to overlook their negative impacts on the environment, as Cooper, O'Mahony and Erfurt (Chapter 1) suggest in the case in Australia? What impact is the development of nature-based thrill products (such as diving or bungee jumping) having on the places visited by backpackers? Is there pressure to invest in infrastructure expansion to provide 'safe danger' for the backpacker?

Alternative voices

One of the problems with charting the impact of backpacking on local communities is the fact that the local voice is seldom heard in backpacker research. Because much backpacking research takes place in developing destinations, where the researcher does not usually speak the local language, this is perhaps not surprising. But this is certainly one perspective that could be explored in a lot more detail.

In addition to the many 'non-Western' suppliers of backpacker services, there are also growing numbers of backpackers from countries outside the main European, North American and Australasian generating regions. Asian backpackers, for example, are now more frequently seen not just in the backpacker centres of Asia, but also in Australasia and Europe. Again the language barrier usually prevents their perspectives being presented, as Vance notes in Chapter 14. In the surveys undertaken for the current volume, for example, Asian respondents were universally underrepresented. The global nomad survey included respondents from Hong Kong and Mexico, but obviously much greater coverage is needed of other countries.

Another voice that is not often heard is that of the supplier of backpacker services. Some research has been undertaken on suppliers in Sydney from the social construction study in this volume, but large differences are likely to exist between destinations. How has the backpacker industry developed in different contexts? What is the role of 'lifestyle entrepreneurs' in creating backpacker products?

The differences between male and female backpackers noted in the contributions to this volume also underline the need for more research on the perspective of women. Do gendered spaces develop in backpacker enclaves? What role do friendships play in the female experience of backpacking? How do women perceive the risks of backpacking? Does real or apparent danger curtail their travel behaviour? Do gender stereotypes have an impact (for example, the stereotype that women are less able to carry heavy rucksacks)? How does the interaction of women with the local population differ from that of men?

The attempts at distinction by backpackers may also have an effect on the host community. How do the 'locals' react to young foreigners arriving and trying to blend in with their surroundings? Is this seen as a compliment or an insult? Is there irritation with the bargaining that seems to be an important part of backpacker culture?

Returning home

The discussion about whether or not backpacking is a *rite de passage* is problematicised by the fact that very little attention has been paid in the literature to the return home. Without some kind of longitudinal study of backpacking, it is difficult to assess how much and in what ways people are changed by the backpacking experience. Did they find themselves, or just a lot of other people living the same hedonistic lifestyle? Do backpackers find it difficult to adjust to life back at home? Perhaps there is a degree of reverse culture shock related to re-entry into everyday life.

There is also the question of how long the changes (if any) effected by backpacking actually last. Do backpackers undergo temporary or more permanent changes in lifestyle (for example, in relationship-forming behaviour and attitudes to authority) following their travelling experiences? To what extent does the backpacking experience have a positive effect on people's lives, in terms of personal development, future employment prospects or increased spatial and social mobility? Perhaps as Binder suggests in Chapter 6, the cultural capital developed through travel can be converted into economic capital on return.

The relationship between motivations for travelling and readjustment may also be interesting. To what extent are people motivated to depart by major events, turning points or life crises (such as divorce, bereavement or career change) and what effect does the travelling experience have on the resolution of these events?

Given the finding of the global nomad survey (Richards & Wilson, Chapter 2) that the most frequently expressed effect of travel experience was that it generated a thirst for more travel, there is also scope for more work on the impact of backpacking trips on future travel plans. Does seeing one country or world region simply lead to a desire to see other countries or regions in order to consume more difference, or are some backpackers returning to the same destinations in order to engage more with local culture?

Change over time

There is a widespread assumption in the literature and in the contributions to this volume that backpacking has changed substantially in recent decades. Some studies (e.g. Westerhausen, 2002) have tried to reconstruct the evolution of backpacker enclaves, but relatively little is known about the changes in the backpacker 'scene' as a whole. What are the major differences between the 'hippies' or 'original drifters' of 30 years ago and the backpackers of today? How do the different generations of backpackers view their experience and each other? Are young backpackers today less alienated, less rebellious and more hedonistic than the veterans of the baby-boomer generation? How do the different generations of backpackers view their own role in the process of changing tourist destinations? Are former backpackers now travelling with their children, and if so, what will these children make of such experiences when they grow up?

The current volume has tended to be restricted to the established backpacker markets originating in Europe, North America and Australasia. But in the future there should be a more significant presence of backpackers from 'new' regions, such as Asia and Latin America. There are already some signs that this is having an effect on the marketing activities of some suppliers, but there should also be significant impacts on the nature of the backpacker 'scene' itself. How will the new backpackers adapt to life on the road? Will they change the face of the existing backpacker (sub)culture, or develop parallel structures of their own? Will their ideas of 'fun' and 'authenticity' differ from those of the current generation?

These areas for research represent just a small selection of potential topics related to the development of the backpacking phenomenon and its impact on backpackers, host communities and the tourism industry. Hopefully some of these topics will be taken up in the future activities of the ATLAS Backpacker Research Group as well as by other researchers. Such research has the potential not just to increase our understanding of backpacking, but also to throw light on many issues that are intimately connected with the growth of the backpacking (sub)culture, such as notions of freedom and constraint, changing identities, the development of global youth culture, 'Otherness' and authenticity. These issues are not just important in terms of theoretical reflection, but also have important practical implications for the tourism industry and for society as a whole.

References

Adler, J. (1985) Youth on the road: Reflection on the history of tramping. *Annals of Tourism Reseach* 12, 335–354.

Almog, O. (1992) Amud-Esh Hadash (Pillar of fire). *Politica* 42/43, 10–13.

Almog, O. (1997) *The Sabra: A Profile*. Tel Aviv: Am Oved.

Anderson, B. (1991) *Imagined Communities: Reflections on the Origin and Spread of Nationalism*. London: Verso.

Andritzky, M. (1986) Nichts wie weg! Jugend und Reisen. In W. Bucher and K. Pohl (eds) *Schock und Schöpfung: Jugendästhetik im 20. Jahrhundert* (pp. 249–252). Darmstadt/Neuwied: Luchterhand.

Anon. (1994) *The Quotable Traveller: Wise Words for Travellers, Explorers and Wanderers*. London: Running Press.

Arkin, W. and Dobrofsky, L.R. (1978) Military socialization and masculinity. *Journal of Social Issues* 34 (1), 151–168.

Ashcroft, B., Griffiths, G. and Tiffin, H. (1998) *Key Concepts in Post-Colonial Studies*. London: Routledge.

Ateljevic, I. (2000) Circuits of tourism: Stepping beyond the 'production/consumption' dichotomy. *Tourism Geographies* 2, 369–388.

Ateljevic, I. and Doorne, S. (2000) 'Staying within the fence': Lifestyle entrepreneurship in tourism. *Journal of Sustainable Tourism* 8 (5), 378–392.

Ateljevic, I. and Doorne, S. (2001) 'Nowhere left to run': A study of value boundaries and segmentation within the backpacker market of New Zealand. In J.A. Mazanec, G.I. Crouch, J.R. Brent Ritchie and A.G. Woodside (eds) *Consumer Psychology of Tourism, Hospitality and Leisure* (Vol. 2, pp. 169–186). Wallingford: CABI.

Ateljevic, I. and Doorne, S. (2002) Representing New Zealand: Tourism imagery and ideology. *Annals of Tourism Research* 29 (2), 648–667.

Australian Tourist Commission (1995) *Backpacking: It's a State of Mind: Opportunities in the Australian Independent Travel Market*. Sydney: Australian Tourist Commission (April).

Barnes, T. and Duncan, J. (1992) *Writing World: Discourse, Text and Metaphor in the Representation of Landscape*. London: Routledge.

Barr, E. (2002) *Backpack*. London: Plume.

Barr, E. (2003) *Baggage*. London: Plume.

Baudrillard, J. (1981) *For a Critique of the Political Economy of the Sign*. St Louis: Telos Press.

Bell, C. (2002) The big 'OE': Young New Zealand travellers as secular pilgrims. *Tourist Studies* 2 (2), 143–158.

Berger, P. and Luckmann, T. (1969) *Die gesellschaftliche Konstruktion der Wirklichkeit*. Frankfurt am Main: Fischer-Taschenbuch-Verlag.

Binder, J. (2003) *Projekt: Driften. Rucksacktourismus als Reaktion auf die Anforderungen spätmoderner Gesellschaften* (working title). Online at: http://www.parapluie.de.

Bird, J., Curtis, B., Mash, M., Putnam, T., Robertson, G. and Tickner, L. (eds) (1994) *Travellers' Tales: Narratives of Home and Displacement.* London: Routledge.

Bocock, R. (1974) *Ritual in Industrial Society: Sociological Analysis of Ritual in Modern England.* London: Allen and Unwin.

Boorstin, D.J. (1961) From traveller to tourist: The lost art of travel. In D. Boorstin *The Image or What Happened to the American Dream* (pp. 86–125). Harmondsworth: Penguin.

Bourdieu, P. (1984) *Distinction.* London: Routledge.

Bradley, M. (1988) Realism and adaptation in designing hypothetical travel choice concepts. *Journal of Transport Economics and Policy* 22 (2), 121–137.

Bradt, H. (1995) Better to travel cheaply? *The Independent on Sunday Magazine*, 12 February, pp. 49–50.

Bras, K. (2000) Image building and guiding on Lombok. PhD thesis, Katholieke Universiteit Brabant.

Brinkley, D. (1994) Educating the generation called 'X'. *Washington Post Education Review* 3, 1–4.

Brown, D. (1995) *Inventing New England: Regional Tourism in the Nineteenth Century.* Washington: Smithsonian Institution Press.

Bruner, E.M. (1989) On cannibals, tourists, and ethnographers. *Annals of Tourism Research* 4 (4), 438–445.

Bruner, E.M. (1991) Transformation of self in tourism. *Annals of Tourism Research* 18, 238–250.

Bruner, E. (1996) Tourism in the Balinese borderzone. In S. Lavie and T. Swedenburg (eds) *Displacement, Diaspora, and Geographies of Identity* (pp. 157–179). Durham: Duke University Press.

Bryson, B. (1990) *The Lost Continent.* London: Abacus.

Bryson, B. (1991) *Neither Here nor There: Travels in Europe.* London: Black Swan.

Bryson, B. (1997) *A Walk in the Woods.* London: Transworld.

Buchanan, I. and Rossetto, A. (1997) With my swag upon my shoulder: A comprehensive study of international backpackers to Australia. *Occasional Paper 24.* Canberra: Bureau of Tourism Research.

Bureau of Tourism Research (1995) Backpackers in Australia. *Occasional Paper 20.* Canberra: Bureau of Tourism Research.

Bureau of Tourism Research (2000a) *Backpacker Market.* Australia: Tourism Queensland.

Bureau of Tourism Research (2000b) *International Visitors in Australia, 1999.* Canberra: Bureau of Tourism Research.

Bureau of Tourism Research (2002) *International Visitor Survey 2002.* Canberra: Bureau of Tourism Research.

Campbell, C. (1999) The Easternization of the West. In: B. Wilson and J. Cresswell (eds) *New Religious Movements: Challenge and Response* (pp. 35– 48). London: Routledge.

Cater, C. (2002) Beyond the gaze: The embodied landscapes of adventure tourism. Presented at the Association of American Geographers Annual Conference, Los Angeles (March).

Carr, N. (1998) The young tourist: A case of neglected research. *Progress in Tourism and Hospitality Research* 4 (4), 307–318.

Cederholm, E.A. (1999) *The Attraction of the Extraordinary: Images and Experiences Among Backpacker Tourists.* Published PhD thesis (in Swedish). Lund: Arkiv Förlag .

Chatwin, B. (1998/1987) *The Songlines.* London: Vintage.

Chatwin, B (1996) *Anatomy of Restlessness: Uncollected Writings* (posthumously edited by J. Borm and M. Graves). London: Picador.

Chatwin, B. (1990/1989) *What Am I Doing Here?* Harmondsworth: Penguin.

Chatwin, B. and Theroux, P. (1985) *Patagonia Revisited.* London: Cape.

Clifford, J. (1992) Travelling cultures. In L. Grossberg, C. Nelson and P.A. Treichler (eds) *Cultural Studies* (pp. 96–116). London: Routledge.

Clifford, J. (1997) *Routes: Travel and Translation in the Late Twentieth Century.* Massachusetts: Harvard University Press.

Clifford, J. and Marcus, G. (eds) (1986) *Writing Culture: The Politics and Ethnography.* Berkeley: University of California Press.

Cloke, P. and Perkins, H. (1998) 'Cracking the canyon with the awesome foursome': Representations of adventure tourism in New Zealand. *Environment and Planning D: Society and Space* 16, 185–218.

Cloke, P. and Perkins, H.C. (2002) Commodification and adventure in New Zealand tourism. *Current Issues in Tourism* 5 (6), 521–549.

Cohen, A. (1985) *The Symbolic Construction of Community.* Chichester: Tavistock Publications.

Cohen, C.B. (1995) Marketing paradise, making nation. *Annals of Tourism Research* 22, 404–421.

Cohen, E. (1972) Toward a sociology of international tourism. *Social Research* 39 (1), 164–182.

Cohen, E. (1973) Nomads from affluence: Notes on the phenomenon of drifter-tourism. *International Journal of Comparative Sociology* 14 (1–2), 89–103.

Cohen, E. (1974) Who is a tourist? A conceptual classification. *Sociological Review* 22, 527–555.

Cohen, E. (1979) A phenomenology of touristic experiences. *Sociology* 13, 179–201.

Cohen, E. (1982) Marginal paradises: Bungalow tourism on the islands of Southern Thailand. *Annals of Tourism Research* 9 (2), 189–228.

Cohen, E. (1984) The sociology of tourism: Approaches, issues, and findings. *Annual Review of Sociology* 10, 373–392.

Cohen, E. (1989) 'Primitive and remote': Hill tribe trekking in Thailand. *Annals of Tourism Research* 16 (1), 30–61.

Cohen, E. (1993) The study of touristic images of native people: Mitigating the stereotype of stereotype. In D.G. Pearce and R.W. Butler (eds) *Tourism Research: Critiques and Challenges* (pp. 36–69) New York: Routledge.

Cohen, E. (1995) Contemporary tourism: Trends and challenges. In R. Butler and D. Pearce (eds) *Change in Tourism* (pp. 12–29). London: Routledge.

Cohen, E. (2001) *Thai Tourism: Hill Tribes, Islands and Open-ended Prostitution.* Bangkok: White Lotus.

Comaroff, J.L. (1992) *Ethnography and the Historical Imagination.* Boulder, CO: Westview Press.

Commonwealth Department of Tourism (1995) *National Backpacker Tourism Strategy.* Canberra: Australian Government Publishing Service.

Commonwealth Department of Tourism (1996) *Building for Backpacker Accommodation*. Canberra: Commonwealth Department of Tourism (produced by P & A Consulting).

Cooper, M.J. (2001) Backpackers to Fraser Island: Why is ecotourism a neglected aspect of their experience? *Journal of Quality Assurance in Hospitality & Tourism* 1 (4), 45–59.

Coupland, N. and Jaworski, A. (eds) (1997) *Sociolinguistics. A Reader and Coursebook*. New York: St Martin's Press, Inc.

Coventry, N. (2002) YHA offers dreams. *Inside Tourism* 427, 4.

Crang, M. (1996) Magic kingdom or a quixotic quest for authenticity. *Annals of Tourism Research* 23, 415–431.

Crick, M. (1991) Tourists, locals and anthropologists: Quizzical reflections on 'Otherness' in tourist encounters and in tourism research. *Australian Cultural History* 10, 6–18.

Crompton, J.L. (1979) Motivations for pleasure vacation. *Annals of Tourism Research* 4 (4), 408–425.

Curtis, B. and Pajaczkowaska, C. (1994) 'Getting there': Travel, time and narrative. In G. Robertson (ed.) *Travellers' Tales: Narratives of Home and Displacement* (pp. 199–215). London and New York: Routledge.

Dann, G. (1996a) *The Language of Tourism: A Sociolinguistic Perspective*. New York: CAB International.

Dann, G.M.S. (1996b) Registers of the language of tourism. In G. Dann, *The Language of Tourism* (pp. 211–252). Wallingford: CAB International.

Dann, G.M.S. (1998) The pomo promo of tourism. *Tourism, Culture and Communication* 1, 1–16.

Dann, G. (1999) Writing out the tourist in space and time. *Annals of Tourism Research,* 26, 159–187.

Dann, G. (ed.) (2002) *The Tourist as a Metaphor for the Social World*. Wallingford: CABI.

De Botton, A. (2002) *The Art of Travel*. London: Penguin.

De Cauter, L. (1995) *De Archeologie van de Kick*. Amsterdam: De Balie.

Dellaert, B., Ettema, D. and Lindh, C. (1998) Multifaceted tourist travel decisions: A constraint-based conceptual framework to describe tourists' sequential choices of travel components. *Tourism Management* 19 (4), 313–320.

Denzin, N. (1997) *Interpretive Ethnography*. Thousand Oaks: Sage.

Desforges, L (1998) 'Checking out the planet': Global representations/ Local identities and youth travel. In T. Skelton, and G. Valentine (eds) *Cool Places: Geographies of Youth Culture* (pp. 175–192) London: Routledge.

Desforges, L. (2000) Travelling the world: Identity and travel biography. *Annals of Tourism Research* 27 (4), 926–945.

DEWSRB (2000) *Harvesting Australia: Report of the National Harvest Trail Working Group*. Canberra: Department of Employment, Workplace Relations and Small Business / Commonwealth of Australia.

DIMA (1999) *Review of Illegal Workers in Australia: Improving Compliance in the Workplace*. Canberra: Department of Immigration and Multicultural Affairs/ Commonwealth of Australia.

DIMA (2000) *Working Holiday Maker Scheme*. DIMA Fact Sheet 55. Canberra: Department of Employment, Workplace Relations and Small Business/ Commonwealth of Australia.

Dominey, T. (2002) Accor Backpackers launched. *Tabs on Travel,* 27 May, p. 2.

Doorne, S. (1994) Symbiosis, integration and the backpacker tourist industry. Unpublished masters thesis, Victoria University of Wellington.

Doorne, S., Ateljevic, I. and Bai, Z. (2003) Representing identities through tourism: Encounters of ethnic minorities in Dali, Yunnan Province. *International Journal of Tourism Research* 5, 1–11.

Edensor, T. (2001) Performing tourism, staging tourism: (Re)producing tourist space and practice. *Tourist Studies* 1 (1), 59–81.

Edwards, E. (1996) Postcards: Greetings from another world. In T. Selwyn (ed.) *The Tourist Image: Myths and Myth Making in Tourism* (pp. 197–221). Chichester: John Wiley and Sons.

Elsrud, T. (1998) Time creation in travelling: The taking and making of time among women backpackers. *Time and Society* 7 (2), 309–334.

Elsrud, T. (2001) Risk creation in travelling: Backpacker adventure narration. *Annals of Tourism Research* 28 (3), 597–617.

Elwert, G. and Waldmann, P. (eds) (1989) *Ethnizität im Wandel*. Saarbrücken: Breitenbach.

Emmons, R. (2000) Peaceful days in Pai. *Bangkok Post, Horizons*, February p. 24: 12.

Erb, M. (2000) Understanding tourism: Interpretations from Indonesia. *Annals of Tourism Research* 27, 709–736.

Erikson, E.H. (1959) Identity and the life cycle: Selected papers. *Psychological Issues* 1 (1), 5–165.

Even-Zohar, I. (1981) The emergence of a native Hebrew culture in Palestine: 1882–1948. *Studies in Zionism* 4, 167–184.

Eyal, G. (1996) The discursive origins of Israeli separatism: The case of the Arab village. *Theory and Society* 25, 389–429.

Farrell, R. (1999) The pre-decision process: Backpackers and their motivations to travel. Unpublished research report, Auckland Institute of Technology.

Featherstone, M. (1987) Lifestyle and consumer culture. *Theory, Culture and Society* 22 (4), 55–70.

Featherstone, M. (1990) Perspectives on consumer culture. *Sociology* 24 (1), 5–22.

Firth, T. and Hing, N. (1999) Backpacker hostels and their guests: Attitudes and behaviours relating to sustainable tourism. *Tourism Management* 20, 251–254.

Fitzgerald, M. (2000) Fear, loathing, and banana pancakes on the traveller trail: Adventures in backpacking. *The Austin Chronicle*, 24 March.

Fodness, D. and Murray, B. (1997) Tourist information search. *Annals of Tourism Research* 24 (3), 503–523.

Forsyth, P. and Dwyer, L. (1995) Employment impacts of inbound tourism, tourism research and education in Australia. In B. Faulkner (ed.) Unpublished proceedings of the Australian National Tourism Research and Education Conference 1994 (pp. 225–234).

Fowkes, T. and Wardman, M. (1988) The design of stated preference travel choice experiments with special reference to inter-personal taste variations. *Journal of Transport Economics and Policy* 22 (1), 27–44.

Fraser, C. (ed.) (1994) *Australia Unplugged: Escape and Discover Down Under*. Australian Tourist Commission, Australia.

Fuchs-Henritz, W. (ed.) (1995) *Lexikon zur Soziologie*. Opladen: Westdeutscher Verlag.

Fussell, P. (1979) The stationary tourist. *Harper's*, April, pp. 31–38.

Fussell, P. (1980) *Abroad: British Literary Travelling Between the Wars*. Oxford: Oxford University Press.

Gallarza, M.G., Saura, I.G. and Garcia, H.C. (2002) Destination image: Towards a conceptual framework. *Annals of Tourism Research* 29 (1), 56–78.

Ganguli, H.C. (1975) *Foreign Students: The Indian Experience.* New Delhi: Sterling Publishers.

Garland, A. (1996) *The Beach.* London: Penguin.

Garnham R. (1993) *A Backpacking Geography of New Zealand.* Wellington: New Zealand Geography Conference Proceedings.

Gartner,W.C. (1993) Image formation process. *Travel and Tourism Marketing* 2 (2/3), 191–215.

Geertz, C. (1983) *Dichte Beschreibung. Beitraege zum Verstehen kultureller Systeme.* Frankfurt am Main: Suhrkamp.

Gibson, A. (2001) Boom time for backpackers. *Weekend Herald* [Auckland], August 25/26, G1.

Giddens, A. (1991) *Modernity and Self-Identity: Self and Society in the Late Modern Age.* Cambridge: Polity Press.

Giesbers, M. (2002) Backpackers: Grand tour of Toeristenvoer? Unpublished MA thesis, Katholieke Universiteit Brabant.

Gilligan, C. (1982) *In a Different Voice: Psychological Theory and Women's Development.* Cambridge: Harvard University Press.

Girtler, R. (1984) *Methoden der Qualitativen Sozialforschung. Anleitung zur Feldarbeit.* Wien: Boehlau.

Gnoth, J (1997) Tourism motivation and expectation formation. *Annals of Tourism Research* 24 (2), 283–304.

Goffman, E. (1971) *Relations in Public.* Harmondsworth: Penguin.

Goodrich, J.N. (1978) The relationship between preferences for and perceptions of vacation destinations: Application of a choice model. *Journal of Travel Research* 16, 8–13.

Gottlieb, A. (1982) Americans' vacations. *Annals of Tourism Research* 9, 165–187.

Graburn, N.H.H. (1983) The anthropology of tourism. *Annals of Tourism Research* 10 (1), 9–33.

Graburn, N.H.H. (1989) Tourism: The sacred journey. In V.L. Smith (ed.) *Hosts and Guests* (pp. 21–36). Philadelphia: University of Pennsylvania Press.

Gray P.H. (1981) Wanderlust tourism: Problems of infrastructure. *Annals of Tourism Research* 7, 285–290.

Gross, P. (1994) *Die Multioptionsgesellschaft (The Multioptional Society).* Frankfurt am Main: Suhrkamp.

Gunn. C. (1988) *Vacationscapes: Designing Tourist Regions* (2nd edn). New York: Van Nostrand Reinhold.

Haigh, R. (1995) Backpackers in Australia. *Occasional Paper 20.* Canberra: Bureau of Tourism Research.

Hall, D. and Kinnaird, V. (1994) A note on women travellers. In V. Kinnaird and D. Hall (eds) *Tourism: A Gender Analysis* (pp. 188–209). Chichester: Wiley.

Hall, S. (1968) The hippies: An American 'moment'. *University of Birmingham Sub and Popular Culture Series16.* Birmingham: University of Birmingham.

Hampton, M.P. (1998) Backpacker tourism and economic development. *Annals of Tourism Research* 25 (3), 639–660.

Hancock, J. (1998) Backpackers, Darwin, and the wet season: What they enjoyed and how to attract more. Graduating Seminar report, School of Hospitality and Management, Southern Cross University.

Harding, S. and Hintikka, M. (eds) (1983) *Discovering Reality: Feminist Perspectives on Epistemology, Metaphysics, Methodology and Philosophy of Science*. Dordrecht: Reidel.

Hastings, J. (1998) Time out of time: Life crises and schooner sailing in the Pacific. *Kroeber Anthropology Society Papers 67/68*, 42–54.

HBTDB (2001) *Hervey Bay Visitor Survey 2001*. Hervey Bay: Hervey Bay Tourism and Development Board.

Hemingway, E. (1993/1952) *The Old Man and the Sea*. London: Arrow Books.

Hemingway, E. (1994/1940) *For Whom the Bell Tolls*. London: Arrow Books.

Hennig, C. (1997) *Reiselust: Touristen, Tourismus und Urlaubskultur*. Frankfurt: Insel Verlag.

Herz, D. (1999) Going east: 19th century German women travelling to the Orient. MA thesis, The Hebrew University.

Hillman, W. (1999) Searching for authenticity in touristic experiences: female backpackers in North Queensland. Unpublished masters thesis, James Cook University.

Hills, J.M.M. (1965) *The Holiday: A Study of Social and Psychological Aspects with Special Reference to Ireland*. London: The Tavistock Institute of Human Relations.

Hirschberg, W. *et al.* (eds) (1999) *Wörterbuch der Völkerkunde*. Berlin: Reimer.

Hofstede, G. (1991) *Culture's Consequences*. London: Sage.

Hoivik, T and Heiberg, T. (1980) Centre-periphery tourism and self-reliance. *International Social Science Journal* 32, 69–98.

Honer, A. (1993) *Lebensweltliche Ethnographie. Ein explorative-interpretativer Forschungsansatz am Beispiel von Heimwerker-Wissen*. Wiesbaden: DUV.

Hooton, A. (1999) Sons of Bazza. *The Sydney Morning Herald Good Weekend Magazine*, 20 November, pp. 34–39.

Hottola, P. (1999) *The Intercultural Body: Western Woman, Culture Confusion and Control of Space in the South Asian Travel Scene*. Finland: Julkaisuja.

Hughes, G. (1992) Tourism and the geographical imagination. *Leisure Studies* 11 (1), 31–42.

Hutnyk, J. (1996) *The Rumour of Calcutta. Tourism, Charity and the Poverty of Representation*. London: Zed Books.

Hyde, K. F., (2000) A hedonic perspective on independent vacation planning, decision-making and behaviour. In J.A. Mazanec, G.I. Crouch, J.R. Brent Ritchie and A.G. Woodside, (eds) *Consumer Psychology of Tourism, Hospitality and Leisure* (Vol. 2, pp. 177–192). Wallingford: CABI.

Israeli Central Bureau of Statistics (2000) *Men and Women in the Mirror of Statistics*. Tel Aviv: Israeli Central Bureau of Statistics.

Iyer, P. (1988) *Video Nights in Kathmandu and Other Reports from the Not-So-Far East*. New York: Vintage.

JanMohamed, A.R. (1985) The economy of Manichean allegory: The function of racial difference in colonialist literature. *Critical Inquiry* 12, 59–87.

Jariyasombat, P. (2001) Thais on a shoestring. *Bangkok Post, Horizons*, August, p. 23: 2.

Jarvis, J. (1994) *The Billion Dollar Backpackers: The Ultimate Fully Independent Tourists*. Melbourne: Monash University National Centre for Australian Studies.

Jaturapattarakij, A. (1999) Cyber-saturation strikes. *Bangkok Post*, August 23, p. 8.

Jidvijak, S. (1994) Worshipping at the altar of hedonism. *Bangkok Post, Horizons*, May, pp. 24–25.

Johnsen, S. (1998) *Jalan Jalan! En Sosialantropologisk Analyse av Backpackere i Nusa Tenggara, Indonesia* (Chapter 1). On WWW at http://www.uit.no/ssweb/dok/Johnsen/Siri/forside.html and subsequent links. Accessed 28.6.02.

Johnston, R.J. (ed.) (1993) *The Challenge for Geography.* Oxford: Blackwell.

Joint Standing Committee on Migration (1997) *Working Holiday Makers: More than Tourists.* Canberra: Australian Government Publishing Service.

Judd, D.R. (1999) Constructing the tourist bubble. In D.R. Judd and S. Fainstein (eds) *The Tourist City* (pp. 35–53). New Haven: Yale University Press.

Jung, C.G. (1956) *Transformation Symbolism in the Mass. Collected Works* 11, 201–299.

Kaplan, C. (1996) *Questions of Travel: Postmodern Discourses of Displacement.* Durham, NC: Duke University Press.

Katriel, T. (1999) *Key Words:Patterns of Cultural and Communication in Israel.* Tel Aviv: Zmora Bitan.

Katz, S. (1985) The Israeli teacher–guide: The emergence and the perpetuation of role. *Annals of Tourism Research* 12, 49–72.

Kerouac, J. (2000/1957) *On the Road.* London: Penguin Classics.

Kerouac, J. (1982/1966) *Satori in Paris.* London: Granada.

Kerouac, J. (1961/1960) *Book of Dreams.* San Francisco: City Lights.

Kininmont, L. (2000) The right mix: Facilities for international backpackers in Australia. Unpublished PhD thesis, University of Queensland.

Klein, M. (1999) The big trip. *The Sydney Morning Herald*, February. Online at www.smh.com.au/travel. Accessed June 2002.

Kucukkurt (1981) Factors affecting travel destination choice: An expectancy theory framework for studying travel behaviour. Unpublished PhD thesis, UMI Michigan, Rensselean Polytechnic Institute.

Laxon, J.D. (1991) How 'we' see 'them': Tourism and native Americans. *Annals of Tourism Research* 18, 365–391.

Lengkeek, J. (1996) *Vakantie van het Leven: Over het belang van recreatie en toerisme.* Boom: Amsterdam.

Lengkeek, J. (2001) Leisure experience and imagination. *International Sociology* 16, 173 – 184.

Let's Go (1999) *Let's Go* homepage. On WWW at http://www.letsgo.com/. Accessed 12.9.99.

Let's Go (2001) *A Budget Travel How-to.* On WWW at http://www.letsgo.com/. Accessed: 28/06/2002.

Levinson, D.J. (1978) Growing up with the dream. *Psychology Today* 11, 20–31.

Levinson, D.J., Darow, C.H., Klein, E.B., Levinson, M.H. and McKee, B. (1978) *The Seasons of a Man's Life.* New York: Alfred A. Knopf.

Lieblich, A. (1989) *Transition to Adulthood during Military Service: The Israeli Case.* Albany: State University of New York Press.

Logan, K. (2000) Service quality at Kiwi Paka YHA. Unpublished masters thesis, University of Otago.

Loker, L. (1993) *The Backpacker Phenomenon II: More Answers to Further Questions.* Townsville: James Cook University of North Queensland.

Loker-Murphy, L. (1996) Backpackers in Australia: A motivation-based segmentation study. *Journal of Travel and Tourism Marketing* 5 (4), 23–45.

Loker-Murphy, L. and Pearce, P. (1995) Young budget travellers: Backpackers in Australia. *Annals of Tourism Research* 22, 819–843.

Macbeth, J. and Westerhausen, K. (2001) *The Development of Backpacker Tourism in Western Australia.* On WWW at http://wwwsoc.murdoch.edu.au/tourism/backpacker.htm.

MacCannell, D. (1973) Staged authenticity: Arrangements of social space in tourist settings. *American Journal of Sociology* 79 (3), 589–603.

MacCannell, D. (1976; 1989; 1999) *The Tourist: A New Theory of the Leisure Class* (three editions). New York: Schocken.

MacCannell, D. (1992a) *Empty Meeting Grounds: The Tourist Papers.* London and New York: Routledge.

MacCannell, D. (1992b) Cannibalism today. In D. MacCannell, *Empty Meeting Grounds: The Tourist Papers* (pp. 17–73). London and New York: Routledge.

Maffesoli, M. (1995) *The Time of the Tribes.* London: Sage.

Malisow, B. (1998) *Film and Loathing in Las Vegas: A Savage Journey to Boredom.* On WWW at http://www.lasvegassun.com/dossier/misc/loathing/ether.html. Accessed 22.5.03.

Maneerungsee, W. (2001) Budget heaven lifts profile. *Bangkok Post,* January, p. 25: 8.

Mansfeld, Y. (1992) From motivation to actual travel. *Annals of Tourism Research* 19 (3), 399–419.

Maoz, D. (1999) Libi BaMizrach (My heart is in the East): The journey of Israeli young-adults to India. Unpublished MA thesis (text in Hebrew), The Hebrew University in Jerusalem

Maoz, D. (2002) *India Will Love Me.* Jerusalem: Keter.

Marcus, G. and Fisher, M. (eds) (1986) *Anthropology and Cultural Critique: The Experimental Moment in the Human Sciences.* Chicago: University of Chicago Press.

Marlowe (1999) *How to Stop Time: Heroin from A to Z.* London: Virago Press.

Marshall, A. (1999) For the road. *The Sydney Morning Herald 'Good Weekend' Magazine,* 17 April, pp. 55–60.

Mayo, E. and Jarvis, L.P. (1981) *The Psychology of Leisure Travel.* Boston: CBI Publishing.

McCabe, A.S. (2000) Tourism motivation process. *Annals of Tourism Research* 27 (4), 1049–1052.

McCafferty's (2002) *McCafferty's.* On WWW at http://www.mccaffertys.com.au. Accessed 31.10.02.

McCulloch, J. (1991) *Backpackers: The Growth Sector of Australian Tourism.* Brisbane: Queensland Parliamentary Library (April).

McCulloch, J. and Murray, J. (1997) *Beds, Boots and Backpacks: The Story of YHA in Australia.* Sydney: Playright Publishing Pty Ltd.

McGregor, A. (2000) Dynamic texts and tourist gaze: Death, bones and buffalo. *Annals of Tourism Research* 27 (1), 27–50.

Mehta, G. (1979) *Karma Cola: Marketing the Mystic East.* London: Jonathan Cape.

Meijer, W. G. (1989) Rucksacks and dollars: The economic impact of organised and non-organised tourism in Bolivia. In T.V. Singh, H.L. Theuns and F. Go (eds) *Towards Appropriate Tourism: The Case of Developing Countries* (pp. 11–22). Frankfurt am Main: European University Studies.

Mellinger, W.M. (1994) Toward a critical analysis of tourism representations. *Annals of Tourism Research* 21, 756–779.

Mevorach, O. (1997) The long trip after the military service: Characteristics of the travellers, the effects of the trip and its meaning. Unpublished PhD thesis (text in Hebrew), The Hebrew University in Jerusalem.

Miles, J (2000) *Review of 'Bruce Chatwin: A Biography' by Nicholas Shakespeare.* On WWW at http://www.salon.com. Accessed March 2002.

Miller, M. (2002) *Jack Kerouac and the Satori Highway.* The Nomad Group. On WWW at http://www.literarytraveler.com. Accessed March 2002.

Mintel (2000) *Independent Travel.* London: Mintel Market Intelligence, Mintel International Group Limited.

Moran, D.M. (1999) Interpreting tourism experiences: The case of structured backpacker tours in New Zealand. Unpublished PhD thesis, Lincoln University.

Moran, D. (2000) Interpreting tour experiences: The case of structured backpacker tours in New Zealand. *Pacific Tourism Review* 4, 35–43.

Morgan, N. and Pritchard, A. (1998) *Tourism Promotion and Power: Creating Images, Creating Identities.* Chichester: John Wiley and Sons.

Mowforth, M. and Munt, I. (1998) *Tourism and Sustainability: New Tourism in the Third World.* London and New York: Routledge.

Muir, R (1994) The New Zealand model: A successful approach to the backpacker market. *'Backpackers: A Growth Market to be Taken Seriously' Seminar Papers.* Melbourne: VTOA Seminar Series.

Munt, I. (1994) The 'other' postmodern tourism: Culture, travel and the new middle classes. *Theory, Culture and Society* 11, 101–123.

Murphy, L. (1998) *NSW and Victorian Backpacker Survey: A Study to Facilitate Backpacker Marketing Strategies for Queensland.* Australia: James Cook University.

Murphy, L (1999) Australia's image as a holiday destination: Perceptions of backpacker visitors. *Journal of Travel and Tourism Marketing* 8 (3), 21–45.

Murphy, L. (2001) Exploring social interactions of backpackers. *Annals of Tourism Research* 28 (1), 50–67.

Neugarten, B.L. (1968) The awareness of middle age. In B. L. Neugarten (ed.), *Middle Age and Aging: A Reader in Social Psychology* (pp. 33–98). Chicago: University of Chicago Press.

Neugarten, B.L. (1979) Time, age and life cycle. *American Journal of Psychiatry* 136, 887–894.

Neuman, W.L. (1997) *Social Research Methods.* Boston: Allyn and Bacon.

Newlands, K. (2002) New Zealand the backpackers' paradise: Preliminary findings of a study of backpackers in New Zealand during Autumn 2002. Unpublished proceedings of the Tourism Hospitality Research Conference. Rotorua, New Zealand.

Nimmo, K. (2001) Willing Workers on Organic Farms: A case study. Unpublished MA thesis, Victoria University of Wellington.

Niyamabha, V. (2002) Eden at a price. *The Nation,* February, p. 2: C.

Noy, Ch. (2002) The great journey: Narrative analysis of Israeli trekking stories. Unpublished PhD thesis (in Hebrew), The Hebrew University in Jerusalem.

Noy, Ch. (forthcoming) Israeli backpackers: Narrative, interpersonal communication, and social construction. In Ch. Noy and E. Cohen (eds) *Israeli Backpackers and Their Society: A View from Afar.* New York: State University of New York Press.

Noy, Ch. and Cohen, E. (eds) (forthcoming) *Israeli Backpackers and Their Society: A View from Afar.* New York: State University of New York Press.

NTTC (1990) *Northern Territory Backpacker Survey 1989/90.* Milton: Kinhill Cameron McNamara Pty Ltd.

Office of National Tourism (1999) *Backpacker Accommodation in Australia: A Ratings Guide.* Australia: Office of National Tourism.

Oppermann, M. and Chon, K. (1997) *Tourism in Developing Countries*. London: International Thompson Business Press.

Ortner, S.B. (1998) Generation X: Anthropology in a media-saturated world. *Cultural Anthropology* 13 (3), 414–440.

Palin, M. (1995) *Hemingway's Chair*. New York: St Martin's Griffin.

Palin, M (1999) *Hemingway Adventure*. London: Orion.

Parr, D.K. (1989) Free independent Travellers: The unknown tourists. Unpublished MA thesis, University of Canterbury, Lincoln College.

Pearce, P. (1990) *The Backpacker Phenomenon: Preliminary Answers to Basic Questions*. Townsville: Department of Tourism, James Cook University.

Pearce, P. (1993) Fundamentals of tourist motivation. In D.G. Pearce and R.W. Butler (eds) *Tourism Research, Critiques and Challenges* (pp. 113–134). London: Routledge.

Perdue, R and Botkin, M (1988) Visitor survey versus conversion study. *Annals of Tourism Research* 15 (1), 76–87.

Perkins, H.C. and Thorns, D.C. (2001) Gazing or Performing? *International Sociology* 16 (2), 185–204.

Plys.com (2002) Interview with Michael Palin. On WWW at http://www.plys.com/~anna/mp_int.html. Accessed June 2002.

Pratt, M.L. (1992) *Imperial Eyes: Travel Writing and Transculturation*. New York: Routledge.

Pritchard, A. and Morgan, N. (2000) Privileging the male gaze: Gendered tourism landscapes. *Annals of Tourism Research* 27, 884–905.

Ragheb, M.G. and Beard, J.G. (1982) Measuring leisure attitudes. *Journal of Leisure Research* 14, 155–162.

Rahav, A. (1995) Generation X. *Otot* 177: 22–23, 35.

Richards, G. (1999) Vacations and the quality of life: Patterns and structures. *Journal of Business Research* 44 (3), 189–198.

Richards, G. (2001) *Cultural Attractions and European Tourism*. Wallingford: CABI.

Riley, P.J. (1988) Road culture of international long-term budget travellers. *Annals of Tourism Research* 15 (2), 313–328.

Ritzer, G. and Liska, A. (1997) 'McDisneyization' and 'post-tourism': Complementary perspectives on contemporary tourism. In C. Rojek and J. Urry (eds) *Touring Cultures* (pp. 96–109). London: Routledge.

Rojanaphruk, P. (2001) Local youth oust backpacker clan. *The Nation*, August 12, p. 4A.

Rojek, C. (1993) *Ways of Escape: Modern Transformations in Leisure and Travel*. London: MacMillan.

Rojek, C. (1997), Indexing, dragging and the social construction of tourist sights. In C. Rojek and J. Urry (eds) *Touring Cultures: Transformations of Travel and Theory* (pp. 52–74). London: Routledge.

Rojek, C. and Urry, J. (eds) (1997) *Touring Cultures: Transformations of Travel and Theory*. London: Routledge.

Roniger, L. and Feige, M. (1992) From pioneer to Freier: The changing models of generalized exchange in Israel. *Archives Europeennes de Sociologie* 33 (2), 280–307.

Ross, G.F. (1992) Tourist motivation among backpacker visitors to the wet tropics of Northern Australia. *Journal of Travel and Tourism Marketing* 1 (3), 43–59.

Ross, G. (1993) Ideal and actual images of backpacker visitors to Northern Australia. *Journal of Travel Research* 32 (2), 54–57.

Ross, G. (1997) Backpacker achievement and environment controllability as visitor motivators. *Journal of Travel and Tourism Marketing* 6 (2), 69–82.

Ryan, C., and Mohsin, A. (1999) Backpackers attitude to the 'Outback'. Unpublished proceedings of the International Geographic Union Sustainable Tourism Study Group & International Tourism Students' Conference (pp. 324–340). Oamaru, New Zealand. August/September.

Ryan C. and Mohsin A. (2001) Backpackers: Attitudes to the 'Outback'. *Journal of Travel and Tourism Marketing* 10 (1), 69–92.

Said, E. (1978) *Orientalism: Western Conceptions of the Orient*. London: Penguin.

Saldanha, A. (2002) Music tourism and factions of bodies in Goa. *Tourist Studies* 2 (1), 43–62.

Schechner, R. (1977) *Essays on Performance Theory, 1970–1976*. New York: Drama Book Specialists.

Schein, E.H. (1985) *Organizational Culture and Leadership*. New York: Jossey-Bass.

Scheuch, E.K. (1981) Tourismus. In F. Stalmann (ed.) *Die Lust an der Erkenntis: Die Psychologie des 20. Jahrhunderts* (pp. 1089–1114). Zurich: Kindler Verlag.

Scheyvens, R. (1999) Backpackers are beautiful: Assessing the potential of budget travellers to support community tourism in Africa. Unpublished proceedings of the Twentieth New Zealand Geography Conference (pp. 278–282). Palmerston North, July.

Scheyvens, R. (2002) Backpacker tourism and Third World development. *Annals of Tourism Research* 29 (1), 144–164.

Schonland, A and Williams, P (1997) Using the Internet for travel and tourism survey research. Experiences from the net traveller survey. *Journal of Travel Research* (Fall), 80–87.

Schulze, G. (1992) *Die Erlebnisgesellschaft. Kultursoziologie der Gegenwart*. Frankfurt am Main: Campus-Verlag.

Scottish Executive (2000) *A New Strategy for Scottish Tourism*. Edinburgh: The Scottish Parliament.

Scottish Executive (2002) *A New Strategy for Scottish Tourism*. Edinburgh: The Scottish Parliament.

Seekings, (1998) The youth travel market. *Travel and Tourism Analyst* 5, 37–55.

Selby, M and Morgan, N (1996) Reconstruing place image: A case study of its role in destination marketing research. *Tourism Management* 17 (4), 287–294.

Selwyn, T. (ed.) (1996) *The Tourist Image: Myths and Myth Making in Tourism*. Chichester: Wiley.

Shakespeare, N. (2001) *Bruce Chatwin*. New York, Knopf.

Shields, R. (1991) *Places on the Margin: Alternative Geographies of Modernity*. London: Routledge.

Shipway, R. (2000) The international backpacker market in Britain: A market waiting to happen? In M. Robinson, M. Evans, P. Long, R. Sharpley and J. Swarbrooke (eds) *Motivations, behaviour and tourist types* (pp. 393–416). Unpublished proceedings of the Reflections in International Tourism Conference, Sheffield, October.

Silver, I. (1993) Marketing authenticity in Third World Countries. *Annals of Tourism Research* 20, 302–318.

Sirgy, M. and Su, C. (2000) Destination image, self-congruity and travel behaviour: toward an integrative model. *Journal of Travel Research* 38, 340–352.

Slaughter, L. (2001) Managing the backpacker market in Australia. Makati: Asia. Unpublished proceedings of the Pacific Tourism Association Annual Conference.

Smith, V.L. (1990) Geographical implications of 'drifter' tourism, Boracay, Philippines. *Tourism Recreation Research* 15 (1), 34–42.

Sollors, W. (ed.) (1989) *The Invention of Ethnicity.* New York: Oxford University Press.

Sorenson, A. (1999) *Travellers in the Periphery: Backpackers and Other Independent Multiple Destination Tourists in Peripheral Areas.* Bornholm: Unit of Tourism, Research Centre of Bornholm.

South Australian Tourism Commission (1999) *Tourism Strategy for the Backpacker Market.* Adelaide: South Australian Tourism Commission.

Speed, C. and Harrison, A. (2000) The Scottish backpacker market: A preliminary study. Unpublished report, Napier University.

Speed, C. and Slater, A. (1999) Backpacker hostel accommodation in Scotland. Unpublished report, Napier University.

Spreitzhofer, G. (1997) Rucksack-Rausch und Freizeitwahn: Drei Jahrzehnte Alternativtourismus in Südostasien. In C. Stock (ed.) *Trouble in Paradise: Tourismus in die Dritte Welt* (pp. 161–170). Freiburg: iz3w.

Spreitzhofer, G. (1998) Backpacking tourism in South-East Asia. *Annals of Tourism Research* 25 (4), 979–983.

Squire, S.J. (1994) The cultural values of literary tourism. *Annals of Tourism Research* 21, 103–121.

Stainton Rogers, R. (1995) Q methodology. In J.A. Smith, R. Harré and L. van Langenhove (eds) *Rethinking Methods in Psychology* (pp. 178–192). London: Sage.

Statistics New Zealand (2002) *Accommodation Survey: January 2002.* Auckland: Statistics New Zealand.

Stein, J.O. and Stein, M. (1987) Psychotherapy, initiation and the middle transition. In L.C. Madhi, S. Foster and M. Little (eds) *Betwixt and Between: Patterns of Masculine and Feminine Initiation* (pp. 285–303). La Salle, Illinois: Open Court.

Stephenson, W. (1978) Concourse theory of communication. *Communication*, 3, 21–40.

Stockwell, A.J. (1993) Early tourism in Malaya. In M. Hitchcock, V.T. King and M.J.G. Parnwell (eds) *Tourism in South-East Asia* (pp. 258–270). London: Routledge.

Strauss, A.L. (1994) *Grundlagen Qualitativer Sozialforschung.* Muenchen: UTB.

Sutcliffe, W. (1997) *Are You Experienced?* London: Penguin.

Taylor, D. (1994) *An Analysis of the 'Backpacker' Segment of the Travel Market for Byron Bay.* Australia: Southern Cross University,

Teas, J. (1988) 'I'm studying monkeys. What do you do?' Youth and travellers in Nepal. *Kroeber Anthropological Society Papers* 67–68, 42–54.

The Nation (2001) Smelling better than ever. *The Nation,* 19 November, p. 19: 7A.

Theroux, P. (1992) *The Happy Isles of Oceania.* London: Penguin.

Theroux, P. (1999) Interview with Dwight Garner. On WWW at www.salon.com. Accessed February 2003.

Thomas, N. (1994) *Colonialism's Culture: Anthropology, Travel and Government.* Cambridge: Polity Press.

Thompson, H.S. (1998) *The Proud Highway: Saga of a Desperate Southern Gentleman 1955–1967 (The Fear and Loathing Letters, Vol. 1).* London: Bloomsbury.

Thompson, H.S. (2000) *Fear and Loathing in America: The Brutal Odyssey of an Outlaw Journalist 1968–1976 (The Fear and Loathing Letters, Vol. 2).* London: Bloomsbury.

Thompson, T. (2002) British Woman found dead in Bangkok backpackers' hotel. *Guardian*, April 7. On WWW at www.guardian.co.uk/archive/article. Accessed August 2002.

Thoms, C. (2002) *BTR Niche Market Report Number 1: Backpackers in Australia, 1999*. Canberra: Bureau of Tourism Research.

Thrane, C. (2000) Everyday life and cultural tourism in Scandinavia: Examining the spillover hypothesis. *Leisure and Society* 23 (1), 217–234.

Tickell, A. (2001) Footprints on the beach: Traces of colonial adventure in narratives of independent tourism. *Postcolonial Studies* 4 (1), 39–54.

Timmermans, H. (2002) Een Onderzoek naar de Invloed van Authenticiteit op de Bestemmingskeuze en de Motivatie om te gaan Backpacken in Zuidoost Azië. Unpublished masters thesis, Universiteit van Tilburg.

TNT/Uni Travel (2003) *Backpackers Uncovered*. Australia: TNT Magazine/Uni Travel.

Tomory, D. (1998) *A Season in Heaven: True Tales from the Road to Kathmandu*. Hawthorn: Lonely Planet Publications.

Tomory, D. (2000) *Hello Goodnight: A Life of Goa*. Hawthorn: Lonely Planet Publications.

Tourism New Zealand (1999) *Understanding New Zealand's Backpacker Market*. Wellington: Tourism New Zealand.

Tourism New Zealand (2000) *Backpacker Boom for New Zealand*. Wellington: Tourism New Zealand.

Tourism New Zealand (2002) No backpack required. *Tourism New Zealand Tourism News* (July).

Tourism Queensland (2001) *International Backpackers Market Fact Sheet*. Brisbane: Tourism Queensland.

Tourism Research Council New Zealand (2002). *Tourism Leading Indicators Monitor Series 2002/9*. Wellington: Tourism Research Council New Zealand.

Tourism Victoria (1995) Backpacker tourism in Victoria: Should we aim to increase this market? If so, how? A discussion paper. Melbourne: Industry Development Branch.

Toxward, S. (1999) Backpackers' expectations and satisfactions: A case study of Northland, New Zealand. Unpublished masters thesis. Christchurch: Lincoln University.

Travellers Auto Barn (2000) *About Travellers Auto Barn*. On WWW at http://travellers-autobarn.com.au. Accessed 15.4.02.

Travel Scene International (2003) *Inside Info File: Backpackers Graduate from 'Great Unwashed' to Australia's Most Wanted With Launch of First Globally Branded Backpacker Network*. On WWW at http://www.travelscene.com.au/in-info-040-dec-02-accor-backpackers-01.html. Accessed 24.5.03.

Turner, L. and Ash, J. (1975) *The Golden Hordes: International Tourism and the Pleasure Periphery*. London: Constable.

Turner, V. (1973) The center out there: Pilgrim's goal. *History of Religions* 12 (3), 191–230.

Turner, V.W. (1987) Betwixt and between: The liminal period in *rites de passage*. In L.C. Madhi, S. Foster and M. Little (eds) *Betwixt and Between: Patterns of Masculine and Feminine Initiation* (pp. 5–22). La Salle, Illinois: Open Court.

Turner, V. and Turner, E. (1978) *Image and Pilgrimage in Christian Culture*. New York: Columbia University Press.

Um, S. and Crompton, J. (1992) The roles of perceived inhibitors and facilitators in pleasure travel destination decisions. *Journal of Travel Research* (Winter), 18–25.

Uriely, N. and Reichel, A. (2000) Working tourists and their attitudes to hosts. *Annals of Tourism Research* 27, 267–283.

Uriely, N., Yonay, Y. and Simchai, D. (2002) Backpacking experiences: A type and form analysis. *Annals of Tourism Research* 29 (2), 520–538.

Urry, J. (1990) *The Tourist Gaze*. London: Sage.

Urry, J. (1994) Europe, tourism and the nation state. In C.P. Cooper and A. Lockwood (eds) *Progress in Tourism, Recreation and Hospitality Research* (Vol. 5, pp. 89–98) Chichester, Wiley.

Urry, J. (1999) Mobile cultures (draft). Department of Sociology, University of Lancaster. On WWW at http://www.comp.lancs.ac.uk/sociology/soc030ju.htm.

Van den Berghe, P. L. (1994) *The Quest for the Other: Ethnic Tourism in San Cristobal, Mexico*. Washington: University of Washington Press.

Van Gennep, A. (1960) *The Rites of Passage*. London: Routledge and Kegan Paul.

VisitScotland (2000a) *Tourism in Scotland 1999*. Edinburgh: VisitScotland.

VisitScotland (2000b) *The Growth, Development and Future Prospects of the Hostels Market in Scotland*. Edinburgh: VisitScotland.

VisitScotland (2001) *Hostel Quality Assurance Grading Scheme Study*. Edinburgh: VisitScotland.

VisitScotland (2002) *Tourism Framework for Action 2002–2005*. Edinburgh: The Scottish Executive.

Vogt, J.W. (1976) Wandering: Youth and travel behaviour. *Annals of Tourism Research* 4 (1), 25–41.

Wallace, B. (1991) Backpack travellers using commercial backpacker accommodation in Queensland. Unpublished masters thesis, Victoria University of Technology.

Wang, N. (1999) Rethinking authenticity in tourism experience. *Annals of Tourism Research* 26 (2), 349–370.

Wang, N. (2000) *Tourism and Modernity: A Sociological Analysis*. Kidlington, Oxford: Elsevier Science Ltd.

Ware, M.P. (1992) Been there done that: A study of winter backpackers in New Zealand. Unpublished BA dissertation, Jesus College, University of Cambridge.

Wayne, S. (1990) *Egypt and the Sudan*. Hawthorn/Berkeley: Lonely Planet Publications.

Welk, P. (2004) *On a Shoestring: Constructions of Identity in the Backpacker Scene*. Bangkok: White Lotus.

Westerhausen, K. (2002) *Beyond the Beach: An Ethnography of Modern Travellers in Asia*. Bangkok: White Lotus.

Westerhausen, K. and Macbeth, J. (2003) Backpackers and empowered local communities: Natural allies in the struggle for sustainability and local control? *Tourism Geographies* 5 (1).

Wheeler, T. (1992) *South-East Asia on a Shoestring*. Hawthorn / Berkeley: Lonely Planet Publications.

Wheeler, T (1999) In defence of backpackers. *Tourism in Focus* 31, 15–16.

Wilderness.com (2003) *Getting Away from it All: But Does it Have Mobile Coverage?* On WWW at http://www.hero.ac.uk/studying/wilderness_com1668.cfm. Accessed April 2003.

Wilson, D. (1997) Paradoxes of tourism in Goa. *Annals of Tourism Research* 24 (1), 52–75.

Wilson, J. and Richards, G. (forthcoming) The social construction of backpacker travel. Unpublished research report.

Wood, R.E. (1979) Tourism and underdevelopment in Southeast Asia. *Journal of Contemporary Asia*, 9, 274–87.

Woodrow, R. (1994) Backpacker strategy plan: A national perspective. *Backpackers: A Growth Market to be Taken Seriously*. VTO Seminar Series. Melbourne: Victoria Tourist Organisation.

Woodside, A.G. and Lysonski, S. (1989) A general model of traveller destination choice. *Journal of Travel Research* 17, 8–14.

WWOOF (2002) *What is WWOOF?* On WWW at http://www.wwoof-australia .com.au/. Accessed 22.5.03.

Zinn, C. and Hall, S. (2002) Backpacker killed in robbery: Teenager on gap year thrown from bridge. *Guardian*, April 12. On WWW at www.guardian.co.uk/ archive/article. Accessed August 2002.

Zurick, D.N. (1992) Adventure travel and sustainable tourism in the peripheral economy of Nepal. *Annals of the Association of American Geographers* 82 (4), 608–629.

Index

General

World Regions

Countries (includes references to nationals of these countries)

Places

Companies/organisations